the
CUBAN
C✦P

the CUBAN COP

Nick Navarro

with Jeff Sadler

TransMedia
Publishing, Inc.
Boca Raton, Florida

Published by Transmedia Publishing, Inc.
6001 Broken Sound Parkway, N.W.
Boca Raton, Florida 33487

Publisher's Cataloging-in-Publication Data
Navarro, Nick.
    Cuban cop:the true story of one tough cop and his rise from an undercover
    narc to a celebrated sheriff /Nick Navarro with Jeff Sadler. – Boca Raton, FL:
    Transmedia, 1998.
        p. ill. cm.
    ISBN 1-890819-01-8
        1. Navarro, Nick. 2. Police—Florida—Miami—biography. I. Sadler, Jeff.
        II. Title.
HV7911.N3 A3   1998   97-62088
363.2' 092   B—dc21   CIP

PROJECT COORDINATION BY JENKINS GROUP, INC.

02 01 00 99 ◆ 5 4 3 2 1

Printed in the United States of America

To my most trusted advisor, friend and partner, my beautiful wife, Sharron—the love of my life. Without her, I could not have accomplished nearly as much during the last 25 years in which we have lived and worked so happily together.

To my sons, Nick and John; my daughter, Diana; and our grandchildren, Eileen, Gabrielle, and Michael.

And above all, to the courageous police officers with whom I have had the honor to serve, especially those brave souls who have made the ultimate sacrifice in the line of duty protecting our citizens, our communities and our property. To those dedicated men and women in law enforcement, I am eternally grateful.

God bless them all.

Contents

Introduction

A Great Day To Be An Undercover Cop

IT WAS A SWELTERING JULY DAY IN STEAMY MIAMI IN 1964, AND I WAS ABOUT TO turn the heat up further on two drug dealers whose case I'd been working on for a few weeks. To them, I was known as Louis Gonzalez, a businessman, who wanted to buy four pounds of marijuana from them. They were Cuban exiles, veterans of the Bay of Pigs, who liked telling me stories about their families: honorable people with a heritage that included fighting in the Spanish-American War.

They may have come from good stock, but these two were no-good bastards themselves. This was going to be their last day on the streets for a while.

I was supposed to meet them at Robert's Drugstore on Flagler and Seventh Avenue. A surveillance team was already there, ready to assist after I met Gustavo Constravas and his partner, Pepe, and completed our transaction.

One of the few rules an undercover cop learns is to always be in control of a situation. In this job, one must understand an unfortunate simplicity: if you lose control, you'll likely lose your life.

I wheeled my Chevy Corvair down Flagler Street, within blocks of the drugstore. As I drove, I noticed Constravas and Pepe at a gas station. I swung the car around and honked the horn, motioning for them to join me. Pepe climbed into the back seat, and Gustavo sat next to me in front.

In those brief moments, I had stopped thinking like a cop, an error I instantly regretted, as I had no way to inform the surveillance unit I'd made contact with the two men. The surveillance unit was where we had pre-arranged the buy - at the drugstore.

Constravas told me to drive. "We heard a few things about you, Louis," he said, "about you being a policeman." Before I could react to that bombshell, he shoved a .45 against my throat. It dug in under my chin and I thought, this is it, I'm a dead man, and it's my own fault.

Constravas told me there had been a change in plans as he pushed the gun in further, forcing my head back. "Drive south," he said, "along the river." I attempted to focus, to concentrate on what I was doing even as I recoiled, waiting for the bullet. I was thinking, what am I doing here with these lowlifes? I could have been anything - a carpenter, a taxi driver, a roofer - anything except an undercover cop.

"Maybe you forgot," Constravas said, "but we're from good families back in Cuba and we can't bring any disgrace to them. What do you think, Pepe? Should we just do it and drop him in the river?"

Pepe agreed while I bargained with God. Please, just let me go home tonight. Just this once.

Because the gun was shoved under my chin, I couldn't see whether Constravas's finger was actually on the trigger yet.

"Yes," said Constravas, "I think maybe we'll kill you. What do you think, Louis?"

What I was thinking was that the more he talked, the less likely he was to pull the trigger. A man like him, convinced I was a cop, would already have fired the bullet. I thought, maybe he wants me to assure him I'm not what someone has told him I am. Okay, I told myself as my heart continued to race, you can gain back control if you do this right.

Constravas was still raving about me being a cop. I waited until he paused for a breath and asked, "Look, can I talk now?"

"Go ahead," he replied.

"Do me a favor," I said, "Don't push my head back so far. It hurts and makes it difficult to drive." I felt the pressure on my throat lighten as the gun receded a bit. I reassured myself, he's not going to do it, he's not really going to shoot.

I told them, "You guys know me. I'm just an immigrant like you are, an exile. I'm Louis Gonzalez. I'm not a cop. You have to be an American citizen to be a cop - you know that. Besides, we've already done business. If I was a cop, wouldn't I have arrested you already?"

Constravas's gun hand dropped a little more. I continued to talk, feeling a little more confident. "Now, if you're finished with all this crap, maybe we can do some business here like we planned. Pepe? Since Gustavo still has this gun in my neck, can you reach into my pants pocket and pull out my wallet?"

"Sure, Louis, sure," Pepe replied. He slipped his hand in my pocket and extracted the wallet.

"Check my IDs, Gustavo. Check that the money is there for this buy. I'm just a businessman like you are. There's $800 there for the four pounds we talked about."

Constravas looked at my green card, my Florida driver's license, and some credit cards, all in the name of Louis Gonzalez. His gun wasn't pressed into my throat any longer, but it was still just under my chin and he hadn't backed off any further.

"The way I see it," I said, "we can do business right now like we said, or you can kill me. But you should know that if you pull that trigger, I'm going to die with my foot on the accelerator, and when this car hits another car or a telephone pole, the cops will arrest you for murder if you're still alive. They won't give a damn about four pounds of marijuana. It'll be the electric chair for Gustavo and Pepe, the family disgraces."

Pepe leaned forward in the back seat. "Gustavo, we know Louis. He's all right. It was this other guy saying he was a cop, but I didn't really believe him. We have to trust someone, Gustavo, why not Louis? He's telling us the truth."

Now I had an ally. I could feel Constravas giving in, too.

He didn't want me to be a cop. "I just didn't want to disgrace my family," he mumbled.

"You're a businessman. I'm a businessman," I told him. "Put the gun away and let's do business."

He finally lowered the weapon and placed it in his pocket. My muscles started to relax a bit, and I drove without thinking about dodging a bullet.

As we made our way back to Flagler and Seventh Avenue, they spent most of the time apologizing to me, trying to win back their compadre. When we got to the drugstore, I was back in control of the situation. I made the buy, signaled the surveillance unit, and pulled my badge and gun from under the seat.

"Narcotics officer!" I snapped. "You should have listened to the other guy."

A few weeks later at the trial, the whole story of the car trip was related, and the drug dealers told of how I'd persuaded them of my innocence. The judge, Julius Martens, listened intently to our testimony. The jury found the men guilty and Judge Martens sentenced them to ten years each. After announcing this, he turned to me and asked if I'd follow him to his chambers.

The first thing he did there was apologize. "Nick, I'd like to have given them more time in jail, but ten years is the maximum I can sentence them for this offense."

"That's fine, Judge. I understand."

"God bless you, Nick. I don't know why people like you risk your necks for the rest of us. But if you didn't, guys like this would still be on the street. Keep it up, sir. We need you." He pressed his hand to my shoulder.

I swelled with pride. It was a great day to be an undercover cop.

the CUBAN COP

One

To Serve And Protect

THE IMAGES JUMPED OFF THE MOVIE THEATER SCREEN. THE GOVERNMENT agent has tailed the criminals to the dock where they are unloading crates of rum to illegally distribute. He circles around behind them and suddenly the boatyard is flooded with light. "U.S. Government!" he shouts. "Don't move! You're under arrest!"

The bad guys freeze and the G-man emerges from the shadows. "Hands up!" he snarls. Out of the corner of his eye, he glimpses a movement. He turns quickly and shoots. A man falls, his gun discharges, and the bullet intended for the G-man hits the wooden dock. There is activity all around now as other agents swarm in and haul the rumrunners off to jail.

Another successful conclusion to an American movie.

I watched countless films of this kind in the late 1930s and 1940s in my home country of Cuba. The image of the government agent always getting his man has stayed with me throughout my life. When I watched those films, it seemed to me that there could be no better career for anyone than to be a government agent in the United States of America. To experience the thrill of the chase was my boyhood dream.

I was born in Jaruco, Cuba, in 1930. Jaruco is small town, just outside of Havana, where my family made their home. My father, Nicholas, Sr., was an engineer who did most of his work with American and British companies. He worked with the Websters, the Penns, and most frequently, the Hersheys from Pennsylvania. Mr. Hershey was a regular visitor and a good friend of my father's.

Hershey's had one of the largest sugar refineries in the world located on the outskirts of Havana, and my father contracted to build the railroad tracks leading to and from the plant. His exposure to American culture allowed him to engage us with stories about our neighbor to the north. He constantly reminded me that there was no nation on earth that offered more than the United States of America.

When I was twelve, a couple of friends joined me in a crabbing venture. We lived close to the sea and would often return from a night's work with a sack full of Morro crabs, a delicacy in Cuba, not unlike the stone crabs Americans enjoy. One night after filling our bag, we were stopped by two police officers in a Jeep. They took us to the police station, asked us what we were doing, confiscated our Morro crabs, and called our parents to come and take us home.

When my father came, the police told him we'd been out prowling, but they conveniently left out the part about the sackful of crabs. They said they'd be willing to forget about the incident this time, as long as it didn't happen again. My father assured them on that point and took me home. When I told him about the crabs they had stolen, he simply nodded and put his arm around me. "Forget it, son," he said. "I guess they need the crabs more than we do."

That was my first exposure to police work in Cuba. My second exposure was far worse.

When I was fifteen, some friends and I were seated at a small, outdoor restaurant, where we were having lunch. A police officer walked in from the street. He was young, maybe in his early thirties, and he carried a gun in a holster at his side. He walked past us and went over to a doorway that led from the bar to a storage room. He opened the door, went in, and turned around, facing me.

The door remained open, and as I watched him, our gazes met. There was an empty look in his eyes and I wondered what he was planning to do. I didn't have to wait long for an answer. He unholstered his service revolver, put the pistol to his head, and blew his brains all over the storage room.

We never found out why. We were questioned as to what we saw and that was all. No one spoke of the matter after that, but it was impossible to forget the blank stare or the image of the shiny uniform soaked with blood.

My father died when I was sixteen, leaving a void for me that my mother and other sister couldn't fill. I missed our talks about America and his enthusiasm for all the years that were ahead of me. My older sister had already moved to the United States with her husband, a native Cuban educated at Cornell University. I continued going to school, as my father would have wished, and entered the University of Havana in 1948.

The revolution in Cuba was a national obsession and the University of Havana was in the center of it. The campus was supposed to be a place of higher learning but by the time I arrived, it was no longer functioning as a true university. The goal of the curriculum at the school was to have the students demonstrate against the wealthy dictatorship and a corrupt government and debate the internal dissension on the island, rather than learn history or science.

I thought again of my father's words about the United States: "You can be whatever you want to be if you work hard and set your mind to the task." I thought about G-Men, about investigations, about capturing criminals and putting them behind bars. It was still my dream to be a federal agent. The United States was a country of immigrants, people who came from other lands to try to realize their dreams. I knew it was what I must do as well.

In 1950, I had a physical exam, secured testimonial letters on my behalf, verified that I had no criminal record, and posted the proper bond. Then I was bound for the United States of America.

❧

MY SISTER DELIA WAS SEVERAL YEARS OLDER THAN I WAS. SHE HAD COME TO THE United States after marrying Louis Hernandez, the son of a wealthy Cuban family. Louis had gone to prep school in New York, then on to the Ivy League at Cornell and ended up with a job in Pennsylvania. Delia and Louis welcomed me to their new country and helped me to feel at home in the unfamiliar surroundings and climate.

I didn't have some of the difficulties most immigrants have when they first settle in America. I spoke the language well by then, glad I had been studious with English when I was younger. It didn't take me long to feel at home in my new environment.

About a year after I arrived, the Korean conflict broke out, and not long after that came the "greetings" notice from the draft board. I responded and was soon inducted into the Army. Basic training was at Fort Meade and the Aberdeen Proving Grounds in Maryland and then at Fort Leonard Wood in Missouri.

Shipped over to Korea in 1953, I joined the Seventh Infantry Division, Thirty-Second Regiment, First Battalion, Charlie Company, for the duration of the year. There were a number of skirmishes and sniper fire was a constant problem, but the major battles had already been fought, and peace negotiations were underway at Panmunjom. While under fire, I continuously made promises to the Lord if He could get me out of this place unscathed. One of the promises I made was to stop smoking. It was the only promise I kept, and the best thing to come out of the war for me.

We were allowed a number of short R&Rs on the air base near Pusan. During these brief respites, we slept outside in tents, an absolute luxury compared to the ground we bedded down on at the front lines. Unfortunately, the breaks would end and it was back to the line of fire. Those brief rests, though, helped us keep our sanity.

My total time in Korea was about nine months. The war ended with a cease fire and I returned to Pennsylvania. After receiving an honorable discharge, I discovered that serving in the military can move you up in the citizenship line. I was able to become an American citizen before I had spent five years in this country. My feelings about becoming an American are difficult to express. My country, right or wrong, is an adage that I believe in. Law and order became the natural extension of that belief for me.

I went home to visit my mother and sister Rosalina in Cuba, planning to stay for a month. But I grew restless quickly, feeling like a fish out of water there. America was my home now and the sooner I could return, the better. I managed to stay in Cuba for only three weeks, then headed back to Pennsylvania.

I went to work for Hans Knoll's Furniture Company, which had secured a contract to supply furniture for United States' embassies throughout the world including the one in Havana. I had married by this time and my wife,

Joan, and I had a daughter, Diana, and a son, Nicky. A second son, Johnny, would be on the way soon.

Checking shipment orders for embassy furniture was not the career I had in mind during the hours I spent in the movie theater, where the adventures of U.S. government agents held me spellbound. To protect and to serve, I remembered them saying, and it seemed like the right career for me. In 1959, old flames were rekindled when I watched a new film, The FBI Story, starring Jimmy Stewart. I truly wanted to be an FBI agent.

I had heard that the city of Miami, specifically the Metro Dade Police Department, needed Spanish-speaking police officers. It wasn't a G-man position, but I would be an officer of the law and in a climate I preferred.

I moved my family down to South Florida from Pennsylvania and, with the guidance of a man named Al Tarrabochia, took all my tests and was accepted into the police academy. While attending the academy, I earned an extra assignment to provide tutelage for a general from the Colombian army. I translated for him and assisted him in addition to doing my regular academy assignments. It required double the effort, but I didn't mind. I felt like I was doing something for the country I'd embraced, and it felt good.

The general had been invited here to observe the methods and training of our police. Little did we know how important U.S. police training would become when Colombia took over the manufacturing of coca paste into cocaine.

I graduated from the academy and was assigned to the south end of Dade County, a large, desolate area, measuring about 40 miles long and 30 miles wide. (It's the area Hurricane Andrew hit in 1992.) There wasn't much to it in 1959 other than a few labor camps, some isolated residential areas, and Homestead Air Force Base.

Dade County, with Miami as its seat, had maybe 750,000 people. Nearby Broward County, with Fort Lauderdale as its hub, was mainly cow pastures and had 45,000 people - the cows seemed to outnumber the residents. In South Florida there was a real mix of people - white, black, Cuban, Mexican, and Jamaican. (Meanwhile back in Cuba, Castro was taking control.)

Mine was the only patrol car at that end of Dade County. Some nights I worked alone; other times I had a partner. I had a gun at my side, a pair of handcuffs, and a certain amount of authority beyond what the common citizen had. It may sound idealistic, but to me there were clear lines between good and bad as defined by the law.

When I became a police officer, I discovered my hatred for criminals and the trauma they brought to honest citizens. I saw an opportunity to right wrongs and eventually stop the wrongs from happening in the first place.

It was important to establish a real tie to the community, and I found that I could easily do this. Meeting people, talking to them, and getting to know them better were things I genuinely enjoyed. People seemed to sense that too.

If officers knew what was going on locally and secured the trust of the people they were trying to help, they often heard things that could lead them to prevent a crime, not just mop up afterward. Second-hand news wasn't good enough. Being among the people was the only guaranteed way to know what was really happening.

This wasn't the undercover job I had seen time after time on the movie screen, where the federal agent infiltrated a group of people, investigated, made the case, and blew the whistle. But it was my first police beat and I was proud of it.

It wasn't long before a side of law enforcement that never appeared on the silver screen made its presence known. I received a call while out on patrol one evening around 7 P.M., that there was a "pedestrian down" along South Dixie Highway. The dispatcher didn't say how seriously the person was injured. I rushed to the scene and found myself face-to-face with a sobbing seven-year-old boy. His brother, who looked to be about three years old, lay in the middle of the street. I examined him immediately, but it was clear the boy was dead. After covering him with a blanket, and knowing that an ambulance was on the way, I went to comfort the bereaved brother. Between sobs, he managed to tell me that he was crossing the street with his little brother, but the three-year-old had pulled away from his hand in a playful gesture and quickly moved a few steps into the street where a car struck him. The boy kept shaking his head, and the tears wouldn't stop. The weight of responsibility was clearly dragging him down, but I didn't know what to say to him. He was despondent; the appropriate words didn't come to me. Not knowing what else to do, I simply held the boy and let him cry. Maybe he expected the policeman to somehow bring his brother back to life. I realized how helpless I could be out there, badge, gun, and handcuffs notwithstanding.

When both boys were taken care of, I returned to my car, where all the composure I'd maintained for the last couple of hours suddenly disappeared. With my face in my arms, leaning against the steering wheel, I cried almost uncontrollably. The picture of the toddler facedown in the street and his weeping brother at my side is an image I will never be able to shake.

But death and life are closely related, and one night a call came through to my patrol car to go to one of the Mexican labor camps where a woman, ironically enough, was in labor. Luckily there were two of us working that night; as a patrolman named Schaefer had pulled duty with me.

We drove to the camp and found that the story was true. The camp was in Florida City and the nearest facility was James Archer Smith Hospital in Homestead, the next town. It was too late to call for an ambulance; the only alternative was to drive her there. Schaefer said, "I've got seniority on you - I'll drive."

With red lights flashing and siren on, we took off for the hospital. We'd laid the woman on her side across the back seat as I sat on the front edge of it. I held her hand and thought maybe we'd get to the hospital in time.

All of sudden, she turned onto her back, lifted her legs, and told me in Spanish that the baby was coming. I said, "Oh, Walt, guess what? We're about to be fathers again." He said he was going as fast as he could. Just like that, the baby's head popped out of the woman's vagina, covered with mucous, blood and other body fluids. This is incredible, I was thinking, and then she gave it one more push and out came the entire baby. I caught it and cradled it in my arms, ever aware what was covering the baby was now all over me.

I had heard somewhere that you have to slap a baby to start it crying, but this one needed no help. He (it was definitely a boy) was already into a hell of a tune. He was a beautiful baby. I put one hand in back of his head and the other on his behind and just held him. The umbilical cord was still attached to him and his mother. It's not every day one participates in a childbirth, and it was an amazing miracle.

Schaefer had called ahead for a stretcher and announced the birth, which was the least he could do. He drove straight to the emergency room door, where the staff was waiting. They took mom, son, and umbilical cord away, leaving me sitting in the car, my uniform dripping. I thought, this Metro Dade patrol officer can do it all.

Of course, not every call involves death or new life. One night a call took me to a recognizable address in Perrine. I'd been there several times before to help settle a domestic dispute. It was a small, wood-frame house that had a couple of cinder blocks for stairs. After arriving at the scene, I ascended the stairs, knocked on the door, and almost immediately found myself staring at the double barrel of a gun.

I faced the barrels and said, "Hey, Willie, what's happening?"

"Oh, boss-man," Willie replied, "let me tell you, this woman of mine is bad news."

"Willie, before you tell me anything, how about if you lower that gun?"

"But I got to tell you about her -"

"Absolutely, Willie, we'll talk about the whole thing. Just put that gun down," I said. "We're friends," I added, "aren't we, Willie? Friends don't poke guns in each other's faces."

The gun barrel dropped. "I'm sorry, boss-man. This woman just drives me nuts."

"It's okay, Willie," I told him, easing open the door and getting my hands on the gun. Willie gave it to me and we discussed his domestic problems for some time after that until I was sure he was going straight to bed after I left.

Another evening, a rookie patrolman was working with me when we were called to a neighborhood saloon. This establishment also featured pool tables, and every Friday and Saturday night the place was packed and rocking. When we arrived I told the rookie I would go to the front door and announce I was coming in - doing that was usually followed by the sounds of knives and guns hitting the floor since no one wanted to be caught with a deadly weapon or a concealed firearm.

I instructed the rookie to cover the back of the saloon. "If they have drugs," I told him, "they usually split for the back door."

I yelled through the front door that the police were here and coming in. The commotion that followed was not only the dropping of weapons. Nine or ten of the patrons made a dash for the back door. The rookie had put his shoulder to the door to hold them back. But the runners came through all at once and knocked the door off its hinges. When I made my way to the back to see what happened, my partner wasn't visible - at least not until I picked up the door. Under it was the rookie, with a ripped shirt and bruises to show for his efforts.

Unfortunately, bruises weren't the worst injury a Metro Dade law officer could get on the streets. One night one of our men was shot in the stomach. When the shooting was reported, a cop named Thompson jumped on a motorcycle to try to reach our downed comrade quickly. En route, he failed to negotiate a turn, the cycle flipped out of control, and he was killed on impact. That was an especially rough night for everyone.

When Castro took over Cuba in 1959, the first major influx of Cubans began arriving in Miami from my native country. The first wave was mostly professionals. They possessed ability, knowledge, and a desire to be successful here. These were doctors, lawyers, architects, engineers, accountants, bankers, and business people, displaced by the turmoil in their homeland.

Here they washed dishes in restaurants, carried luggage at the airport, and cleaned rooms in hotels - anything to make a few dollars to live on. At night, they went back to school, in some cases to learn English, in others to secure a degree from a U.S. school in their chosen professions. These people literally changed the face of Miami and Dade County. New businesses sprung up, houses and apartments were built, residential and business areas were expanded, and the sidewalks were no longer rolled up in the summer.

This massive migration impacted the police as well, for along with the many professional people were those that intended to take the criminal path. It became our job to identify those most likely to attempt a criminal venture. Metro Dade started to add officers, and specific departments grew.

I was eventually transferred to the vice squad, where my Cuban background and accent were thought to be an asset. I worked on a number of cases all over Dade County. This was markedly different from the patrol beat, and it was during this time that I began to create, learn, and perfect a number of undercover personalities that would be alter egos for me for a substantial portion of my law enforcement career. Perhaps it was all the movies I'd seen as a kid, but playing a role to catch criminals was natural for me.

There was an establishment in Miami Beach that we called a "clip joint," where male patrons would pay exorbitant prices for refreshments and also have the opportunity to pay even more for entertainment of the female variety. One night, a Japanese businessman, raging about the overcharging, pulled out a gun and started shooting at people. We responded to this problem by sending me in undercover to play the big shot, get overcharged and solicitated, and then signal the troops to make the arrests.

The clip joint was called the Place Pigalle and it featured an exotic dancer named Zorita, who performed onstage with a snake. I went in, played the high roller, bought some champagne, was propositioned several times, received the overpriced bill, and gave the signal for the raid to begin. Police officers crashed through the doors and panic took over. The women making the propositions started heading for the exits, muscling out the patrons who were attempting to do the same thing. Tables were overturned, glass broke everywhere, chairs were damaged, and general chaos erupted.

Forgotten in this melee were Zorita and her snake, who were performing at the time of the raid. The commotion scared the snake, which constricted in fear and caused Zorita to begin choking from the stranglehold. As she tried to wrestle the snake off of her, she shouted for help, all of which went largely unnoticed because of the excitement on the main floor. As the place emptied, the snake finally relaxed and Zorita managed to get her breath back. She began screaming at me, saying I could have gotten her killed. I replied that it was her snake and the last thing I wanted to do was interfere between a woman and her snake. She uttered a few expletives in response to that sentiment.

In any undercover work, there is a line one shouldn't cross. When the work involved drugs, the line for me was not taking any. With prostitution, it was sleeping with a suspect.

In order to break up one prostitution ring we knew of, an undercover cop would call a woman and give her the name of the person who referred him. This code name prompted her to invite the cop over. We then would mark the bills and once she accepted them, we could make the arrest. I proceeded on one of these assignments with a backup team waiting outside for my signal. A pretty, young, dark-haired woman invited me in, took me immediately to the bedroom, and started to disrobe.

"Wait," I called. "Don't you want me to pay you first?" Which was all I wanted to do - give her the money and make the arrest.

"You can pay me afterwards, darling," she answered as more clothes came off.

"I'd rather do it now, if it's all right with you," I said. Panic was beginning to set in. She has to take this money, I thought, I can't get into bed with her.

She relented. "If you insist," she said, holding out her hand, into which I deposited two twenties and a ten dollar bill.

As soon as she took the money, I breathed a sigh of relief and said, "You're under arrest. Get dressed," and ran to the door to let in the other detectives.

They moved in. The woman had made little attempt to get dressed at this point but demurely covered up when the officers followed me into the bedroom.

"Let's go!" I snapped.

"Why?" she asked. "Who are these men?"

One of the other officers asked where the money was. I went to the dresser where she had put the bills down. No money.

"What did you do with the money?" I demanded.

"What money, darling? I love you. What's money got to do with it? We were just about to make love this afternoon when you let these men in."

"What are you talking about? I gave you two twenties and a ten and I want to see them now."

She simply shrugged.

One of the other officers said, "We have to find the money. No money, no case."

I had paid her $50 out of my own pocket, which in 1961 was the better part of my paycheck. I turned on her. "Listen, I don't know where you hid the money, but I'm going to find it if I have to take this room apart piece by piece. Where would you like me to start?"

Something in my look must have caused her to relent. She reached down and proceeded to remove the three bills from inside her vagina, a hiding place we might not have thought of checking. She offered the bills to me, but I could only look down on them in amazement. I turned to one of the officers and said, "You take it."

Narcotics were also part of the vice squad's domain and it was while working on undercover drug cases that I came to be noticed by the Federal Bureau of Narcotics (FBN), the forerunner to the Drug Enforcement Agency (DEA). The Metro Dade Police Department, in cooperation with the federal government, detached me from the vice squad to work with the FBN. The demand for a Spanish-speaking undercover cop to work narcotics with the FBN was high, Metro Dade saw this as a chance to play good Samaritan to the federal government. There were only three other officers in FBN's Miami office at the time, so there was more than enough work to go around.

I became Louis Gonzalez and Ramon Trippino, among other identities that I used interchangeably. I had identification papers and an attitude and I hit the streets running. I was a businessman, but my sole business was drugs. I moved around in a number of circles, ear to the ground, and caught several violators in the process.

If a drug distributor asked me too many questions about my background, I'd always say, "What are you? A cop? I'm here to buy dope from you, that's all. Are you here to sell me the stuff or write a book about me? I don't want to be your friend. I only want to do business."

I didn't want any close relationships with these guys. I told them not to waste my time with social bullshit, "Let's just do the buys and go home." The less I said, the better. The more I talked, the more likely I was to make a mistake. The margin for error in this job was minimal.

My attitude fit the role I was playing, because a high roller drug buyer wasn't the type to make small talk with the in-between distributor. It was simply a matter of telling the would-be violator that my last connection was lost and I needed a new one. They had the stuff I needed, I had the money they wanted. That was the only relationship to make with these guys.

While I played the buyer, I never assumed the role of the user. I hated drugs and the effects they had, and I wasn't about to sample any of the wares. Many dealers asked me to, but my reply was always the same: I buy and sell, I don't use the stuff.

In 1963, the FBN agents convinced me to join them full time. My dream of becoming a federal agent was realized the day I was sworn in by U.S. Federal Court Judge Dyer. I was now in a job where every day could be my last if I made a mistake - I saw a federal agent get killed over a $50 buy - but it was the kind of work I loved doing and to me the rewards of seeing criminals taken off the streets far outweighed the risks involved. As long as agents remained focused on their objective, success rates were high.

The narcotics cases we handled often involved the Mafia, an arm of organized crime whose existence FBI Chief J. Edgar Hoover refused to acknowledge.

In the course of our investigations, we arrested Carmine Galente, Vito Genovese, and Joe Valachi and deported Lucky Luciano. We were involved in these cases only because these organized crime figures were trafficking in drugs. After the Valachi hearings, though, the FBI assumed control of the cases.

I was working undercover with a group of Latinos, mostly Cubans, when one of them told me about this great new shipment they had coming in from California. It was Mexican heroin, the guy told me, the sweetest stuff ever made. I said to bring it to me and I'd consider buying some.

This shipment was fresh, and I do mean fresh. Smugglers had brought it over the Mexican border by filling individual condoms with one-eighth kilo of heroin, inserting the condoms into their anuses and entering the United States. When my contact brought me a couple of sample condoms, the smugglers' feces still coated their outsides.

I looked inside one and all I could see was a dark, muddy substance. "What's this crap?" I demanded. Actually, that's what I thought it might be.

"Oh, man, this is the best stuff, the highest purity heroin in the world. Go ahead, touch it, feel it."

"In the first place," I told him, "I don't touch this shit. In the second place, this stuff looks awful. I don't understand it. My buyers won't understand it. They want white heroin, not brown."

"You don't understand, man, this is the best stuff and we want you to introduce it into the market here. You can take these two on consignment and sell them. See what your people think of it, only don't let them shoot it until you've cut it four or five times. If you don't, they'll probably die, man, this stuff is so pure."

I wrapped the condoms in a couple of napkins and took them to the lab. The contents tested at 95 percent purity, the highest in heroin I'd seen at the time. We ordered some more Mexican heroin from this distributor and busted him and his connection.

I worked on another case that involved a group of Cubans who were going to bring me a large quantity of marijuana to buy. I was to meet two of them in downtown Miami. I had been playing the big shot and wanted to take the role to the limit, so I asked the agent in charge, my boss, Gene Marshall, if I could borrow his Cadillac for the operation. He agreed as long as I returned it immediately afterward. I drove to an outdoor cafe where the two men were sitting. One of them stayed in his seat; the other came over, opened the driver's side door and said, "Move over, I'll drive." I let him. Big mistake.

My gun and badge were under my seat, but they were out of reach now. This guy was running red lights and the surveillance car had lost us. This never would have happened to Jimmy Stewart, I thought.

We ended up in southwest Miami, where "Driver of the Year" pulled up to a two story apartment building. "Wait for me here," he told me, "I'll get the stuff."

He went upstairs and brought down two suitcases containing fifty pounds of marijuana. I had vacated the passenger seat and was standing by the trunk. I had pre-arranged a signal with the surveillance team: when I verified that I had the marijuana and opened the car trunk, the agents would come rushing in. I was hoping they had picked up our trail again. I opened the suitcases, checked each of the twenty-five pound bricks, and then opened the trunk.

Nothing happened.

I waved the trunk door a couple of times. No police officers came to the rescue.

"All right," the dealer said, "you saw it, now close the damn trunk. Where's the money? I thought you said the money was in the trunk."

"While you were upstairs, I moved it to the car," I told him, "so nobody would be suspicious." There actually wasn't a dime anywhere near the Cadillac. "Let's get back in the car."

I went to the driver's side, trying to regain control of the situation. He got in on the passenger side and demanded the money. "Where is it?"

"You know," I said, as calmly as I could, "I see some people over here I don't like. I'm going to drive away from this place." The guy was getting restless, but he let me drive away. I didn't know where he'd grabbed the suitcases, but two or three of his confederates might have been hanging around the building, watching us.

Satisfied that I'd found a reasonably quiet spot, I pulled the car over and parked it.

"Okay. Where's the money?" he growled.

"Under my seat," I replied, and I pulled out the badge and gun. "You're under arrest. Don't even think about moving. I'm going to drive back to pick up your friend, and if you make any kind of movement, this gun is aimed right at your balls. Comprende?"

Shocked into silence, the dealer was afraid to even nod his head, but he understood my message. We drove the twenty-five blocks or so back to the out-door cafe where his partner was still seated. The surveillance car was back there, too. The other dealer got up and started to walk over to the Cadillac.

"Don't say one word," I snarled at the guy in the front seat.

"I'm not saying anything," he managed to answer, looking fearfully at the gun and then his crotch.

The other man came over and I told him to get in the back. He complied, then asked, "How did everything go?"

"Great," I answered, flipping open my badge. "I am a federal narcotics agent and you're under arrest. Don't make a move or I'll kill you."

The man's face paled. "You're a narcotics agent? Oh, shit!" And that's exactly what he proceeded to do, all over his pants, the back seat, and the floorboards of Gene Marshall's Cadillac. He apparently had some kind of bowel disorder. I thought, "Oh, no, not my boss's car!"

The surveillance team ran up. "What's going on? Are you okay?" they asked before the smell hit them. Then they exclaimed, "Jesus Christ! What happened!"

"What do you think? Mr. Dealer here in the backseat just shit on himself."

One of the agents shook his head. "How are you going to explain this to Marshall?" How, indeed? I was terrified.

We took the two back to be booked, showered the one guy off, disposed of his clothing and gave him a pair of janitor's coveralls.

I took the car to the best car wash in town and, while they could get the stains out, the stench remained. I tried every variety of deodorizer available, but the smell seemed permanent. Finally, I returned it to Marshall.

"Here are the keys," I told him, "but I don't think you're going to want this car back."

"Why not? Did you have an accident?"

"You could say that."

He opened the door, got one whiff, and said, "You'll be driving this car for awhile, Navarro." He was not a happy man. (In 1965, Gene Marshall would be convicted for selling out to the underworld and given fifteen years in prison, a far more traumatic situation than what happened to his car.)

That cured me of using a fancy car to play the high roller. I stuck to my Chevy Corvair, and if anyone asked, I told them it was a loaner and that my Rolls was in the shop.

I worked most of my cases alone, except for the surveillance team that provided backup. After some time I was assigned a partner. The man's name was
Jerry Miller and he was due to transfer in any day.

In the meantime, I was close to finishing a case involving one of the largest
cocaine dealers in the country. I had arranged a buy for two kilos of the drug
and designated the location, which I called in to the office to obtain surveillance assistance. I didn't go into the office that day, but my new partner
arrived just as the surveillance team was preparing to leave. They asked if
he wanted to go along and he agreed.

The buy was to take place on a street off of Biscayne Boulevard. I parked
my car, spotted the surveillance team, and called over the three violators to my
car. They handed me the cocaine, which I looked at briefly, then I advised
them that the money was in the trunk. I raised the hood, the pre-arranged signal, and the agents rushed in.

I didn't know who Miller was as he ran up, but thought he could have been
an agent who had tagged along from ATF (Alcohol, Tobacco and Firearms).
Apparently, no one had told him who I was, either, because he grabbed me by
the back of the neck and threw me against the car. I was wearing a new pair of
Air Force style sunglasses that had cost me $30 and when Miller flung me
against the vehicle (and added a boot in my ass), the glasses went flying over
the top of the car and shattered in the street.

One of the agents said to Miller, "Hey, easy, buddy. That's your new partner, Nick Navarro."

I mumbled, "You son of a bitch, you are going to buy me a new pair of sunglasses." He brushed me off and apologized for the kick he gave me.

"The kick I can handle," I told him. "But those glasses set me back thirty
bucks."

"I'll make it up to you," Jerry assured. He did, too. He brought a new pair
of Air Force glasses for me and took me out to dinner.

It was an inauspicious way to start a new partnership, but we had our share
of successes together. What I remember most is that Miller is the only federal
agent I ever shot.

We were working with an informant who was setting up a buy. The informant was wearing a wire and as soon as Jerry and I heard the transaction take
place, we rushed the car, pulled the dealer out, and noticed a semi-automatic

pistol in the guy's belt, cocked and ready to fire. I carefully extracted it and placed it on the seat in our car. We took the dealer to the county jail and booked him.

We then headed to the office (we were located in an old post office building), where we needed to clean up a little. We were expecting an internal security investigator who was in town to do an audit.

I carried the cocked semi-automatic pistol inside and Jerry told me I should release the trigger before the gun went off. I pointed it at the ceiling, but in the process of trying to secure it, the gun discharged. The round went up, hit the ceiling, ricocheted and hit the wall, and then the floor, and then I lost sight of it.

All of a sudden, Miller exclaimed, "You shot me. Thanks a lot."

"I shot you?" I couldn't believe it. The bullet had grazed his knee after it hit the floor, but the round had lost most of its punch and hadn't done any real damage to Miller.

"I'm sorry I missed," I told him, "I was aiming for your head."

Most of our work was in Dade County. Broward County was still a sleepy residential area, with its population explosion still five or six years away. However, we did manage to set up and arrest a Broward County bar owner named Porky Baines for selling marijuana. He ran a club in Fort Lauderdale off of Federal Highway and Oakland Park Boulevard, an area that today is a mass of buildings, restaurants, and shops, but was quiet then. The bar was called Porky's and was later made famous in a series of movies by the same name.

In 1965, I experienced the first downside to working as a federal agent: a transfer. It's one of those things you must accept if you work for the federal government. After I'd worked two years in Miami, the FBN decided I was needed more in their largest office in New York City.

When I moved my family to New York City, it was mutual hatred at first sight. The city looked like a sprawling, dirty, urban mess to me, probably because Miami, by comparison, was spacious, clean, and still largely rural. The differences in climate don't need elaboration.

We picked Staten Island to live in because it reminded us somewhat of South Florida. It was not built up much at that time; in fact, the Verrazano Bridge (where, every fall, more than 20,000 runners start the New York City marathon) had not yet been completed. We lived in an area called Grimes

Hill, near Wagner College, where we could watch the boat traffic going in and out of the harbor. Many days I took the ferry to work, and I developed a special relationship with the lady I passed each way - the Statue of Liberty. She always reminded me of where I'd come from and the progress I'd made in this country. I never tired of that sight, and it often brought a lump in my throat.

The New York City office was the largest of all FBN locations, with 55 to 60 agents stationed there. In addition to our offices in the United States, we had branches in Mexico City, Lima, Istanbul, Rome, and Paris.

Our undercover operations here often grew into major cases, involving several countries and tons of contraband. As the cases became more involved, the paperwork increased and the field time decreased. The kingpins were well isolated and often untouchable. To contact sources close to them, we usually used informants. Using information from informants was different from gathering it ourselves. We had to sit back and document their work, rather than create it ourselves. I learned an entire new side of law enforcement over the next couple of years.

The best known case we handled was the French Connection affair, run by New York City detectives Eddie Egan and Sonny Grasso. It was a long, tedious task, involving different countries, networking, a lengthy waiting game, and mountains of paperwork before the case finally broke. We didn't capture all the criminals, but there was a multitude of arrests as a result. Our agency was called in because of the lack of resources at NYPD. It was a total office effort but not the largest bust we handled.

Another case involved the arrests of Brazilians, Italians, French, and Americans and the seizure of ninety-seven kilos of heroin smuggled in by a U.S. warrant officer who was stationed in France. Among those arrested were several organized crime figures.

In another situation, we arrested two police officers from Sydney, Australia, who smuggled heroin inside corsets. The corsets were difficult to spot if they were pulled tight enough, thus making them a good smuggling apparatus.

When I was working undercover in New York among the Hispanic and Latin communities, I spent a lot of time in an area called Needle Park, near Seventy-Second Street and Amsterdam. It was a park composed almost exclusively of dealers and addicts. I was supposed to meet a couple of the dealers in a bar nearby to conduct a transaction. I was in the place ahead of the appointed hour, sipping a beer (one was my limit and I had learned to nurse it a long time if I had to), when a lady came running out of the bathroom yelling, "There's a dead woman in there, I can't wake her up." I went inside and there was a young girl, blond, beautiful, no more than sixteen years old, probably from the Midwest, with a needle and syringe still sticking out of her arm. She was dead, no question, and I couldn't help thinking that this could be my daughter.

She had track marks all over her arms and no identification. She was probably a prostitute who had long forgotten the city she left or ran away from. She would be buried in an unmarked grave. I was outraged. Here was someone's daughter, someone's granddaughter, someone's sister, someone's niece - a human being, for God's sake.

Anytime somebody says we should legalize drugs, I think of that girl. It's difficult to convey this image in a courtroom where a jury or a judge can't see or feel the impact of drugs on the street.

Working in New York was more dangerous than working in Miami because of the depth of corruption within the city's own law enforcement ranks. There was a real concern that our covers could be blown at any time by our own side. We were careful how we handled busts. More often than not, I would be thrown in the police car with the dealers and placed under arrest myself to protect my identity. That move had an added benefit, too.

If I was captured along with the guys I had set up, I could try to obtain even more information on the way to the station. They'd be somewhat frightened by all that had transpired and I'd tell them, "Look, if I can make bond, is there anyone I can go see for you?" and find another potential arrest. Or, I'd tell a dealer that I'd need another connection when I got out, and ask if he knew anybody he could trust. I picked up a number of new leads that way.

I had several sets of identities, criminal records, whatever I needed. Because so many ethnic groups were represented in New York, it was a good place to try out several different disguises. I had one problem, though. There was a NYPD cop named Bermudez who looked almost exactly like me. This topic would come up occasionally and, of course, I would truthfully deny I was Bermudez, but I hated for any of the people I was working with to use the term "cop" and my name in the same sentence.

One day I received a phone call from an informant who told me to go up to the Bronx where he had a dealer set up to deliver three ounces of heroin. I didn't have a car that day, so I asked for volunteers to loan me a car. An agent named Clarence Cook tossed me his keys.

"It's not a Cadillac, is it?" I asked.

"No, T-Bird."

I asked another agent, Leo Thomas, to act as backup. He followed me to the Bronx. The informant and suspect approached the car and got in, the dealer in the front seat, the informant in the rear. We discussed the transaction. I was about to make the buy and signal Thomas when all of a sudden we heard, "605 to Group Six, 605 to Group Six," coming from the glove compartment.

The dealer nearly jumped through the roof. "What the hell is that?"

"What the hell is what?" I said, as calmly as possible.

"This is Group Six. Go ahead, 605," the glove compartment squawked. With that, the dealer hit the street running. He may have reached Syracuse by sunset.

I opened the glove compartment and, sure enough, there was Cook's police radio, still turned on. The informant said he never saw the dealer after that.

I was in demand for assignments other than undercover. The Treasury Department often asked me to teach at the department's training academy in Washington, D.C. My specialty, naturally, was undercover work. Jerry Miller, my old partner from Miami, was frequently assigned there at the same time, so we'd exchange war stories and get reacquainted every so often.

Promotion from a GS-9 to a GS-11 usually took two years, but the department decided to promote me in one year. I had to document the number of cases I had handled, the arrests, the teaching assignments, the overtime, and so forth. As I was putting these records together, excited about this unexpected advancement, it struck me how little I'd been home during the last year.

At that time, my marriage was a little shaky, and if I wondered why, I didn't have to look any further. I never punched a time clock, but there were a lot of twenty-hour days and countless nights away from home in my records. No wonder things were a little rocky at home. I was never there. My problems at home and the city itself were starting to get me down.

I realized that all the hours spent at work could be wiped out in a heart-

beat, and I walked into these types of situations so often. On a recent assignment, I was with a drug dealer to set up a buy and, convinced I was a cop, he
drew out a .25 before I could react, stuck it in my side, and pulled the trigger.
The gun misfired and I grabbed it before he could try again. I'd sidestepped
death by a stroke of sheer luck.

Later, I infiltrated a group of Cuban heroin and cocaine dealers working
with an informant. Unfortunately, one of the dealers was from Miami and he
recognized me as a federal agent. The informant was beaten and tortured to
find out the truth. He stayed silent, at a high price. He had been well
entrenched and trusted, and it was now his word against the Miamian's. The
Cubans wanted the informant to get me over to their place to confront me
with this knowledge. If I was really a federal agent, they'd kill me.

The informant went straight to the agency and told them the story, adding
that the Cubans knew where I lived in Staten Island. The agent in charge,
George Halpin, called me in and said he was going to send me to school in
Washington, D.C., and he thought it might be a good idea to take my family -
to visit my wife's relatives in Pennsylvania perhaps.

"George, I teach at that school. Why do you want to send me as a student?"

"The agency wants you to go, Nick. What can I tell you? I think you should
consider taking your family, too. That's all I was suggesting."

This was unusual. The agency rarely made any suggestions about family
and whether to take them along on a trip. I questioned him further and he
finally told me the story about the Cubans. "Basically, Nick, they intend to kill
you and perhaps your family, too. We want you out of town. You're too valuable to lose."

I volunteered to take my family to Pennsylvania and come back to try to
flush these guys out, but Halpin wouldn't hear of it. I was D.C. bound again.
The agency did round up the Cubans with the informant's assistance, and it
wasn't too long after we'd left when it was considered safe for us to return.

Personally, I'd had enough of New York. I wanted to put down some roots,
preferably in a climate and area I liked. The problem was I couldn't do it as a
federal agent. I had asked for any number of transfers back to Miami, but my
requests were always denied. Even if I did get transferred back, there was no
guarantee I'd be in Miami forever. Transfers were a way of life for a federal
government agent.

As much as I hated to turn my back on the dreams of my youth, my desire to return to a better environment triumphed over my desire to be a federal agent. I would be happy as long as I could remain in law enforcement, I'd be happy no matter whether the agency was local, state, federal, or otherwise.

When I was with the FBN in Miami a few years earlier, a University of Miami law professor named Bill Reed was part of a blue ribbon committee investigating corruption in Miami and Dade County. I had been one of the agents assigned to work with the committee as a liaison, helping to identify those involved in criminal enterprises. In 1968, Reed had just been named by Governor Claude Kirk of Florida to head up the state's first Florida Bureau of Law Enforcement (FBLE), an investigative branch of the state police, which combined the Florida Sheriff's Bureau in Tallahassee with some smaller law enforcement agencies.

Reed contacted me to see if I was interested in relocating back to Miami. Hell, yes, I was interested - anything to get back to Miami. In addition to my personal preference, I felt a change of scenery could be just the thing to help my marriage along. Reed wanted me to use my undercover expertise to train a group of agents in a new branch of law enforcement as well as handle operations myself. He said he'd match my current salary.

My family and I left New York City and the federal government behind and headed south, back to the sunny climate of South Florida.

In 1965, when I transferred to New York, there was a moderate amount of drug trafficking in Dade County. When I returned in 1968, cocaine and heroin were flowing freely.

A man I had arrested in Miami a few years earlier, Armando Dulzaides, had become a fugitive and escaped to South America, but he was recaptured in the American zone in Panama. He was extradited back to the United States and sitting in a cell in a federal penitentiary in Atlanta, Georgia. The only person he would talk to was me.

What he told me was amazing. A chemist by trade, he had helped some Colombians set up a laboratory to extract cocaine hydrochloride from coca paste that was being imported from Peru. Once the cocaine was made, it was sealed inside secret compartments of suitcases to smuggle it into the United States. Dulzaides helped draw a diagram of how the cocaine was concealed and it led to the successful confiscation of the drug in Miami, New York and

San Juan, Puerto Rico. Dulzaides also put the bureau on notice that Colombia was becoming a major cocaine trafficker.

The objective of the FBLE was to assist local law enforcement agencies with their more complex cases. The hard-to-solve drug and homicide cases generally fell under our jurisdiction in the late 1960s. We used a special crime lab that had been set up in Tallahassee and typically had resources the local agencies didn't.

In one instance, a Hollywood (Broward County) police chief asked for our help on a case involving the murders of two women. Our investigation into the case led us back to a well-known thief, Jack "Murph the Surf" Murphy, reputed to have stolen the 563 carat Star of India diamond, among other items, from the American Museum of Natural History. Since the stolen items were eventually returned, Murphy was never prosecuted for that crime.

Murphy was a painter and a musician - a talented guy, who, unfortunately, channeled his abilities into activities on the wrong side of the law. The murders of the two women in Hollywood led right to his doorstep.

As the case unfolded, we put together the details. Murphy and his partner, a tough-guy karate expert named Jack Griffith, along with two women from California, had stolen a substantial amount of negotiable bonds. The two women had become involved because they were trying to raise money to help get their boyfriends out of prison in California. As time wore on and Murphy insisted the bonds be left alone since they were hot, the women became restless. They didn't understand why the bonds couldn't be moved and confronted Murphy with the demand to give them their share.

Murphy wasn't about to do any such thing. He and Griffith killed the two women and took them on a boat ride on Whiskey Creek, off the Broward intracoastal waterway. The creek is small and was used quite often by rumrunners in the 1920s. Located within John Lloyd State Park, it was a very secluded spot and not often traveled by boaters. The men slit the girls' stomachs to keep them from bloating, tied cinder blocks to their legs, and dumped them overboard.

The creek rises and ebbs with the tides, and at one low tide, a rare boater passed and spotted a foot sticking out of the water. The bodies were recovered and identified, and we started our investigation. Murphy was tied into the murders through an informant for the FBN who was living and working in the

Virgin Islands and who'd heard through his sources about the negotiable bond job and the women's subsequent murders.

I was waiting for the indictment and trailing Murphy on a daily basis so we wouldn't lose him. He drove away from his residence one morning and I followed as usual. He turned down a side street, and when he saw that I, too, had made the turn, he wheeled around and pulled up next to me.

"I've noticed you've been following me around and I wanted to save you some trouble," he said. I simply sat there and listened. "I'm going to exchange a pair of shoes for Connie (his girlfriend), then I'm going to my attorney's office on Lincoln Road in Miami Beach. I'll keep you in sight. Okay?"

What could I say? I agreed.

After the stop at the store, Murphy pulled into the parking lot of his lawyer's office building. He went upstairs and I sat and waited for him to return. And waited. And waited some more.

After about three hours, my heart sunk as I realized it had been way too long. Murph the Surf had given me the slip. I rushed upstairs to Jack Nagel's office and found the lawyer waiting for me, a smile across his face.

"Sorry to do this to you, but Murph knows about the indictment and he wanted to put some things in order without you on his back. I promise he'll return to town in a couple of days and surrender to you."

Losing him was embarrassing, but Murph kept his word. He surrendered two days later, and the jewel thief went down for murder. Later, he sent me a painting he'd done in prison. It was great work, but it's difficult to look at the painting without seeing an image of those two women, stomachs slit open, cinder blocks tied to their legs. A criminal can't be excused even if he happens to be a good artist.

Narcotics busts were prevalent and I continued my undercover routine. One time, while pretending to be a guy just in from Panama, I met a dealer in a room at the Columbus Hotel in Miami. He was acting paranoid the minute he walked in. He checked the room thoroughly, looking under the bed and in the bathroom, and I asked him what was up. The agents working with me were in the next hotel room.

He said we had to be very careful, there was a Cuban narcotics officer named Navarro that was busting everyone in town. I told him I wasn't worried about any agent busting me.

"Just be careful," he warned. "He's your height, he has some graying in the temples like yours, he's about your weight. In fact, you look a little like him."

I waved him off and we concluded the transaction. When we busted the dealer, I said, "Guess what? I am him."

About a year after joining the FBLE, I accepted a promotion to supervisor of the Orlando office in Central Florida. It was the first time I was officially in charge of a group of agents, and I welcomed the challenge. It was my opportunity to run the operation from the top down, within our sphere of influence, and train undercover people in what I'd learned - information that could be put directly to use in their field work.

Probably the biggest bust we had was at a tiny airport in Spruce Creek, just south of Daytona Beach in Volusia County. It involved a smuggling ring we'd been making a case on for some time and it all came to a head on a hot July evening in 1971.

We had staked out the Spruce Creek airport for about four weeks knowing this was one of the places the group liked to bring in dope. On a Saturday afternoon, our patience was finally rewarded. A plane landed and two men unloaded nineteen burlap sacks and then disappeared into the woods. The plane took off. The pilot was actually a Customs agent and my informant was on board as well. That evening, a pickup truck slowly approached the field, with no headlights on, and made its way toward the abandoned sacks. The driver was joined by the two men who'd been waiting in the woods all this time. They loaded the sacks into the pickup truck and headed toward a hole they'd cut in the airport fence. We bolted out from behind our hiding places and ordered them to halt.

They opened fire, which we immediately returned. One man quickly gave himself up, while his associates made a dash for it. We chased them into the woods and gunfire erupted from one of the suspect's AR18 automatic rifle. Agents' guns sounded in retort and it was quite a shoot out for a time; it was hard to see, and the danger of a stray round was imminent. After about fifteen minutes, we caught one of the two men. The search for the last man took nearly fourteen hours, but we finally found him in neighboring Port Orange.

The nineteen sacks contained 1,100 pounds of marijuana, which had a street value of over a million dollars at that time. We grabbed a few weapons, too, including the rifle. Almost every one of our busts included the confiscation of firearms. It was scary to think how well armed the criminals were in this country.

That same year, 1971, my friend Bill Reed left Florida to take the number two position in the FBI under Clarence Kelly, Hoover's successor. This left me in another quandary.

I liked what I was doing. It was great to be back in Florida. But the person appointed to take charge of the FBLE after Reed left, a man named Trolstrep, did not possess the same views on law enforcement that I did. He wasn't a team player and didn't share the same objective of catching criminals, focusing instead on the small parts of the operation rather than the ultimate goal. Taking direction from him would be virtually impossible for me.

After twelve years on the job, I was at another career crossroad.

Two

Building An Organized Crime Division

W ITH BILL REED OFF TO WASHINGTON, D.C., AND TROLSTREP THE NEW Florida Bureau of Law Enforcement's head, it was re-evaluation time for me again.

The move back to Florida had not solved my marriage difficulties. The type of work I did, the danger involved, the long hours, the time away from home - none of that had really changed. I loved my family and wanted them to love my work as much as I did, but it wasn't meant to be. It was, unfortunately, not an unusual story - that of a police officer whose marriage suffers and ultimately fails. The job seemed to simply grab me and not let go, and I didn't fight it.

I decided to attempt a return to the federal ranks. When I began working for the FBLE in 1968, a couple of government people had contacted me to persuade me to return to federal law enforcement. When I called them in 1971, the reception was still warm and they still remembered my accomplishments. The job door was open. After some discussion, the government confirmed by letter the offer of a GS-14 rank, which paid $17,700 annually. In 1971, this was decent money. I would be assigned to Dallas, Texas, whose climate was not much different from the Florida weather I loved.

During that time, I had also inquired about a position in Broward County that was being created by Sheriff Ed Stack. I had met Stack a couple of times during my work with the FBLE when a case took me into Broward. He had received a $360,000 grant to establish a new unit - an organized crime division that would take cases that were too small for the federal government and too large for local enforcement agencies in and around Fort Lauderdale. This unit would handle the mid-level trafficking cases as well as other organized crime situations.

Stack was a lawyer from New York state. He owned property in Pompano Beach, located in Broward County, including a hotel. He relocated to South Florida in the 1960s and eventually became mayor of Pompano Beach. In 1968, then Broward County Sheriff Alan Michel was indicted on gambling charges. Michel was acquitted and ran against Stack in the next sheriff's election, but by that time Stack was entrenched, Michel's reputation damaged and Stack won easily.

Stack called me to set up an interview for the position of head of his new Organized Crime Division (OCD). He was familiar with my reputation as an experienced undercover cop and thought I might be the perfect choice to run the type of operations he had in mind. Our interview went well. Stack was a reformed alcoholic and had a ruddy complexion to prove it. With a short, thin build that contrasted with his Irish temperament, he was a thoughtful, intelligent man who wanted to eradicate the serious drug problem developing in South Florida.

He was impressed enough with my credentials and the way I handled the interview to offer me the position of head of the new unit. My problem was that now I had two jobs. Stack solved my dilemma after he reviewed the letter from the feds offering me Dallas and $17,700. He agreed to match the federal offer.

I was thrilled. My salary would be $17,700 and I would get to stay in Florida! There was no hesitation in accepting the job. So in October 1971, Broward County was my new destination and the worry about transfers was removed. The new unit was a Broward County unit and it was going to stay that way. I was back in South Florida - home again.

Fort Lauderdale was beginning to grow. The Cuban influx in Dade County was having an effect on all of South Florida. It was becoming a real melting pot. A large number of Central and South Americans were coming in, while our neighbors to the north in Canada were also contributing their share of immigrants. Relocation from other parts of the country, particularly the northeast, eventually gave us the third largest concentration of Jewish people in the country. It was a fascinating population mix, and the entire area was taking shape all at once. What used to be distinctly different regions in Dade, Broward, and Palm Beach Counties were now joining to form one large urban sprawl across county lines. In New York City, you can drive in and out of five different buroughs, often without knowing that you've crossed any lines. The same was becoming true for these three South Florida counties.

The organized crime unit was a hush-hush operation from the beginning. Cloaked in secrecy, we were housed off site, separated from the rest of the Broward County Sheriff's Office (BSO). Our first location was the old Governor's Club Hotel, where we took the upstairs suites. The Gore family, who owned the hotel and also controlled the Fort Lauderdale News and Sun Sentinel newspapers, had agreed to lease the county the necessary space. Only Ed Stack knew where we were, a situation we deemed important to protect the identities of the undercover cops I would have working for me.

Stack and I developed some stringent requirements to select the best people. Our initial group consisted of twelve officers, who came to be known as the Dirty Dozen. I brought in a couple of men from Brevard County who had worked with me in the Orlando office of the Florida Bureau of Law Enforcement. We also had two women in the unit. It was, in our estimation, a formidable team.

For some of them it was the last chance before being dismissed from the force, but I welcomed the challenge of molding these individuals into good undercover officers. They had talent, but usually had difficulty with supervisors; they were loners who resented the everyday bureaucratic intrusions that the sheriff's office often holds. I didn't care about their past supervisory problems. They would have a long leash with me, which I wouldn't pull in as long as they were successful. There were no clocks to punch, no set hours, no rigid structure. Instead, their job was to make cases and then arrests, using the law enforcement techniques they all possessed. I would keep an eye on each one, but only to sense signs of trouble that might put their lives in jeopardy.

I believe nearly anyone can be trained to be an undercover cop. Most successes in this job come from an inner drive to exterminate, within legal restraints, the criminal element. The Dirty Dozen all harbored that drive. The rest of the job was networking: meeting people, finding out who was dealing and then setting them up. At all times, an undercover cop has to have control of the situation. To be in control, a cop must be firm, though not rigid; never backpedal or pussyfoot around; be direct; and trust no one. Losing control often means losing one's life.

It was theater, life imitating art, a role played to achieve the desired result - an arrest. One must never forget, however, that it is only a role, that an undercover operative is, first and foremost, a police officer, regardless of the disguise. There is an inherent danger that a cop will get so comfortable with the part being played that he or she will cross the line and be more underworld than undercover. It was my job to look for signs of this danger and pull that officer off the case. If someone wanted to take the part of a biker to infiltrate a motorcycle gang, that was fine. The long hair, the tattoos, the leather outfits were all okay as long as he remembered he was a cop.

I trusted all my people and never had a problem with them. Honest mistakes were made, of course, but I wanted them to learn from these mistakes and not make the same ones again. A mistake in our line of work could be the last one we ever made.

Networking in the criminal underworld helped us make cases. Once we arrested someone, we tried to turn that individual into an informant in an attempt to move up the criminal ladder. If we could use a good informant, the success rate for scuttling an entire operation, instead of only one or two people in it, were much higher. We tried to achieve a domino effect; one person was arrested, became an informant, and led us to someone higher up on the criminal organizational chart, and then this person would give us someone even higher. We would pursue this avenue as far as we could take it.

Informants were often critical to an operation's success. But because they were usually criminals themselves who had agreed to help in exchange for a reduced sentence or even complete forgiveness of their past illegal enterprises, they were often the weakest links in the chain of any operation. Running such an operation was a delicate business that was learned only by experience. The more times we worked with informants, the better we could identify good candidates for this type of duty. We often had to work with people who we'd normally never associate with, but they could produce some solid arrests.

It was through informants that we often progressed from the "one gram of marijuana bust" to the eventual twelve-ton bust. As we continued to be successful at arresting the lowest criminals on the underworld ladder, we were able to make bigger and higher profile arrests, confiscating drugs and money. It was highly unlikely we could get to the kingpin, as that person was well insulated from the inner workings of our operations, but our unit deterred millions of dollars in drugs from entering the country and quickly moved from midlevel cases to large busts the federals usually made.

I didn't try to corner the market on the glory of our unit's successes. In almost every major bust, I involved old friends of mine from Customs, the new DEA (created out of my old unit the Federal Bureau of Narcotics), the ATF, and even the Secret Service. I had a good rapport with these agencies and we all shared a common goal - keeping the criminal element off the street.

Our organized crime unit, however, was not necessarily accepted by other police departments. The chief of police in Fort Lauderdale thought we were infringing on his territory when we followed cases into his city limits. He and others like him just didn't understand what we were doing. We weren't trying to make any other departments look bad, we were simply following the criminals in the cases we were working on, wherever they led us.

One night, I was doing surveillance on a case with one of my undercover investigators, Phil Lindsley, a big black man who had been a boxer while in the Marines. Lindsley was waiting for a pre-arranged drug delivery, and we were set to make some arrests once the deal was made. The buy was set up in a white Fort Lauderdale neighborhood and as Lindsley waited, he was approached by two Fort Lauderdale police officers who told him to move along. Lindsley replied that he would as soon as his informant showed up. The Fort Lauderdale cops didn't know who Lindsley was, since his identity and our organization were a well-kept secret, and he told them little, as he hoped to see the dealer pull up at any minute. This didn't please the Fort Lauderdale police. When they request someone to move, they don't want to hear anything else.

Apparently, after sizing up the ex-Marine boxer, they called for backup and soon there were six police officers gathered around Lindsley. There goes this bust, I thought. Lindsley must have thought the same thing because he then

told the cops who he was and what he was doing. Of course, he had no identification with him, working undercover, and the police officers refused to
believe he was really a cop.

I could see that the situation was deteriorating fast, but before I could
make a move, Lindsley was battling the six cops - and the Fort Lauderdale
police weren't winning. He laid out a couple of them before I could get over
there with my ID and straighten the mess out.

Stack met with Fort Lauderdale's Chief Johnson to settle this matter. He
described our assignments and made it clear we were not going to relax our
efforts to pursue criminals. This type of operation was new and it would take
some time for the local municipal forces to become familiar with it, but our
success rate spoke volumes for us. Some of the police chiefs never got comfortable with it, being more accustomed to protecting their turf themselves,
but the rank-and-file law enforcement officers loved our results. The compromise between Stack and Johnson was to have two Fort Lauderdale police officers assigned to our unit and to keep the lines of communication open on
some of our cases.

An example of this cooperation was the case of Fred Chapman, a criminal
who had been arrested fifty-three times in Dade County but had not been convicted. His streak was broken when he crossed the Broward County line.

He owned a country estate in Broward where he counted each week's take
from his gambling enterprises. Having probable cause that the dirty money
was in Broward County, we obtained a search warrant and discovered
Chapman with $138,000. The feds took over the case from that point, and
were able to bring him to trial and get a conviction. In Dade County, they were
zero for fifty-three with Chapman, but in Broward County we were one for
one. This was the kind of result I liked.

The man who wrote out the search warrant was a legal advisor to the sheriff's office, assigned to our OCD unit, named Bob Butterworth, presently
Florida's Attorney General.

Butterworth was part of a two-man legal team working for the state attorney's office. His associate was Ken Jenne (now a state senator) and the duo was
affectionately referred to as Batman (Jenne) and Robin (Butterworth). One
night, Butterworth and I were working on obtaining a search warrant I needed for an early morning raid. Progress was slow and I felt Butterworth needed

some extra motivation or we would never have the warrant finished in time for a judge to sign it that night. I told him I was going out for a couple of hamburgers and since he was working hard on the warrant, I would treat. I left, but only after locking the door from the outside and taking the inside key with me.

I drove around for a short time then called him from a phone booth.

"Hey, Bob, how's it going?"

"Great. Where are the burgers?"

"Well," I answered, "I have to admit I didn't exactly play fair with you this time. In fact, you're locked in the office as we speak."

I heard him slam the phone down and rush to the door. He returned and growled, "You SOB, Navarro. What made you pull a stunt like that?"

"Relax, Bob, relax," I told him. "I'll be back with the food soon and I'll trade you the burgers for a finished search warrant."

A few more expletives came out of Butterworth before he agreed to finish it in haste. All things considered, he did an excellent job on the warrant, which was signed in time for the search to be conducted as scheduled.

Drugs were fast becoming the biggest problem in South Florida, most of our initial work was drug related. We didn't ignore other organized crime and were successful in bringing down other enterprises as well, but narcotics was where the action was.

One case led to a Florida International University professor who was manufacturing Quaaludes by the millions in a laboratory he had built in his house in Homestead, Florida. We had word that a lot of students were becoming violently ill from ingesting these pills. It turned out the professor was lacing the Quaaludes with PCP and the overall dosage result was so strong, it was making people sick. One of our undercover cops, posing as a student, infiltrated the group around this professor, and eventually made a buy from him, and discovered the location of the lab. We obtained a search warrant, made the raid, confiscated the lab, and arrested the man who went from instructor to prisoner in the blink of an eye. He had no previous criminal record, this being his first and only venture into crime.*

FOOTNOTE: *Miami Herald journalist Edna Buchanan (now a noted author) chronicled this story and others about our department for her paper. She was far more objective in her reporting than many of her colleagues who covered the crime scene in South Florida.

One of the many dangers of undercover work with criminals involved with narcotics is the rip-off. It was not uncommon for drug dealers to try to walk away with both the drugs and the money, leaving dead bodies in their wake.

One close call involved two of our undercover officers and a Metro Dade cop, who had set up a $50,000 cocaine buy from a man representing a group of Jamaicans. One of our cops, a female, was wired so the surveillance team outside could hear what was transpiring.

After our team was inside the apartment where the deal was to take place, the Jamaican edged his way over to a closet and opened the door to reveal another man with a gun. Rather than kill our operatives, the drug dealers bound them and demanded the money. The surveillance team knew the deal had gone sour and rushed the apartment. The agents inside freed themselves from the ropes that had loosely tied their wrists and opened fire at the fleeing suspects, who had run the minute they heard the agents outside their door. Bullets were flying everywhere, killing one of the Jamaicans and wounding the other. However, in the confusion, a bullet from the gun of one of our men in the surveillance team struck one of the undercover officers. He survived, fortunately, but it took a long time for the agent who fired the shot to shake off the trauma of having wounded a fellow officer.

Our well-kept secret operation was becoming famous around the Broward County Sheriff's Office. Whenever I reported to Sheriff Stack in his office, I used the cover that I was a Bell & Howell salesman to prevent anyone from knowing who I was. I think his secretary started to have her suspicions, however, since Ed Stack rarely, if ever, spoke to salespeople himself, and our meetings lasted much longer than a sales call should have.

Stack's secretary's name was Sharron Watkins, an attractive redhead whose appearance made the trips up to see Stack infinitely more bearable. I was now divorced and was definitely interested in getting to know Sharron better.

She seemed to be a terrific secretary, always keeping Stack's head above water, handling his appointments like clockwork, keeping the Broward County Sheriff's Office well organized and efficient. I was impressed with her and when she finally found out who I really was, I began pestering her for a date. She was recently divorced, but she kept putting me off. This old bowser doesn't know when to quit, though, and succeeded in wearing her down until she agreed to a date.

Sharron was not only a past homecoming queen but a model who appeared in several ad layouts by Coca-Cola, Hertz, and Nestea. She was in Life magazine and was even featured on a Kodak billboard that hung in Grand Central Station. She had turned to modeling as a second choice; her childhood dream was to be an FBI agent - my kind of woman. Unfortunately, the FBI wasn't hiring women when she wanted a job.

I knew from the minute I saw her outside of Stack's office that she was the woman I wanted. She felt the same way I did, and within a year or so after that hard-earned first date, we decided to get married.

Ed Stack was licensed to perform marriages so we asked him if he'd marry us. At first he agreed, but a month before the wedding, he opted out. He explained that he had a bad record: he had married eight couples and seven of them had since divorced. He thought with my Latin temperament and Sharron's Irish heritage, the marriage already had long odds, and he didn't want to make them any longer. A minister married us instead and I can honestly say it's the best thing that's happened in my life.

Success continued in my work as well as my private life. I had maintained contact with an informant from New York, a Canadian who used to live off the earnings of some of his "girls." He had been a reliable source for me in New York and was now doing his part in South Florida. One of his girls had met a guy who could supply up to two kilograms of heroin and also had obtained several million dollars' worth of stolen airline travel tickets through the robbery of a travel agency. When my informant passed this information along to me, I told him to set up a buy, which he arranged to occur at the Diplomat Hotel. I decided to handle the case personally. I brought along an undercover operative, Sandy Klukey, who agreed to pose as one on my girls in need of a "hit." I wore a thick pair of prescription glasses, which I'd recently found out I needed.

Once inside our hotel room, we didn't have long to wait before a knock came and we were joined by my informant and the targeted violator. I had carried a suitcase in with me, filled with bills to the tune of $100,000. Waiting in a connecting room were backup officers. When the dealer came in, I recognized him immediately, a fellow Cuban who had been a Miami policeman with me. His name was Martin Garcia. I thought, oh, no, we're sunk. He'll know me for sure.

But he didn't. I watched him carefully as we talked, but the dumb bastard had no idea who I was. It had been at least ten years since we'd seen each other and I was wearing thick glasses, but, hell, the man was a cop. I thought of our previous associations while on the Metro Dade police force. There weren't that many Cubans on the force, so we tended to know one another. Garcia and I had an occasional beer or Cuban coffee together, but nothing more than superficial conversation. He had been fired while I was still in Miami working at the Federal Bureau of Narcotics. In fact, after that happened, I went to see Garcia and tried to make an informant out of him. He had said he would let me know if he learned about any illegal enterprises, but I never heard from him. Until now.

Garcia said he didn't have the heroin with him but wanted to count the money first then return to his source to pick up the drugs. His source, he said, was a man named Angel Vigo. My heart did another somersault. Angel Vigo! I'd arrested him only a few years ago, in 1968. I remembered it vividly because we pulled him out of bed when he was making love to his wife. They were so involved in what they were doing, they never heard us come in the bedroom. Then - arrestus interruptus! I was sure Vigo would recollect that incident, too. This whole deal was beginning to make me nervous.

Garcia said it would take him a couple of hours, but he'd be back and make the exchange: his heroin for my cash. Out the door he went. We had a unit on the street, but they lost Garcia. Unlike in the movies, it's difficult to follow someone in an automobile without them knowing it, so the chances of losing a tail were often better than maintaining contact.

Garcia didn't want to take the informant back to the source, so the three of us sat in the hotel room, waiting for a former police officer turned drug dealer, who may have recognized me after all, to call back.

Three hours went by without a word. He probably recognized me and, with good cop instincts, didn't betray his knowledge, figuring he had only one chance to get out of there. The surveillance team wanted to leave after four hours had elapsed, but I convinced them to wait another hour longer.

At four hours and thirty-five minutes, Garcia called, saying he was on his way and would be up in a few minutes. What he and Vigo had probably done was cut the heroin one more time to make an additional sale later. Greedy SOBs!

The surveillance team on the street called us when Garcia pulled into the hotel parking lot and told us another man had driven in right behind him. Vigo, I wondered? I described Vigo to the cops and they confirmed he was in the parking lot, too. Vigo handed Garcia a bag, and up the elevator came my old associate, while his source remained downstairs.

Garcia came in and handed us the bag, and Sandy Klukey immediately started begging for some of the heroin. Pleading desperately, she said she needed a hit now. I gave her some of the heroin and she took a syringe out of her purse and went into the bathroom. While Garcia thought she was using it, Sandy actually tested it. When she came out, she said it was real good smack. I said to Garcia that it was time for me to pay up, based on that recommendation, which was the signal for the back-up team to charge in. As they did, I drew my gun and said, "Martin Garcia, you're under arrest for trafficking in narcotics. Turn around while I pat you down."

I frisked him and when he turned to face me he said, "I'm the dumbest son of a bitch on the face of the earth. Nick Navarro! Now I remember you! Let's make a deal, Nick. I can be your informant. We can work together."

"Thanks, but no thanks, Martin. You had an opportunity to be an informant once. Sorry, no job openings today."

The team in the street captured Vigo and we booked both men for drug dealing. What a waste! Garcia, a man who once had something going for him, now only listened to the sound of dollar bills. Well, it had landed him where he belonged - off the streets.

Our police activities were not confined to land. We had a number of successes on the high seas, too. Boats were a common form of transportation to bring drugs into the United States.

A couple of my undercover operatives were approached by some smugglers and told that if they wanted to make a buy, they would have to acquire two medium-size boats, sail them out beyond the three-mile territorial limit, and make contact with a mother ship from Colombia called the Escopesca. When they hooked up with the ship, there would be 24,000 pounds of marijuana that could be offloaded onto our crafts.

My operatives agreed to see what they could work out, regarding transportation and money. I felt there must be some way to discourage these huge shipments from coming in and contacted some people in Customs. They did some quick research and cited a 1929 law still in existence called the Hovering Vessels Act. Enacted to capture rumrunners during Prohibition, this statute permitted the seizure of a ship on the high seas if it was carrying contraband bound for the United States or unloading contraband bound for our shores. This seemed to fit the situation we had. The Customs agents concurred and agreed to participate in the deal.

We arranged for two medium-size boats for our undercover agents, contacted the middle men, and waited for word on the Escopesca's arrival. When the ship approached, we were ready with its coordinates. A team of my operatives and Customs agents set sail for the rendezvous.

The Escopesca was a 175-foot freighter that carried illegal drugs for a number of destinations besides Fort Lauderdale. The size of our crafts did not accommodate all twelve tons as pre-arranged, but the crew offloaded what we could take. As soon as we verified that it was marijuana, contact was made with the Coast Guard, which had agreed to play a role in the boat's capture.

The crew members were stunned. Thinking they were safe in international waters, they had been conducting ship-to-ship transfers for some time. Citing the act, we hauled the ship and crew to port - the ship to be impounded, the crew to be deported.

These high seas seizures became more commonplace once we knew more about the Hovering Vessels Act. We plucked a number of boats from the Atlantic and Caribbean, at times having to fire across a boat's bow to prevent it from entering Cuban waters. Drugs were confiscated in huge amounts and we slowly became known as the International Sheriff's Office of Broward County.

The smugglers got the message. The Americans involved were arrested, the foreign nationals returned to their countries after learning a lesson: Don't bring contraband into the United States. The great majority of these seized ships were sunk off our coast, thus contributing to the artificial reef program we've established offshore.

While ships were popular, a more common method for drug smuggling was a night landing of an airplane in the Everglades. We had identified about eighteen or twenty possible landing strips in the swamplands that dominated western Broward County. All a pilot needed was a flat, dry piece of land of reasonable length and the aircraft could be put down and the contraband unloaded.

On a regular basis, we'd search the Everglades in the daylight to look for the freshest tracks, which indicated the more popular landing spots. Once a target was pinpointed, we'd stake it out. You haven't lived until you've spent a few sleepless nights out in the middle of the Everglades, surrounded by alligators, snakes, mosquitoes, and God knows what else, just waiting for a plane to land. Fortunately, there were never any false alarms. If a plane landed out there, it was for only one reason.

One coordinated operation out in the Everglades was called "Operation Trick or Treat." It was October, harvest time for Colombian marijuana. We'd received word that the growers had a good crop and that planes would be flying in on a regular basis. We made a score of arrests over a couple of weeks as we tracked and seized several aircraft bringing in contraband. One of the pilots told us that, to the smugglers, we were the most hated department in the United States. Believe me, we wore that hatred as a badge of honor.

Not all of the planes landed successfully out in these swamplands. Flying at night with no lights anywhere and very little turf to negotiate made for some landing mishaps that were as successful in slowing drug traffic as catching the planes that did manage to put down safely. One such crash involved the Zion Coptic Church in Miami Beach, a well-known and wealthy religious cult that claimed smoking marijuana to be its sacrament.

Let me tell you that any group that is an open advocate of drugs is going to come under scrutiny from our offices. This cult was good at smuggling in contraband for distribution to its followers, and we hadn't been successful in thwarting its illegal activities. Sooner or later, though, I knew we'd get a break.

The church's leader was Thomas Reilly, who called himself "Brother Louv." He ran the operation from a bayfront mansion along with Carl Swanson, a law school graduate who functioned as the church's executive director. Marijuana smoking was part of their worship service and smuggling their main source of income. Smoking marijuana, they claimed, brought them closer to God. A couple of arrests had led nowhere as there was never enough evidence of smuggling activities to get a conviction.

One Sunday evening, Swanson and a pilot, also a member of the church, were flying a two-engine Cessna into South Florida with 2,000 pounds of marijuana as cargo. Flying in over Boca Raton during the early morning, the plane clipped a 175-foot unlit radio tower belonging to the Doby Brick Company, located just west of the Florida Turnpike. The impact killed Swanson instantly and severely damaged the plane. Somehow the pilot was able to continue flying, with Swanson lying dead in his lap, for an additional twenty or so miles before he belly landed in the Everglades and made his escape, leaving the marijuana and his nearly decapitated co-pilot behind. There were Jamaican newspapers aboard the aircraft, which probably indicated the plane's point of origin (Jamaica was the home base for the Zion Coptic Church worldwide). The crash put an abrupt end to the church and its smuggling activities.

News of our successes was reaching the underworld. During one buy that I made from a group of five men, one of them told me to be very careful as the sheriff had these new super-narcs and you never knew who or where they are. He went on to say he'd heard these super-narcs had made sixty-five arrests already that year.

"Oh, really?" I replied, and began pointing at each one of the men. "Well, you are 66, 67, 68, 69, and 70. Congratulations! You're under arrest."

But our popularity had its drawbacks. The criminal world worked overtime trying to identify our headquarters in hopes of being able to stop our undercover operations. At one point, we moved three times in twenty-one months to remain clandestine.

Another problem we had was with defense attorneys' depositions we were required to make. We were asked questions about our home address, how many times we'd been married, where our children went to school - personal data that was likely not relevant to anyone or anything involved in the case. The defense attorneys claimed that information about our lifestyle revealed prejudices and inclinations that may have influenced our actions. But we knew the questions were an attempt by a defendant to learn more about the undercover cop who'd made the arrest possibly to achieve some future revenge.

The situation posed a serious dilemma. If we didn't answer the questions, we could face contempt-of-court charges. If we did reveal personal information, it could put our families' lives in jeopardy. We were left with a decision whether to let a case go if we considered the defendant dangerous enough to do something rash with the personal information obtained. This meant dismissing a case where many hard, long hours had been put in to make the arrest. Being put in this type of no-win situation was difficult for all of us.

The federal government continued to reach out in an effort to return me to its ranks. In an attempt to reorganize the fight against narcotics to make it more effective, several departments were combined. The bureau of Drug Abuse Control, which generally worked on cases involving only amphetamines and other pills; my old group, the Federal Bureau of Narcotics, which handled marijuana, cocaine, heroin, LSD, and PCP busts; and the branch of the United States Customs office that handled narcotics were rolled into a new unit called the Drug Enforcement Agency (DEA).

Its first head was an old neighbor of mine from Staten Island, John Bartels, who had been working most recently as a federal prosecutor in Newark, New Jersey. He invited me to Washington, D.C., to see if he could entice me to come back to the federal team. It was good to see him and I knew he'd do a great job of getting the DEA off and running, but I was happy with what I was accomplishing in Broward County and respectfully declined his offer. I told him that I would keep his South Florida DEA office well informed of our activities and would find many future occasions where we could work on cases together.

My unit worked around the clock, and none of my operatives ever felt there was such a thing as "off duty." One evening, several of us were at Broward General Hospital, checking on one of our men who had been injured. While sitting in the waiting room, two of my men struck up a conversation with some other individuals. As it happened, the conversation turned to drugs. One of the men mentioned he had some drugs in his truck, so my operatives arranged for a two-ounce buy while they were waiting for news about their injured comrade.

Two ounces may not sound like much, but a drug dealer is a drug dealer, and we wanted them all off the streets. There is a "ladder of success" for these criminals, too: today it's two ounces, tomorrow it's two tons. It's better to get the person off the street now before further damage is done.

They went out to the truck and the buy was made, but the seller got nervous and floored the gas pedal, nearly running down my two operatives. Before the buy, my men had recruited a couple of other cops for surveillance, and these back-ups jumped out of their car and shot out the truck's right front tire. The truck screeched to a halt and the dealers were arrested immediately. No one was hurt except the truck, which died of an acute flat right front tire.

After the arrests, my men returned to the hospital to tell their stricken friend that they had dedicated this bust to him.

The organized crime unit began to attract media attention. While we were conducting a series of raids of suspected bookmakers in the city of Hallandale, a reporter from a local television station, Jim Malone from Channel 10, turned up after receiving a tip. As the arrests were being made, he kept nagging me for a quote. I told him I was an undercover cop and didn't need my picture broadcasted throughout South Florida.

"Come on, Nick," Malone said. "You're more of an administrator now since you're the head of the unit. I promise never to interview any of your people. Only you."

"You need a quote? Talk to Ed Stack," I replied.

"I don't want Stack, Nick, I want you. Stack doesn't know exactly what's happening on the front lines. You do."

I could see I wasn't going to get rid of Malone by arguing with him, so I went to a phone and called Ed Stack's office. Naturally, Sharron answered, and I told her what Malone wanted. After checking with Stack, she came back on the line and told me it was okay to talk to the reporter. "Give him the quote," Stack had said. "The sheriff's office can use the positive publicity."

Jim Malone got his live quote, and I made my first appearance on the nightly news in 1975. I was now this newscaster's "front line" contact and I would slowly become a regular on television, reporting our police efforts.

Sheriff Stack continued to give me a tremendous amount of flexibility in conducting the affairs of the OCD. He never told me to back off and supported our efforts from the sidelines 100 percent. He was pleased with our success rates and felt we were making a difference in Broward County, especially in narcotics.

I know we diverted a lot of contraband that otherwise would have been sold to the citizens of this country. I can't tell you what percentage of illegal substances we were seizing since I have no way of knowing how much was coming in. I'm always amazed by statistics that reveal some department's or agency's action is responsible for taking thirty-five percent (or some such number) of drugs off the street. How can the agency know that? It's not as if the criminals publish records of their successes. We simply focused on winning every battle we could and felt secure in the knowledge that every ounce of drugs we pulled off the street most likely meant someone's life would be saved.

The organized crime unit had come a long way since its birth in 1971. Neither Ed Stack nor I could have envisioned the success this division would have and the reputation it would build, locally and nationally, in five years. I had a solid group of operatives, undercover cops who other supervisors couldn't handle but who were stellar performers out on the front lines of the crime war. We were making an impact on drug trafficking, gambling, prostitution, and other illegal activities being conducted in South Florida.

Sharron and I had planned a two-week Christmas holiday in North Carolina at the end of 1976 and I was looking forward to the rest. I brought Sheriff Stack up to date on our activities before leaving and he seemed as pleased as always with our results. Sharron and I left for what we thought would be a quiet, uneventful couple of weeks skiing in the mountains.

It's amazing how wrong one can be.

Three

Reassignment
And Return

Tstack. First, he loved politics. He had been Florida campaign chairman for Richard Nixon in 1968 and 1972 and an influential
Republican supporter of Democratic Governor Reubin Askew. He then
switched political parties and was state gubernatorial campaign chairman for
Democrat Robert Shevin, Florida's Attorney General.

Second, he badly wanted to unseat Republican Herbert Burke for the
Twelfth District Congressional seat of the U.S. House of Representatives.

Third, he was obsessed enough with his desire to be a congressman that he
made some decisions that were clearly politically motivated. Somehow, some
way, I drifted into his political firing line. Our Organized Crime Division had
achieved some remarkable exposure with a series of excellent results, and
since 1975, I had been available, with Stack's blessing, to talk to reporters
about the cases we had brought to closure. In my mind, I believed this publicity showed the sheriff in a very favorable light. Ed Stack's interpretation,
however, was much different.

In December, 1976, Sharron and I were in North Carolina for a relaxing
end of the year skiing holiday. It seemed like forever since we'd had a respite,

47

and the cases and the hours seemed particularly long that year. The condo in which we were vacationing had no phone, which was fine with me. We weren't expecting to hear from anybody. It was, therefore, a surprise when we received a message that Ed Stack had called the main hotel, leaving word to call him back.

Since Sharron was Stack's secretary, we both assumed the call was for her - probably something Ed couldn't find or a message he couldn't decipher. It was snowing heavily in the mountains that day and it was a hearty trek to the main building from our condo. Sharron made the trip and returned to say that Stack wanted to speak with me, not her.

"What for?" I asked.

"I don't know," Sharron replied. "He wouldn't tell me. Something to do with one of your cases, I'll bet."

"I guess." A hundred thoughts were bouncing around in my head: one of my officers was down, a case got screwed up, they needed my advice for a trial. It could be anything, but it had to be important, as I'd never heard from Stack while I was on vacation before.

But Stack, after I had reached him and exchanged season's greetings, seemed to be in an upbeat mood. I couldn't imagine what he wanted.

"Nick, ol' buddy," he said as I watched the snow come down outside the window. "You've done a lot for Broward County and we're extremely proud of your accomplishments."

He paused, and I wondered briefly why he would call me to tell me that.

He cleared his throat. "You've had great results, Nick, but your services are no longer needed in the Organized Crime Division."

I wasn't sure I heard him right. Could the weather have fouled up this connection?

"I have another assignment for you, Nick, that's very important. I'll give you a complete rundown when you return from your trip."

I could barely speak. "I don't understand," was all that I managed.

"Sure, it'll be an adjustment, but I have a position that calls for the kind of strengths you have. We'll talk about it when you come back. Happy New Year."

That was it. Short and sweet. Ed Stack's Christmas gift to me.

I stood there in a state of shock. No one had ever relieved me of my duties before. I had just seen Stack a few days earlier. Why didn't he tell me then?

Why now? Couldn't this have waited until my vacation was over? I tried to recall every word of the short conversation to see if I'd missed anything, but that was it. The year was about finished and so was I as head of the Organized Crime Division. If this new assignment was so critical, why not let me know briefly what it was?

I trudged back to the condo, brushed the snow off my clothes, and gave Sharron the news. She was equally taken aback. As Stack's secretary, she generally knew what was going on, but this bombshell had caught her by surprise, too.

I had met with Stack the day before I left to bring him up to date on our caseload. He seemed pleased, as always, although I was never sure how much of what we did, or the everyday dangers it represented, were absorbed by Stack. Still, he had let me run the department and I had willingly and routinely passed along the credit to him.

Sharron speculated that this move might be politically motivated. Stack was planning to run again for Congress, she pointed out, and maybe viewed me as a threat.

"To run for office? I have no desire to do that."

"Well, honey, I know that and you know that, and I really think that Ed knows that, too. One of his advisors must not like the publicity you're getting as head of OCD."

"What publicity?" I protested. "Everything I do and say is meant to put the department and, by inference, Ed Stack, out in front in the public eye in a positive light. I don't want the publicity."

Further speculation was useless. Whatever the motivation, Stack seemed bent on reassigning me. It was not the most cheery of holidays for Sharron and me. When I returned after the first of the year, Stack explained that, after five years, my public exposure has created undue risks for me. OCD's success was more than a little perturbing to the underworld and the sheriff felt that an interdepartmental rotation was in order. I was becoming well known, Stack told me, and not only with those on the right side of the law.

I was to switch jobs with Captain Ed Roehling, who was in charge of the Internal Affairs Division. Roehling would be the new head of OCD and I would assume his position. I would be asked to consult on OCD matters from time to time.

Of course, it was not as simple as that. I found out later that there had been a cutback on government funds and the lease on OCD's headquarters was running out. Stack meant to bring the unit back inside the Broward County Sheriff's Office, but in my opinion, that would doom it.

Internal Affairs was about as far away as one could get from the public eye. The investigations done by this unit were very low profile. Stack told the media the position needed a sensitive touch in handling and that I was perfect for the assignment. He is, after all, a politician.

It would be an adjustment, but I didn't see any way to refuse it. Fort Lauderdale Police Chief Leo Callahan called me with words of encouragement and advice, suggesting I take the new assignment. "These things have a way of working out, Nick," he said. So Stack made me a captain and I was in charge of Internal Affairs.

I wasn't head of the Internal Affairs Division for too long. In June 1977, Stack re-assigned me again, this time as liaison to the State Attorney's Office. A statewide probe of pornography peddlers was being conducted with the ultimate objective being the arrest of several organized crime figures believed to be key distributors of the illicit material. I was part of a strike force that included detectives from Fort Lauderdale, Pompano Beach, and Hollywood. We would be handling surveillance and raids, and it felt like I was back in charge of the Organized Crime Division. State Attorney Michael Satz wanted more arrests, and those, I figured, I could give him.

Convictions were something else again. It was not easy to enforce pornography laws since a Supreme Court ruling gave judges the power to decide whether material was obscene or not by applying a "community standards" test. It wasn't an easy assignment, but we had a good conviction rate. I remained restless, though. It was, finally, the unlikeliest of jobs that returned me to doing what I do best.

Some time back, the Broward County Commission and the Airport Authority, following some union problems, contracted with the Broward County Sheriff's Office to provide security at the Fort Lauderdale/Hollywood International Airport. Known around the office as "Siberia," it had long been the last posting an officer was given if, apparently, he or she couldn't handle anything else. Being transferred to the airport was generally a career killer. Thoughts like these began churning in my mind when Sheriff Stack informed me about the need to have a capable supervisor out there.

Anyone else in my position would probably have refused. I was nearly a twenty-year veteran and had been a success at the federal, state, and local levels of law enforcement. The airport was a vast wasteland in which one merely passed the time until it was feasible to retire.

But the airport was something else, too. It was a preferred point of entry for drugs being smuggled into the country. After years of seeing the effects illegal substances have, I saw the airport assignment as an opportunity to make a difference in the drug war again. I told Stack I'd take the job. From his point of view, I was probably even less likely to attract any attention at the airport than as part of internal affairs. Stack misjudged the publicity I would get, but that publicity would show him in a positive light.

I was transferred out to the airport as a captain, at my same salary, a rank higher than any of my predecessors in the job had carried. Captain or not, what I headed up was, in essence, a leper colony. The individuals working airport security had long since lost sight of their mission and played the role of outcast to the hilt. For a few days after this reassignment, I simply went to the airport to observe the operatives in action. Their appearance was not up to par, they acted dull and listless and I was certain that tons of contraband had found its way though the airport under their not so watchful eyes.

I decided that what was needed here was not fresh troops, only a rekindling of the flame in the existing ones. I felt I could inject some pride in them, which would go a long way in turning this operation around.

At our first meeting, I chastised the group for their appearance, saying the uniform of a Broward officer should make one feel proud to wear it. An officer who looks sharp, I told them, will act sharp and might shake the confidence of the criminals who were laughing at us right now. I even made them wear their hats.

I told them I wanted the airport to be a showcase of security and the envy of other airports around the country. We were a key entry point for drug smugglers, I advised, and it was time we turned the tables. I said that I had reevaluated their positions and would be redesigning the posts to make the officers more effective. We would be, I assured them, as much of a success as the Organized Crime Division had been. Be proud, I said, look proud, and do your jobs. I couldn't ask for anything more.

In a short period of time, the difference was amazing. The officers felt more effective in their redesigned unit, more utilized than they had been in the past. They were good officers and now was their chance to prove it. "Siberia" had been transformed into the "Riviera." Soon the personnel department was receiving transfer requests asking for assignment to the airport.

Soon after my transfer, I went to Sheriff Stack with an idea. The DEA had developed a profile of people that were likely transporters of drugs or high amounts of cash. It was an adaptation of the Sky Marshals' "profile of skyjackers" idea, which a DEA agent out of the Detroit office had modified for drug smugglers. It listed obvious characteristics that could be spotted, traits that suggested an individual was involved in some kind of illegal courier activity. Truthfully, I was skeptical, especially since the concept had not been tested in the courts yet. (It's difficult enough to catch criminals without having the court release them because of our arrest procedures.) But Broward County was certainly a source area for drugs, and this was a chance to make smugglers think twice before trying to bring in their contraband through our airport.

I asked Stack for four additional officers. Since the profile is still in use today, I don't want to reveal it in its entirety, but the obvious signs of nervousness - glancing around, sweating - are sure indications that something is amiss, and it's usually not a fear of flying. Using the profile won't likely help one identify a professional courier, but the amateurs become easy to spot.

In one instance, a man carrying a suitcase and three bundles rushed up to the counter at the last minute to buy a ticket. When our officer explained that he was a narcotics specialist and asked if the man minded being searched, the suspected courier broke into a cold sweat. He agreed to the search of his suitcase but not his person. The suitcase contents looked ordinary, but when the officer picked up a shaving cream container, it didn't feel right. While shaving cream did indeed spurt from the top, the bottom of the can was false and opened to reveal two vials. The man was arrested and searched, and $30,000 was found stuffed in various pockets of his clothes.

Many similar arrests were made. Court dates were set and convictions returned. We were confiscating more drugs than many narcotics units across the country. Of course, Broward County was a hot point of entry, so the opportunities were there for us and we tried to make the best of them. Eventually, some defense attorneys charged that we were violating their clients' constitutional rights. A couple of our cases were thrown out of court, but the majority of them stood. We were not using just the profile characteristics, but their use in conjunction with our experience at spotting couriers was giving us an unparalleled success rate. We were not stopping ordinary citizens nervous about flying or paying cash for their tickets. There was a lot involved in spotting a criminal, and we were becoming experts at it.

One Fort Lauderdale lawyer, hoping to show we were stopping anyone displaying certain characteristics, tried to match the profile as he moved through the airport. We didn't stop him. We knew an attorney when we saw one, too.

The people we stopped were like the two men who were waiting in line to buy Delta Airline tickets. They changed lines several times while carefully guarding their carry-on luggage. They paid cash for the tickets and were subsequently stopped by an officer. After they agreed to a luggage search, the suitcases were opened and a significant stash of marijuana was found. Like I said, after a while one can tell who's dirty and who isn't.

The operation was so successful that we were observed by officers representing airport security in San Francisco, New York, Los Angeles, and Miami. We were also called on to testify before a select committee of the U.S. House of Representatives investigating the drug smuggling business.

Sheriff Stack thought that his Congressional opponent, Herbert Burke, was trying to make him look bad before the election; a poor report by the committee could severely damage the sheriff's campaign. I assured him that our success rate was significantly high and that this investigation would help him, not hurt him.

My words turned out to be prophetic. The committee was impressed with our results. The sheriff asked if I minded if he claimed credit for the idea. I told him to go ahead; it didn't matter to me. Making the arrests and getting convictions were my bottom line. I didn't need the bonus points with the committee. The chairman of the committee, Lester Wolff from New York, praised Stack and his office for the results to date.

It wasn't only drugs we were turning up. We found weapons of all varieties as smugglers tried to move them through our airport.

In one instance, we stopped two men who were carrying heavy-duty magnums. When we were transporting them to jail for booking, a routine check of the Florida Crime Information Center revealed an outstanding warrant on the men for second degree murder in Dade County. As soon as they got to the station, they made their one phone call to well-known attorneys Fred Haddad and Ray Sandstrom to advise them of their plight. We, in turn, called the Metro Dade police. I advised them to get up here in a hurry as I wasn't sure how long these men could be detained. The attorneys found a magistrate, Judge Herring, and convinced him that these men were okay and managed to get their bond set at $5,000. The attorneys quickly posted bond and the order was issued to release the men. I told the jailer to do all he could to delay the process. "Just stall," I said, "We only need a little more time."

The two attorneys confronted me and said, "What's the holdup? We've posted bond. Let these men go."

"That's not possible yet, I'm afraid," I answered. "Just give us a few more minutes. Paperwork. You understand that we have our procedures."

"That's bullshit, Navarro. Now, let these guys go or we're going back to the judge."

"It won't be but another hour, gentlemen. Make yourselves comfortable. We're moving as fast as we can."

"An hour! No way!" Off they went, back to Judge Herring.

The attorneys told the judge I was holding the two men illegally and that I didn't care about the judge's authority or the men's constitutional rights. Judge Herring was not pleased about this and he came down himself to see what the problems were.

I explained that we hadn't finished processing the men through yet. The judge told me that if I didn't let them go immediately, he would hold me in contempt of court. Haddad and Sandstrom were encouraging the judge to do so, then a reporter happened along. It was turning into a free-for-all.

"He has no respect for the courts at all," the attorneys complained. The judge's face was getting redder by the minute as I simply stood there like a statue. I finally decided to tell the judge my story.

I explained that I was waiting for two Dade police officers who had a warrant for the arrest of these men on second degree murder charges. Fortunately, just as I was telling this to the judge, in rushed the Dade police. Thank God! The judge gave me a contempt of court citation anyway, which was of little consolation to the attorneys. Later, Judge Herring called me to his chambers and ripped the citation up, explaining that the attorneys had painted an unrealistic picture of these men. He assured me that we were on the same side and appreciated the stance I'd taken. I told him I was certainly not trying to defy his authority and knew that he wasn't aware of all the facts. By that time, the two men were already headed to Dade County Jail.

The publicity accorded our presence at the airport achieved some unexpected side effects. Pickpocketing and the theft of luggage or other personal belongings at the airport slowed to a trickle. Criminals took their activities elsewhere. Why take a chance that the person whose pocket you just picked might be an undercover cop? This made life easier for the innocent traveler.

In 1978, an election year, Stack's campaign got an even bigger boost than our committee testimony when his opponent, Congressman Herbert Burke, was arrested for disorderly intoxication and resisting arrest at a nude dance joint called the Centerfold Club. The publicity surrounding this incident, along with Stack's positive image based on the success of the Broward County Sheriff's Office that year, especially at the airport, won Stack the election. Finally, he would be headed to Congress in the first part of 1979.

It was a strange feeling. I had been with the Broward County Sheriff's Office since 1971 and Stack had always been sheriff. We had no idea who would be appointed to fill the position until the next election in 1980. Whoever it was, I would have a new boss.

A number of names surfaced as potential candidates. Ken Jenne, now a state senator and formerly the "Batman" half of the team that worked in the state attorney's office for us back in 1971, was mentioned. So was Major Ken Collins, uniform division commander who had been with the BSO about ten years. The former chief of police for Lauderdale Lakes, Albert Kline, was a possibility.

The man Governor Reubin Askew eventually selected had not been among the early candidates. Currently a circuit court judge, following his stint as the "Robin" half of the state attorney's team, Bob Butterworth was selected to succeed Stack as the sheriff of Broward County.

Personally, I was pleased. Butterworth and I had worked well together when he was the liaison between the Organized Crime Division and the State Attorney's Office, notwithstanding the time I locked him in my office until he'd completed a warrant for me. He was well organized and hard working, two assets that were important in his new job. He would be a good sheriff.

Ed Stack didn't leave without controversy, however. The day before he was to depart for Washington, D.C., and his new job, the soon to be ex-sheriff handed out several promotions to, apparently, close friends and political allies. This action followed an agreement on a new labor contract with a maritime union affiliated with a large labor organization that had made sizable contributions to Stack's campaign against Burke.

The promotions involved about a half-dozen people, one of whom was advanced from sergeant level directly to captain. Another promotion involved me directly. Edward Schmidt, then sixty-four years old, who had spent a number of years in security at Kennedy Airport in New York and now was loosely affiliated with Internal Affairs, was moved to the airport to be chief of operations. This meant I would be reporting directly to him. Ed Schmidt was "loosely affiliated" with Internal Affairs because what he did was drive Sheriff Stack everywhere. The sheriff did not drive himself. There was some speculation that it was due to past difficulties with alcohol and the possible loss of his driver's license in the state of New York before he ventured down to Pompano Beach. Schmidt wasn't Ed Stack's first chauffeur, but he was the first one Stack had promoted to head up security at the airport.

The labor union contract came under scrutiny, as it seemed to be politically motivated - a charge that Stack denied. It was formally with the Federation of Public Employees, but the force behind it was the National Marine Engineers Beneficial Association (MEBA), which had donated $15,000 to the sheriff's congressional election bid. Unquestionably, Stack was a political sheriff; the line between his political and law enforcement roles had long since blurred. Stack himself did not mind the tag of political sheriff, as he felt it was part of the job description.

He may have crossed the line with the union contract. Some of his subordinates came forward and said they had lobbied officers and other employees in the BSO to sign union authorization cards. Major Collins, whom reportedly had been recommended by Stack to the governor to succeed him, told of a conversation between Stack and MEBA national official Charles Browne in which Browne reportedly asked Stack what MEBA was getting for its $15,000. Browne apparently obtained a position for his friend Schmidt within the BSO. In addition to his chauffeur duties, Ed Schmidt was also the intermediary between Brown's aides and Stack's. Browne had told Collins that he would have the support of organized labor in the 1980 sheriff's campaign if, as Stack believed, Governor Askew would appoint Collins to fill the sheriff's slot. Browne was considerably upset when Butterworth was Askew's pick and not Collins.

With all of this information coming out on the eve of Bob Butterworth's first day as sheriff, it was no wonder he was on the job at 5:30 A.M. The first thing he did was to rescind all of Ed Stack's final promotions pending a full review. Next, he ordered a complete investigation into the labor union fiasco. He told everyone, including the media, that the BSO would no longer be called "Manhattan South," a reference to the name the office had earned because of Stack's preference for former New York police officers.

The next week, Sheriff Butterworth began to assert his new authority. He ordered about two dozen personnel moves, including a reassignment for Captain Albert Kline, a man mentioned as a possible candidate for the sheriff's job only a few days earlier, and the formal transfer of Ed Schmidt to the airport, but not as its head. I would remain in charge of airport security.

I was absent for most of this flurry of activity. Ed Stack had said nothing to me about any changes he was making, including the promotion of Schmidt to head of airport security. I did attend Butterworth's swearing-in ceremony, which was held at Parker Playhouse in Fort Lauderdale. The next day I left on a planned year-end holiday to London with Sharron.

While we were there, I received a telegram from the new sheriff that he had rescinded all the promotions Stack had recently made, including Schmidt's.

Included in this message was the news that I was still captain, but that Butterworth had other plans for me when I returned from my trip. Happy New Year!

I thought, oh, no, what now? It was getting to the point where I was afraid to leave town. Another New Year's Day was spent wondering what was in store for me.

It was a pleasant surprise, actually. In our first meeting, in January 1979, the new sheriff apologized to me for the way Ed Stack had shuffled me around the last couple of years.

"I'd like you to come back and take your old job as head of the Organized Crime Division. Does that interest you?"

Interest me? I never wanted to leave it in the first place, but Stack hadn't given me a choice. I would be back where I belonged. Ed Roehling, my replacement as OCD head, was transferred by Butterworth to the Criminal Warrants Division.

What I found when I returned was somewhat discouraging. Stack had brought the whole unit back under the BSO umbrella, and now the entire department knew who all the undercover officers were. The officers that remained in OCD had been reduced to flushing out petty crime. It was time to bring this unit back up to its previous high standards.

Promising more men, Butterworth moved us back outside the BSO down near Port Everglades. There we could maintain our accustomed secrecy in pursuing organized crime. The sheriff publicly stated that he hoped this move would not only have a positive effect on crime but also smooth relations with other agencies, as I was well known and well liked. I appreciated the support Butterworth was showing and was determined to produce results.

At this point, we were in a losing battle to keep drugs off the streets. Despite our modest success at the airport, tons of contraband were finding its way to our shores. The demand was high. To this day, I truly don't understand why kids view drugs as an escape. What are they escaping from? I was from Cuba and I knew what it was like for people to grow up with no aspirations, in a country where they could only get so far. But here in America? You could be anything you wanted here. Why escape with drugs?

As long as the demand was high, smuggling would flourish. Smugglers had the advantage: they had money, equipment, boats, planes, guns, and fewer and fewer legal restraints. I remember arresting a man in Miami in the early 1960s for possession of a ten-dollar matchbox of marijuana. The judge gave him ten years in prison. Now, we can bust a guy for bringing in ten tons and he'd end up walking out of court, laughing his ass off at us. It's tough to win a battle against those odds.

That didn't mean, however, that I wouldn't wage the fight. I had about forty-five people working for me in 1979, and we went about the business of undercover work again - turning criminals to work as informers for us, playing the various roles that must be played. It wasn't long before we had a string of operations underway that closed with arrests and seizures of a wealth of drugs, money, and guns.

In one case, we eliminated the tail end of a drug smuggling operation run out of Colombia. One of my undercover officers had infiltrated the group and was acting as a middleman for a well-connected local buyer. "Mr. Well-Connected" turned out to be me. Using the name Don Nicholas, I met the sellers along with my officer. We made the buy, with a couple of the criminals kissing my hand in respect. We arrested and booked them and were able to make simultaneous raids on other locations of this ring, netting fourteen arrests, three guns, and seven vehicles.

This was the job I wanted to do. Working with my officers every day, each of them dedicated to taking these criminals off the street, was what law enforcement was all about. Sheriffs seem more interested in the political aspect of their position, but what law enforcement essentially came down to was removing the criminal element from our everyday lives.

Our operations turned up planes loaded with drugs. I also made an arrangement with Nova University, a local school, to concentrate on the water entry of illicit drugs originating from the shores of South America. We set up shop in the university's ocean sciences facilities and brought in agents from Customs and other state and local agencies. We'd had success seizing ships before under the Hovering Vessels Act and I wanted to stop as much of the smuggling that occured on the water as we could.

There had been a marked increase in the sale of hashish, if our busts were any indication. In 1978, only thirty-seven pounds of hashish were seized the entire year by South Florida agents. In the first quarter of 1979, over 1,100 pounds had already been confiscated. Quaalude use was also on the rise, and marijuana and cocaine continued to maintain their lofty positions here.

A man we suspected of being a drug dealer had booked a flight on National Airlines from Palm Springs to Fort Lauderdale, due to arrive at 5 P.M. He had also made return reservations for a flight to Los Angeles, due to leave at 5:45 P.M. Who flies all the way from California to simply turn around and fly back forty-five minutes later? Sure enough, between flights, the suspect took a package from a man standing near a restaurant close to the National Airlines gates. The package contained 7,000 Quaaludes. Earlier that day, we had confiscated a suitcase that contained over 100,000 of the pills.

The hashish seizures were even more alarming. Traditionally, hashish, a concentrated derivative of marijuana made by pounding resin out of the leaves, is manufactured in Turkey and Afghanistan, but the shipments we were intercepting came from South America. If the South Americans had figured out how to produce hashish, it simply added to our woes here in South Florida. Quaaludes, we knew, were being manufactured in Colombia.

In 1979, my former country made its own contribution to our crime problems when Fidel Castro emptied his jails during the infamous Mariel boatlift. The time and personnel of many of our allies in the drug war were diverted to patrolling the Florida Straits, and we were left to our own devices for a time in the "water battle." Of course, we had more criminals to worry about with this new influx into South Florida. The process of separating the criminals from the genuine immigrants would take a considerable amount of time. In the interim, crime was destined to rise.

Despite these developments, we managed to turn OCD around within the year. By the end of 1979, I was comfortable with the people and the operations we had. BSO had received some positive publicity as a result of OCD's rebirth, and Sheriff Butterworth was looking good heading into the 1980 election year. He certianly wanted to continue serving as sheriff.

In 1980, he took a rare "active" role in a three-month-long investigation of a pornography ring that we were about to close out. We had centered the investigation on a one-story white stucco nameless storefront in Hallandale, part of unincorporated Broward County. Through un-dercover police work, we had determined that the building was a warehouse for sado-masochistic devices and pornographic films made on site. Young female dancers had been used in various torture depictions involving electric shocks, chains, whips and assorted other implements.

The owner was William Zinn, a fifty-one-year-old Hollywood man. Having enough probable cause, I was concluding a buy to finalize Zinn's arrest. He was to sell me about $7,000 worth of videocassettes and photographs that I would then distribute throughout the northeast United States. Zinn had the market in Florida and California. Once again, I was "Louie" Gonzalez. This time, though, when I went to make the buy, I took along the sheriff, who I introduced to Zinn as Bobby, my partner. Zinn didn't recognize either one of us, although if I'd brought President Jimmy Carter along, the chances he would have recognized him still would have been only about 50/50.

Zinn had previously given me some sample cassettes to view. I had taken them to Broward Circuit Court Judge Daniel Futch, who, after reviewing them, declared the material obscene. I complained to Zinn about some of the flaws in the tapes and he agreed to fix them. By the time "Bobby" and I met with him, he had erased the flaws and was quite proud of his efforts.

I congratulated him on his handiwork and, with Zinn's help, we loaded the material into my car and completed the transaction. Now it was Butterworth's turn.

"By the way," he said, "there's one thing we haven't told you. We're with the Broward County Sheriff's Office. In fact, I am the sheriff."

Zinn was astounded. "You're the sheriff! What the hell are you doing out arresting me?"

In truth, we were glad to conclude this investigation. Zinn had been approaching young girls, many of them runaways, about modeling lingerie, and one thing led to another. The more they did, the greater the pay. Some of the girls didn't look older than fourteen or fifteen. Zinn's operation grossed nearly a million dollars a year.

In 1980, a program started up that I personally became involved in. It didn't involve arrests or seizures. Instead, it was a fund to help officers in distress. Called the 10-24 Foundation (after the code signaling that an officer needed assistance), it was meant to fill a potential vast financial gap a police officer could face in certain situations. If an officer is wounded in the line of duty, a paycheck is still issued. If an officer is killed, his family receives money from the state and the county insurance program, but if he is stricken with a disease, he is on his own.

The foundation was precipitated by an officer's battle with leukemia. At thirty-two years old, Detective Charles "Warren" Wolfe was battling for his life. He was undergoing bone marrow transplants at John Hopkins Medical Center in Maryland and was incurring a large amount of travel expenses in doing so. His wife was pregnant with their first child and the bills were piling up. The foundation was established to raise money to help when officers faced this sort of hardship.

We held dinner fund-raisers and appreciation nights at local sporting events. The money started to come in. Professional wrestler Eddie Graham heard about the foundation and donated $6,000 from one of his matches held at the Sportatorium in Hollywood. One of the officers who helped set it up, Captain Joe Pierce, would need the foundation's assistance less than two years later during a bout with cancer he would eventually lose. Over the years, a number of fellow officers have been helped through the foundation.

The Broward County Sheriff's Office was by then Butterworth's baby. He had started several social services programs to work on the rehabilitative side of law enforcement, an attempt to fit former criminals back into society. He hadn't entirely eliminated politics from the position, and Ed Stack would have thought it humorous that, during the 1980 election, a number of officers within the department volunteered to help in Butterworth's campaign effort.

While Stack was losing his bid to serve another term in Congress in 1980, Butterworth gained a huge margin of victory over Republican candidate Earl Oltersdorf. Stack left the sheriff's office with a $16 million budget and 765 employees. By 1981, Butterworth's budget was $40 million with more than 1,100 employees. Crime was growing in South Florida and the increases in money and personnel were necessary to keep it in check. Additionally, Butterworth seemed to view the sheriff's office as a place to prove the value of a number of social programs he had developed with volunteers while he sat on the bench as a circuit court judge.

During this time, we were able to pass a law through the state legislature in Tallahassee that allowed us to use confiscated property and money in any way we saw fit. While some legislators saw a potential for abuse, the majority viewed the law as giving police the ability to use the smuggler's own wealth against them. Confiscating funds meant being able to buy better equipment and materials that wouldn't normally be approved under the usual state budget process. Fort Lauderdale Vice Mayor Robert Cox wasn't too excited about us keeping all of the confiscated funds and instead suggested that the cities and counties should use the money in any way they saw fit. He didn't see the benefit of letting the police buy "toys." To me, he was another politician who would rather control these funds himself then let them be used by someone else.

Our organized crime unit continued its success rate. In June 1981, we raided a marina and confiscated fourteen tons of marijuana. In May, a high-speed motor boat chase ended in the seizure of over a million methaqualone tablets. In March, we found thirteen pounds of cocaine brought in by an airline passenger from Vancouver, British Colombia. Still, the drugs continued to pour in. We received some criticism that we focused too much on narcotics, but the spillover crime from trafficking was being checked, too. Any number of burglaries, for example, could be traced to a perpetrator who needed money to buy drugs. Slowing down the flow of drugs can cut down on these types of crimes, too.

We seized another mother ship on the high seas in 1981. The Jean Anne was offloading about 7,500 pounds of marijuana into five boats when we showed up. One of the men involved in that illegal enterprise was a former police officer from Pembroke Pines, a suburb of Broward. He was around during the Escopesca capture but apparently had forgotten that we're not beyond seizing a whole ship.

We utilized informers as often as we could, despite the fact that some of them were disreputable. They were effective, though, in helping to compile evidence on the "bigger fish," and sometimes we had to dance with the devil on this job. We listened to their stories and tried to discern what was truth and what was fiction. The rules were simple. We'd take the information, test it, separate the real from the counterfeit, and then attempt to verify it. If it couldn't be verified, we didn't act on it.

One of our informants, Peter Foster, had worked a few operations for us. In one, he went to the Bahamas to bring back a load of drugs and information. He called me and said he was getting a little nervous about the deal, but I assured him that if he got into trouble in the Bahamas, I could help him. This seemed to make him feel better. So he went, and the operation was a success.

Foster made another trip of the same variety, but this time to Colombia - a different story. He went entirely on his own. We were not aware who he was going to see or what he was going to do. If he managed to get some information, we would use it, but we never told any of our informers we wanted them to make these "runs" in other countries.

Apparently, Foster was arrested during his sojourn in Colombia. I received a cryptic phone call from an employee of the State Department saying there was a man in jail in Colombia who said he worked for us and he wanted to verify this information. Over the phone, there was no way to verify who was calling. A number of scenarios flashed through my mind. This could be one of the dealers calling from Colombia or a corrupt policeman in that country or almost anyone. If I confirmed Foster was working for me, I could well be signing his death warrant. If it really was the State Department, it was likely the department could secure his release and transport him back to the United States. I denied any knowledge of him. He was eventually freed and returned to the United States. He sued the sheriff's office, but I told him we were only acting in his best interest. If I had confirmed him to a drug dealer, I wouldn't be talking to him now. He didn't accept this explanation and instead complained of abandonment, but no one from my office had ever sent him on a mission to Colombia; the trip was his own idea. We would never ask an informant to make such a trip. It was simply too dangerous. The insurance company that underwrote BSO's liability coverage eventually settled with Foster.

The drug wars touched celebrities, too. Country singer Larry Kosa and his brother were arrested one evening following their attempt to buy cocaine from undercover officers. In the search, we turned up the usual material associated with people in the drug business: expensive cars, substantial cash, and an array of guns. This time we also found something unusual: full Ku Klux Klan garb, bearing a leader's insignia. We found out it belonged to Larry's brother, Lou (given name Arthur), who was a member in good standing of the Klan. While Larry did the singing, his brother ran an airplane rental company in Florida. The take for that evening's work was ten high-powered handguns, three Mach-10 submachine guns, a silencer, 10,000 rounds of ammunition, $72,000, two Corvettes, a Rolls Royce, and one white hooded robe.

These stories were duplicated night after night, day after day, with no end in sight. If I hadn't concentrated on the individual operations running twenty-four hours a day, seven days a week, the apparent futility of it all would have worn me down. I figured that one less drug dealer or user on the street was saving someone from grief. I took consolation in that knowledge.

About this time we had focused on an island close to our shores that was a prime stopover point for planes and boats bringing drugs into America. We found that more than a few trails led to the same location, and scouting operations revealed the type of activity normally associated with smuggling.

The island was not part of the United States, but then again, I was merely pursuing criminals wherever they went. The invasion of Bimini was about to begin.

Four

The Invasion of Bimini

THERE ARE SOME 700 ISLANDS IN THE BAHAMAS CHAIN IN THE SOUTH Atlantic Ocean. Two of these islands, North and South Bimini, lay only fifty miles east of Miami. By day, these islands are a tourist habitat; beaches, fishing, numerous water sports are available to vacationing travelers. On clear nights, the lights of distant Miami can be seen to the west.

Paradise? Perhaps. But not only for tourists. Bimini, by the late seventies, had acquired a well-deserved reputation as a drug smuggling steppingstone to the United States. Planes bringing in contraband from Central and South America could stop off in Bimini and either refuel before attempting a run into the United States, or offload their cargo to vessels or aircraft meeting them on the island of South Bimini.

There was historical precedent for this type of illegitimate operation. During the U.S. prohibition era of the 1920s, rumrunners used to work out of the Bimini islands, bringing in illegal alcohol to the U.S. mainland. The smugglers had swapped booze for drugs and worked hard at keeping up the supply to meet the demand.

While daytime in Bimini is for tourists, the night is owned by criminals. The noise of aircraft and speedboats can and does go on for most of the evening. The Al Capones of the twenties had yielded to the Colombians of the seventies.

By 1979, a number of undercover drug operations were being handled by my Fort Lauderdale Organized Crime Division, so it was inevitable that at least one of them would lead to South Bimini as a supply point for a group of drug dealers operating in the United States. But when several of our ongoing investigations all pointed in the same direction, it was obvious we had a big problem. This information indicated a major supply route for drugs being brought into this country. My quest became a simple one in theory: cut off this supply route and put a major dent in the drug trafficking to the United States.

Practically speaking, this wouldn't be an easy task. Bimini, after all, is a sovereign state. Diplomatic relations were a delicate enterprise, and I wasn't sure what kind of cooperation I would get from my own State Department, let alone the Bahamian government. But the drugs were being smuggled into Broward County and this I was dedicated to stopping. If the trail led to Bimini, then that is where I would go.

With Sheriff Butterworth's encouragement, I set up a special team to handle airport/seaport drug smuggling. The members included officers from several municipalities located near the water in Broward County, such as Hallandale, Hollywood, Pompano Beach, Deerfield Beach, and Fort Lauderdale. I asked U.S. Customs for its participation, especially in view of the Bahamian involvement. The officer assigned from the Fort Lauderdale unit was Cherokee Paul MacDonald (now a writer), who was a terrific cop. Hollywood assigned Jim Harms, now deputy chief of police for Cooper City (in Broward County). U.S. Customs sent Hal Sagar. I assigned Ian Griffith and Sandy Ledigal from the Broward County Sheriff's Office.

This new unit, attached to my Organized Crime Division, now shared a similar status with my other units: Narcotics, Vice, Gambling, Pornography, and Intelligence.

We leased space from Nova University's oceanographic research facility and arranged for the use of a boat that had been donated to the university. We had several other boats available as well.

As this new unit acquired intelligence about sea smuggling operations, it became clear that all routes led to Bimini. The stories we heard from informants or other prisoners made Bimini sound like Dodge City of the Old West. Worse, many of these tales indicated that much of what was going on was being done with the blessing of the Bahamian government.

Based on this information, I sent a couple of officers over to Bimini on a fishing exhibition, literally. Their instructions were to fish and observe for a few days and then come home.

The officer-fishermen stayed at The Complete Angler Resort, a well-known tourist stop on North Bimini. The fishing waters near the resort were quiet during the day, but at night the sound of speedboats and airplanes was constant. My officers couldn't believe the activity. The island of South Bimini resembled some of the islands in the Pacific during World War II, with plane and boat wreckage everywhere, often riddled with bullets.

According to one of the officers, who had visited Bimini before, the architecture had changed on North Bimini. Broken-down wooden homes with no indoor plumbing were being replaced by stucco dwellings with all the amenities, including air conditioning. It was obvious where the money was coming from to bankroll this transformation.

I met with some DEA people I knew, along with Customs agents. Both organizations were aware of the problems in Bimini. According to some confirmed sources, Carlos Lehder, a high ranking official within the Colombian cartel, was buying up property in the Bahamas while donating Mercedes to members of the Bahamian ministry.

Bimini had become the transfer point for drugs coming from Colombia to the United States. The DEA's and Customs' hands were tied, since these were national agencies required to work through the State Department, which refused to sanction any type of action against the Bahamas.

"What about me?" I asked them. "What about the Broward County Sheriff's Office? I don't believe I'm bound by the same shackles that you are."

They agreed that the BSO, as a local law enforcement agency, might not have to follow the same protocol. I could tell that the idea of my officers following the criminals from Broward County to the Bahamas was appealing to my federal friends.

They agreed to supply information to me about operations they were told about - news that I could act on as I saw fit. They would deny giving me any information but this wouldn't be necessary, I assured them, since I would never mention their names. I promised to keep them informed of all the activities of my operatives, while warning them about trusting too many people with this information. It was difficult to know where Colombian informants were, but Customs and the DEA seemed like places the drug smugglers would attempt to have a source.

So we went to work. One of our first operations involved an undercover operative talking with a drug smuggler who needed a boat. We provided the boat, and the smuggler sailed our officer to Bimini for the offloading of bales of marijuana. Once back within U.S. territorial waters, the smuggler was arrested and questioned, which led to the arrest of five other individuals. Nearly 20,000 pounds of marijuana was confiscated. This was the first of many seizures of this magnitude.

As more of these operations were conducted, the extent of Bahamian government corruption surfaced. In several instances, I personally informed Bahamian authorities about the activities going on within their island chain and asked for their help. Either nothing was done or operations were closed and moved to another part of the Bahamas. Bahamian police assistance would have been extremely helpful in our operations, but not knowing who to trust made it almost impossible to work with them. Now they were tipped off as to the U.S. police interest in their islands, and drug smugglers were guaranteed to be more careful in working with any Americans. For these criminals, shooting first and asking questions later was often a preferred method of business.

Anyone hanging around Bimini long enough had the opportunity to participate in smuggling if he or she wanted. I had officers over there as "fishing" tourists who received an offer to rent their boat for a few hours for a substantial sum of money. When the sheriff's office participated in such deals, arrests were made once back on American soil, and significant amounts of drugs, destined for our streets, were taken.

We were doing a drug run with smugglers every other week out of our port operations. We had gutted the inside of one of the boats to make it look like a legitimate smugglers' craft. One of the cases we worked on in conjunction with the Florida Department of Law Enforcement involved this boat and the dangers that are inherent in any undercover operation.

The smugglers loved the boat and set it up for a run to Bimini to pick up a load of drugs. Five of my officers were on the boat along with seven well-armed drug dealers. Ian Griffith, who could handle the boat well, was the captain, and he set sail flying the Bahamian flag.

I had informed the local commandant of the U.S. Coast Guard about the operation but asked him not to share this information with many of his people. I didn't trust everyone in the Coast Guard either, I'm afraid.

Not long after the boat took off, we received an emergency call from the Coast Guard saying that our vessel had radioed a distress call - someone on board was in need of medical attention. What happened? was my first question. The commandant hadn't received any further information. I told him to use his discretion and extract the injured person from the ship and have him flown to Broward General Hospital.

I was in a state of panic. I was unaware of both the extent of the medical attention needed for the crew member and the status of my other four operatives, if, in fact, it was one of my people who was down. The injured party could have been a smuggler, but somehow I doubted it. I honestly didn't believe the operation was blown yet, either, or there likely would have been no radio call.

When I arrived at Broward General to await the helicopter bringing in the victim, I was confronted by several reporters already on the scene. The media monitors our radio frequencies to get leads on developing stories. I called them all over to a secluded room and told them that the injured person was part of an undercover operation in progress and that other officers were still involved whose lives could be in danger if any of the story surfaced at this time. "This small story is not worth anyone's life," I told them, "so no print or television - yet." I promised they would get the full story when the operation was brought to a conclusion.

All of them agreed to these conditions, except one writer from the Hollywood Sun-Tattler. He said he'd have to call and check with his editor first. I said that was fine and that I would accompany him to hear what he had to say to his editor. As we walked over to the phones, he told me he wasn't sure he'd be able to kill this story.

I grabbed his arm and stared him down. "Look, I've made a legitimate request to you to hold your story. If someone gets hurt because of you, I'm going to hurt you like you've never been hurt before. Consider this a promise. I'm not going to get angry. I'm not going to shout. But if you persist and one of my people gets shot, you're next."

He called his editor and gave him an accurate description of our conversation. He kept glancing nervously at me, wondering if I was going to do him bodily harm at any moment. He definitely had gotten the message. I meant it, too. If this reporter's story cost any lives, I would reach down his throat and rip his heart out.

The editor apparently understood the message, too, as he killed the story. The reporter hung up, relieved. "You'll get the story when everyone does," I promised. "No one will scoop you."

When the helicopter landed, the victim turned out to be Ian Griffith, but he wasn't as injured as I'd feared. He had been in the engine room, doing some mechanical work, when the boat hit a wave and sent him crashing into the machinery. He cracked his forehead and dislocated his shoulder, thus prompting the distress call. The boat had continued to the Bahamas after Ian was carried off. He didn't think that any suspicions were raised, especially since the drugs hadn't been picked up yet. The smugglers were no wiser, Ian assured.

He turned out to be correct. The smugglers were concerned for Ian's safety right up until they returned from the Bahamas with our officers. We arrested them in the United States on drug trafficking charges, and they suddenly had a lot more to worry about than Ian's health.

The intelligence being gathered on Bimini was producing excellent information about where drug shipments were bound and allowed us to make arrests on our end. I didn't want any of the agents over there to become directly involved with smuggling, only to obtain as much knowledge as they could. If they were approached about a buy, I told them to get in touch with a couple of operatives here who would pose as smugglers.

One such call came in and officers Cherokee Paul MacDonald and Rick Riggio were dispatched to handle it. They flew to Bimini, met with the drug dealers, and started negotiating. The dealers turned out to be Bahamian Customs and Immigration officials who said they had a cocaine stash on Andros Island. They wanted Riggio and MacDonald to fly them from South Bimini to Andros to pick it up. My men agreed.

When they arrived on Andros, they were greeted by a uniformed Bahamian official with several stars on his shoulder, probably the local chief of police. He told the operatives how many kilos of cocaine he had available for sale and was ready to conclude the deal immediately. MacDonald declined, saying the money was not here but in the United States and that's where he wanted to make the buy. He said they were here to explore the possibilities of a deal, take back a sample to test, and if it was legitimate, negotiate the arrangements.

The Bahamian officer was not pleased with these revelations, and as he vented his rage, Riggio and MacDonald hopped back aboard the plane and took off, leaving the fuming man at the end of the runway. The Bahamian officer must have written down the identification number of the plane because he radioed ahead to U.S. Customs that two drug smugglers were on their way back to the United States at that moment. Riggio signaled in his flight plan to land at Pompano Beach's small airfield. He called in to us as well and I went down with a couple of others to meet them and find out what they'd learned.

When we arrived, we saw about a dozen Customs officials armed with rifles and shotguns, obviously waiting for an airplane to land.

I looked around the room and waved. "Hi, fellas. Who are you waiting on?"

One of the leaders replied, "We're waiting for this bunch of smugglers to come in from the Bahamas and we're going to bust their ass."

"Really?" I said. "That's a coincidence because I'm waiting for a couple of my operatives to get in from the Bahamas, too."

Of course, we were both waiting for the same plane. When Riggio and MacDonald disembarked from their plane, they were surrounded by Customs officials, each pointing some type of weapon at them. I broke in quickly to identify my undercover agents and all was settled before the situation got out of hand. In fact, the Customs agents applauded what we were doing because they were not allowed the latitude to do it themselves.

An operative on North Bimini became involved with a group that, again, included officers from the Bahamian government. These policemen had confiscated 400 kilos of cocaine and wanted to sell it, promising that they could get as much as they wanted, when they wanted. We arranged the buy from stateside, actually withdrawing a million dollars in cash from a cooperating banking institution to conclude the deal. Minutes before the arranged buy, we received a phone call saying that the sellers didn't want to finish the deal on American soil so the deal fell through, but the corruption of the Bahamian officials was very evident.

I decided to place an operative in Bimini in a semi-permanent living arrangement that would make him seem less suspect to wary Bahamian officials dealing drugs. I tagged the operation "Houdini" and assigned one of my top officers. A friend of his owned a house in Bimini where he could live, and he had already been a regular visitor as a fisherman.

We loaded his boat with transmission devices and an antenna tuned to our frequency to enable easy communication. He was a student on leave when he sailed to Bimini. The islanders seemed to accept that explanation and left Houdini to himself.

Every morning, he would do some reconnaissance, on foot or by boat, checking out the latest boat and aircraft arrivals. He heard horror stories about bodies washing ashore, headless corpses, Colombians shooting Colombians, and Colombians shooting Cubans. It became obvious that there was no honor among these thieves.

While Houdini was doing his daily run, I would send Rick Riggio out by aircraft to pick up Houdini's broadcast, which included coded messages that the other undercover operatives faithfully delivered to Houdini each day. Various names were assigned to specific types of sea and air craft to disguise the message from anyone who happened to be on the same frequency. There could be no mistakes, or we'd lose Houdini.

This was a superior intelligence operation and we tracked down a number of these air and sea craft when they put in the United States, usually on a drug-running mission. We would then notify the appropriate unit - whether it be Customs, the DEA, or the Coast Guard - to make the arrests. It wasn't important who made the final arrests, only that the arrests were made. Higher authorities in all of these organizations were interested in my source for this intelligence, but I merely said that we picked it up routinely in questioning arrested dealers.

Houdini continued to do his job. With the $70,000 high-powered "cigarette" boat and his $150 sunglasses, he was well known on the island. The intelligence he continued to transmit was incredible. During the height of the Colombian marijuana harvest, smuggling flights arrived every day. It was so crowded on the small island that if one more aircraft had landed on South Bimini, the island probably would have sunk beneath the weight.

Everything came to a head during an undercover operation that finally exposed the Bahamian corruption running rampant throughout the islands.

A group of men that we believed were Cuban bought the largest home on South Bimini, a sprawling estate with a large dock and direct access to the

Atlantic Ocean. Their nearest neighbor was several hundred yards away. We started calling it the "Cuban House." Houdini confirmed that it was a smuggler's haven. A tall tree near the dock was stripped of its limbs and a strobe light placed on top to signal boats inbound from South Florida. Boat traffic was extremely heavy in the few hours before dawn. Any complaints made in person to the group living in the Cuban House brought forth gunfire in response. If someone happened to witness something he or she shouldn't have, that person would most likely be killed. It was not unusual to find a boat covered with blood and full of bullet holes and a corpse or two - mostly innocent tourists who were in the wrong place at the worst time. The dealers killed their own as well. One pilot who used to smuggle contraband regularly out of Bimini finally quit when he refused to pay the "protection fee" of $100,000 since it didn't ensure that the gun battles over drugs would cease.

We arranged a drug deal with a ring that included Bahamian Customs, immigration, and police officials. I dispatched several operatives to the Bahamas to buy more than 800 pounds of cocaine. The source of this cocaine was apparently confiscated drugs that the Bahamian officials had been holding for their own disposition. Because the deal was to be concluded on foreign soil, I alerted Bahamian officials about this buy and about the Cuban House, which I urgently encouraged them to raid without hesitation. They were somewhat taken aback by all of this news, but agreed to assist us. Their raid netted the arrests of five American citizens, six Bahamians (none of whom were officials) and one Colombian national. However, the raiding party ignored the Cuban House.

I was furious. I told the Bahamian police that if they didn't raid that damn house, I'd do it myself. They agreed again to handle it. They were 150 miles from South Bimini at that moment but said they'd have a boat leaving within a few minutes. They needn't have bothered making the trip; while en route, the Cuban House disappeared in an explosion that precipitated a massive fire that destroyed the house. By the time Bahamian police arrived, there were no residents, no aircraft, and of course no house.

Our secret was out. The Bahamian government complained to the U.S. Ambassador, who blasted the State Department, which prompted a department official to contact me. He asked me, "Who the hell do you think you are, the International Sheriff's Office of Broward County?"

I replied, "I have a duty to my country, not to the Bahamas. If the drugs were staying there, that would be one thing. The Bahamians could work it out for themselves. But the drugs are coming over here and being sold on our playgrounds. I took an oath to protect and defend the United States and its citizens - not the Bahamians, not Colombians, not Cubans."

After that speech, the State Department official said that was fine, but I was not to go near Bimini again. I said that if he told me where I couldn't go, I'd tell him where he could go. That conversation didn't accomplish much.

While under fire we had the support of Sheriff Butterworth. He told State Department officials that we simply followed the crime trail. These were major busts, he pointed out, that were successfully putting a chokehold on some of the drug traffic coming into the country. We can't buy an ounce of marijuana, make a few arrests and say we're fighting the drug problem, he concluded.

We had community support as well. Local prominent citizens and banks raised $840,000 for us to use as a "flash roll" while playing the part of dealer on Bimini. Having the money added to our operatives' authenticity, directly leading to major arrests and seizures.

I pulled Houdini out of Bimini after the Cuban House blew up. It was time. He had been there for almost a year with fantastic results, and since our unit's actions were no longer a secret, his days were limited at best. He had earned some time off.

Without the support of any of the major federal agencies, except in a clandestine manner, I thought I would make public our charges of corruption within the Bahamian government. Otherwise, the drugs were likely to keep flowing - it would be "business as usual" on Bimini.

A former South Florida newscaster named Brian Ross was with NBC in Washington, D.C., and I contacted him with the story about the Bahamas. He was interested and convinced his news producer to do the story. The day he arrived back in South Florida to begin gathering information, he asked when he might expect to see some action.

"How about tonight?" I asked. "Is that too soon?"

"Nick!" he answered, "You set me up!"

Sadly, I shook my head. "Didn't need to do that, Brian, we get drug shipments all the time. A couple of smugglers are bringing some stuff in from

Bimini to Pompano Beach tonight according to our operatives on the island. A Hollywood lawyer and five others are involved."

We made the bust. Brian was impressed. He filmed the action, then flew with his producer, Ira Silverman, to Norman Cay, the island that Carlos Lehder, leader of the Medellin cartel, had purchased. All the footage he got would be broadcast in Washington, D.C., home of the State Department, when he returned.

Brian Ross's story caused a ripple that grew bigger and led to NBC's Today Show inviting Bahamian Prime Minister Lynden Pindling over to answer my charges of corruption within his government. He was offended and refused to come, but Brian would not back down from the story.

The whole affair prompted a Congressional investigation, which I attended and testified at, Houdini didn't want to compromise his identification, so he didn't go. I told the Congressional committee about a time when we had confiscated eighty bales of marijuana and loaded them on a Bahamian Defense Force gunboat, since we were in the Defense Force's jurisdiction. It was later reported that only twenty-five bales were loaded. This was one of the ways Bahamian officials ended up with drugs to sell. I wasn't accusing every officer in the Bahamas of corruption, but the ones that were involved were making it a nightmare for those that were not.

I accused Bahamian police officers of not arresting drug traffickers. I said that Colombia had bought out the islands and that the drug smuggling industry would continue to flourish unless something drastic was done. My operation was a dire measure needed to combat this insidious invasion of my country.

I was not very popular in the Bahamas. Most of the Bahamian ministers, as one might expect, denounced me as a liar and charged that we had violated their nation's sovereignty and had, in actual fact, invaded their island. The Congressional committee didn't seem to believe the Bahamians' denials and their insistence that they were aggressive in combating drug traffickers.

After the Houdini case, the DEA, U.S. Customs and the Coast Guard received more flexibility in handling these types of situations. They made some arrests, even though it seemed like the arrests were of drug dealers who didn't cut the government in on its "fair share of proceeds." It was the beginning of the end for the current era of Bahamian politics.

Prime Minister Pindling finally ordered a blue ribbon commission to investigate the charges that his cabinet was corrupt and involved in drug smuggling. Pindling was represented by famed attorney F. Lee Bailey.

I was one of the individuals called by the committee to testify in 1984. A panel of judges from other British Commonwealth nations asked questions, along with attorney Bailey. In truth, I was nervous about testifying. My accusations had made me no friends over in the Bahamas and I was concerned for my safety. I didn't want to spend any nights there, so I arranged for a private jet to take me over and back on the same day. Bailey asked the usual attorney-type questions about my charges against Pindling. "Did you ever see the prime minister accept a bribe?" "Did you ever see the prime minister in the company of a known drug dealer?" I answered truthfully that I hadn't, but I pointed out the glorious mansion Pindling was having built that seemed incredibly expensive for someone on a government salary, even a prime minister's. "Do you mean to tell me," I asked, "that the prime minister is the only virgin in a house full of prostitutes?"

I gave my testimony and flew back home. After much deliberation, the inquiry into Prime Minister Pindling's government resulted in the indictment of Kendall Nottage, the minister of Youth Sports and Community Affairs. He was, apparently, the sacrificial lamb because no other charges were filed, despite evidence that Pindling's own spending far exceeded his income and he had made several large bank deposits that were unexplained. They may not have been drug related, but it wasn't clean money. Pindling denied any wrong doing and instead pointed his finger at us. Americans are the principal drug smugglers, he said, the principal crooks of the world. Pindling was dirty and I knew it.

Nottage's undoing came from being involved with a trust financed primarily by money from U.S. fugitive banker Robert Lee Vesco. One of my officers had spotted Vesco in Nassau in 1981, but attempts to extradite him failed. Nottage and Pindling also jointly owned an aircraft charter firm based in Fort Lauderdale, which made one wonder what those planes could have been used for.

The commission's revelations shocked Bahamians and eventually led to Pindling's ouster. Our U.S. ambassador was also replaced. Best of all, drug traffic from Bimini slowed to a crawl. When we ran a few operations within Bahamian territory in the late 1980s, we did so with full cooperation and assistance from the Bahamian police force. I'd like to believe that our 1979-81 undercover efforts on Bimini led directly to the changes that were made in the Bahamian government's attitude toward drug dealers. To believe that the people of the Bahama were not affected, that all the drugs were coming to the United States and not being distributed to their own children, was naive at best. Drugs will corrupt and destroy unless you address the issue. Ignoring it will not send the problems away. When the Bahamians started kicking the Colombians out, I knew they'd turned a corner.

I hoped we'd sent a message to the underworld, too: there was no place they'd be safe, no haven in which to hide. To protect our county and our country, our Organized Crime Division would go anywhere it had to. I was proud of this unit, of the people dedicated, as I was, to stopping the flow of drugs on our streets no matter what it took. These officers weren't watching the clock or scrutinizing their paychecks. They simply wanted to serve and protect in the best way they knew how.

It would be some time before anyone dealing drugs in the Bahamas could look at a passing speedboat and wonder if he had just been spotted by the Broward County International Sheriff's Office.

∽

IT WASN'T LONG AFTER THE BIMINI INVASION THAT VICE PRESIDENT GEORGE BUSH and I had a difference of opinion on the ABC-TV show "Night-line" before a national television audience. He had created a highly publicized task force to prevent drug smuggling in South Florida, and had brought in a number of agents from all over the country to our community. He placed in charge a retired admiral named Murphy who, quite truthfully, if hit in the face with a bale of cocaine might not have known what it was. After a few months, the vice president was ready to declare the war against drugs in South Florida a victory and went on national television to do so.

When the vice president calmly said that the word from the task force was that smuggling was now under control, I countered with the comment that in South Florida all the evidence pointed to business as usual, every addict was getting what he or she needed, there was no panic in the streets, and if anyone was in control, it was still the drug criminals.

Vice President Bush was not pleased to hear this. He cited evidence from his drug task force as to its results. I could only apologize and give him my view from the front lines. Marijuana prices had actually come down, I told him, hardly an indication that the stuff was scarce. I wanted desperately to tell the American people the same thing as the vice president, I said, but it wasn't possible. I had seen no slowdown at all. Despite a string of busts we had made ourselves and the virtual shutdown of the Bimini source.

A year later, the task force closed its doors and quietly left town. Most of what it did in the Fort Lauderdale office was to process evidence seized by Coast Guard and Customs patrol services. We rarely saw anyone from the task force and its presence didn't alter anything we did in the way of drug investigations.

In October 1982, Sheriff Butterworth was appointed by Governor Bob Graham to head up the State Highway Safety and Motor Vehicles Division in the state capitol of Tallahassee. I was sad to see Butterworth go, as we had a good working relationship and OCD had brought him a number of successes along with the controversies. It was the second change at the top in less than four years.

For Butterworth's successor, Governor Graham reached out to the circuit court bench, just as Governor Askew had done when he selected Butterworth, and chose Judge George Brescher as the new Broward County Sheriff. Sheriff Brescher was a soft-spoken gentleman with a law background, and he'd been an excellent judge just as Butterworth had been. Like his predecessors, his knowledge about front-line law enforcement was not strong, and it likely meant that he would rely on his department heads for input and direction. Sheriff Brescher settled in, kept me in my position as head of the Organized Crime Division, and left me to report directly to him as Sheriffs Stack and Butterworth had done. That was fine with me.

At about the same time, several things happened.

First, the state of New York was about to pass a confiscation law similar to Florida's whereby criminal property seized, whether it be cash, cars, boats, planes, etc., could be retained and used by law enforcement agencies to fight crime. The law was working well in Florida and I was flown up to testify at the New York hearings. I advised that in the last two years, Florida had confiscated about $5 million from drug dealers, $4 million of which was used to build a new jail and the remainder utilized to hire more dispatchers for the 911 emergency communications department. I encouraged the legislature to pass the law.

Second, I was approached by film producer Martin Bregman about a film he was going to make with director Brian DePalma and actor Al Pacino. It was called Scarface, only it wasn't about Al Capone and Chicago, but based on the influx of Cuban criminals to South Florida during the Mariel boat lift. What Bregman needed was someone to act as a technical advisor on the film, some-one who knew about drug dealers and understood the South Florida scene. I told him I'd be glad to do it and he said that he would like me to instruct Al Pacino in the ways of Cuban drug dealers. Having impersonated a few of those in my time, I was certain I could do it.

Al Pacino and I didn't get off to a great start. The first day he showed up to work with me, he was dressed like a street bum. I told him if he wanted to tag along, he would have to look better than that. I waited until he changed clothes and we began our work. I'll say one thing for Pacino, he learned fast. There were plenty of drug dealers on our streets and he studied their every move.

A number of people were concerned about the image this film would give to South Florida and, in particular, the Hispanic community. Those fears proved to be unfounded. There was nothing remotely attractive about cocaine or drug dealing in the movie. The Hispanic characters in the film that were portrayed in a good light outnumbered those that were on the wrong side of the legal system. It was a great experience for me, having been a movie fan since I was a child, and I was grateful to Martin Bregman for the opportunity to assist in the film's making.

In 1983, a Florida grand jury report criticized the Broward police chiefs' anti-racketeering unit for its ineffectiveness in dealing with organized crime. As a result, State Attorney Michael Satz vowed to form another independent operation that would be composed of officers from all of the Broward County police forces with a specific agenda to battle organized crime. The Broward sheriff, George Brescher, favored my appointment to head up this task force but caught some flack from others because they found someone who was more low key and less controversial. Besides, these critics said, I was better known for narcotics enforcement.

While most of our work involved drug arrests, I also ran units with several other divisions in my department that investigated organized crime every day. During the reports about this so-called special unit, my office had begun a new undercover investigation into a loan shark/bookmaking ring. We were constantly "getting in the face" of organized crime for a variety of offenses, not only narcotics.

My division was also currently being audited for the first time since it was formed in 1971. I had set my own controls against corruption within the unit and I was confident we could account for every dime allocated to the Organized Crime Division. Neither Sheriff Stack nor Butterworth had seen the necessity of an audit, but Sheriff Brescher, who didn't know me as well, ordered it as, I believed, a matter of course.

The year 1983 had been an interesting one for me. It was the first full year under a new sheriff, we had forced a foreign government to pay attention to a corruption problem within its ranks, the vice president's drug task force had quietly slipped out of town after declaring victory only a year earlier, I had tutored Al Pacino on how to behave like a drug dealer for a feature film, and my division underwent its first audit.

Twenty-four years after joining the Metro Dade police force, I was still doing the work I loved. I was beginning to think about retirement within the next three or four years. I still had time to do something in the private sector before I retired, and I had to admit to a curiosity about what it would be like to work outside the constraints of government.

For now, though, I was intent on continuing to build the Broward OCD into the finest unit of its kind in the country. We had acquired a national reputation and were in constant communication with similar units, offering advice and expertise.

I had no way of knowing that an interesting and rewarding police career was about to take another ride on the roller coaster of politics.

Five

A Stitch in Time

Broward County Sheriff's Office

PERSONNEL ORDER #83-90
ISSUED: November 29, 1983
EFFECTIVE: November 19, 1983
The following personnel actions shall become effective on the date
above indicated:
Bower, Donald, Lieutenant, is re-assigned from Internal Affairs to
the Organized Crime Division reporting to Director Edward Pyers.

Navarro, Nicholas, Major, is re-assigned from Commanding Officer
of the Organized Crime Division to Administrative Duties as
assigned by the Sheriff.

Peart, Charles, Lieutenant, is re-assigned from the Department of
Strategic Planning to the Organized Crime Division reporting to
Director Edward Pyers.

Pyers, Edward, is re-assigned from the position of Counsel to the
Sheriff to Director of the Organized Crime Division.

George Brescher, Sheriff of Broward County

IT WAS THE WEDNESDAY BEFORE THANKSGIVING, NOVEMBER 23, 1983, WHEN I walked into Broward County Sheriff George Brescher's office for a meeting he had called between the two of us. Brescher had been sheriff for about thirteen months. He was a former county judge who was a nice man, a decent human being, but who knew little about the job of law enforcement.

I had no beef with Brescher, though. As head of the Organized Crime Division, I reported directly to him just as I had with previous Sheriffs Stack and Butterworth, updating him frequently on all the various cases we were working on.

I had no idea what the meeting was for, having given Brescher a briefing the previous Friday on the division's current caseload. He started the conversion by telling me that I was the most professional law enforcement officer he had ever met and what a terrific job I'd done for Broward County.

This was trouble. Nobody in this office ever started a conversation that way without ending it on some kind of sour note. Still, I never expected to hear what came next.

"Nick," he said, "there are a few changes that need to be made, you know, in streamlining the office, and they include removing you from the Organized Crime Division."

"What?" I was stunned.

Brescher, obviously uncomfortable, said that he had some pressures on him and this was just one of the moves he had to make.

It felt like I'd been hit in the face with a two-by-four. "What pressures?" I asked.

He didn't give me a specific answer. "Just pressures," he said. Then he told me my options: first, going back to the airport as head of security, where I'd been in 1977 and 1978; second, teaching at the police academy; or third, become Commander of District 3, an area of North Broward. He told me to go home for Thanksgiving, take some time to think about my options, and let him know next week which position I wanted.

Just like that. Thanks Nick. So long. It's been good to know you. Words failed me. I felt I was one of the main reasons for OCD's success, and being asked to leave it again was mind-numbing. Brescher had openly said he was happy with the work we were doing. So happy, apparently, that he was going to transfer me into some dead-end job for the rest of my career.

I walked out to my car in a daze and sat in the front seat thinking, this is it? This is what twenty-four years in law enforcement has for you at the end of the rainbow? I couldn't go home and face Sharron yet. I had to go somewhere to sit and absorb this news. I drove to a deserted spot, put the car in park and sat there, a multitude of thoughts going through me.

I shook my head. No, this isn't right. This can't be what the good Lord has in store for me after all of the scrapes I'd been shoved into and managed to escape. The hard work and dedication to making this community, my community, safe for its citizens. There had to be something more than "See you later, Nick. You've been such a good cop we're putting you out to pasture."

Then it struck me that I'd been in this same movie before: Christmas 1976. Stack picked Christmas, Brescher opted for Thanksgiving. What is it with these guys and holidays?

I remembered hearing that Stack's move to reassign me was politically motivated. Although he had been sheriff of Broward County for some time, he was constantly running, unsuccessfully, for congress. Some people had him convinced I had become too popular as head of the organized crime unit and would use this widespread recognition to run for sheriff against him. In the political arena, people think that everyone else has a political motive. High profile, which I guess I was, is equated with those ambitions.

Those people didn't know me very well. I had no interest in politics whatsoever and wasn't running against Ed Stack or anyone else. All I wanted to do was bust the bad guys and, in the process, make the sheriff's office look good. I was content and never thought or cared about the sheriff's office for myself. I didn't care who got the credit as long as we were taking drugs and criminals off the streets.

Did Brescher have the same ideas as Stack? That I was going to run against him? I thought about the scene the weekend before when the local media sponsored a "roast" of the area's politicians and celebrities. It's called the Yellow Feather Awards and both Brescher and I had been invited to attend. It's usually an entertaining evening; everyone has a lot of laughs. I had no idea that the two of us were destined to win awards that night that would ignite a series of events and change my future.

Mine came first. The local press corps handed me their High Profile award for being the best known undercover agent and the public official most adept at getting himself publicity. They called me "ol' Scarface," in reference to the Al Pacino movie. Everybody, including me, had a pretty good laugh about the award.

Later that evening, Brescher received his award, given to honor the individual who had distinguished himself by being indistinguishable, the Yellow Feather Everybody Should Be So Lucky Obscurity Award. In presenting the award, the press called Brescher "an obscure former county judge who, after a number of unremarkable years on the bench, disappeared from sight entirely last October 16" - the date he was appointed sheriff of Broward County. The award received a lot of laughs, but I wondered how well Brescher took it. Looking back on the incident, sitting in my car, I wondered even more.

Brescher was rumored to make some of his decisions only after consulting with a group of advisors nicknamed the "Kitchen Cabinet," led by its "godfather," none other than former Sheriff Stack, then in his early seventies. Among its members were Chief Circuit Judge John Ferris, County Court Judge Larry Seidlin, Brescher's top assistant, Sharon Solomon, and Brescher's head of Internal Affairs, Mike Fufidio. Could they have convinced Brescher to make this change? Could history really repeat itself like this? Did Brescher think I was going to run against him for sheriff, too? Is that what started this?

The longer I sat there, the angrier I became. I'd worked hard all those years for the sheriffs and this was how it was going to end - reassigned to some thankless role for the last couple of years before retirement? It was ridiculous. Happy Thanksgiving to you, too, George.

I finally went home and told Sharron. Equally taken aback by this news, we spent almost the entire holiday weekend discussing our options. We really weren't financially ready for me to retire, but I wasn't going to choose one of Brescher's three options. Ed Stack may have told Brescher, "Hey, Nick accepted a reassignment before; he'll accept one again." Wrong, Ed. Bad advice. The circumstances were different and reassignment wasn't in the cards for me. By the time the weekend was over, the decision was made. First thing Monday morning, I was back in Brescher's office.

I told him each of his options was considered carefully but my final decision was to take option four: I quit. These were difficult words for me to say, having never quit anything in my life. From Brescher's startled reaction, I could see he didn't expect this from me, either.

I shook my head. He never did understand what the job I had been doing meant to me.

I asked him who he had in mind to replace me as head of the organized crime unit, just as a matter of curiosity. He said he hadn't completely decided, but was leaning toward Ed Pyers.

Ed Pyers! He was counsel to the sheriff's office and didn't know the first thing about law enforcement. A prosecutor who rarely won his cases was taking over. What a travesty! My resignation was in the mail.

Even so, that night we were wrapping up a big case we'd been pursuing for some time, and I went to work as usual. Sharron talked to the media when word leaked out I was being removed. While Brescher was forcing me out, I was still making arrests on his behalf. Brescher just didn't understand that I wanted to be a law enforcement officer, not a politician. I felt bad for the people I worked with, who were going to still be there after my departure, and knew life would be difficult for them. But I had to resign. Brescher's alternatives were unacceptable.

Brescher held a press conference the next day, Tuesday, to announce his personnel moves. Naturally, there was a flood of questions about my removal. Brescher told the reporters he had no problems with me (which was true), but that it was simply time to remove me from a job I'd had too long. He went on to say the job has tremendous temptations and stress and more than ten years is a long time to be subjected to that kind of pressure.

What stress? I felt as good that day as when I first started the Organized Crime Division back in 1971. Temptations? That sounded like a cheap shot. I've never been tempted to take one nickel. All of the drugs and money we'd come in contact with were dirty. There was blood all over them. To my dying day, I can say I was never tempted to take any.

So what did he mean? He emphasized the honesty and integrity of my successor, Ed Pyers. But why bring any of this up at all? If the man was going to question my personal integrity, he was going to have a problem with me.

Late in the day, Brescher publicly apologized for any misconceptions he may have raised about my honesty. But the damage had been done. Doubts had been planted in people's minds. I would never forgive this man for those comments.

My resignation was made effective a few weeks in the future, allowing for the amount of vacation and sick leave that I had accumulated. I went home, thinking I'd never see the sheriff's office again.

∽

THE PHONE CALLS AND VISITS STARTED ALMOST IMMEDIATELY. NICK, WHAT ARE you going to do? What's going to happen? How do you feel?

One of the first calls I received was from my former boss in the sheriff's office, Bob Butterworth, now Florida's State Attorney General. He told me this move would set law enforcement back twenty years in Broward County. Newspaper columnist John DeGroot and his wife came over and they started encouraging me to run for sheriff against Brescher in next year's election. Similar suggestions came from the community as a whole. The support was overwhelming.

That would be ironic, I thought. Brescher removes me because he thinks I was a political threat, which wasn't true. I leave office because of this removal and run against him for sheriff. The idea was interesting.

The encouragement continued. Jack Hamilton, president of Fort Lauderdale's Democratic Club, told me I had to run. So did Ed Houston, former head of Barnett Bank; Carl Mayhue, the liquor chain magnate; car dealer Jimmy Bryan; trucking executive Ralph Sessa; attorney Steadman Stahl; and industrialist Jack Holcomb. These were some big financial hitters who promised to support my campaign if I decided to run. They told me I'd be doing a great service to Broward County.

That's how the seduction started. They made it sound as if life would come to an end for everyone unless I could come to the rescue. After a while, I began to believe it. When Bob Butterworth, a man I trusted and respected, said, "Nick, you have to run for office, it would be the right thing for the community," my mind started to buy into the idea. Then, Don Knight, a man I didn't even know and who owns a lumber supply company in Fort Lauderdale, put up a big sign in front of his store that said, Navarro for Sheriff. The local media interviewed him and he said that, although he didn't know me, he thought I seemed like a top-notch drug-enforcement type of guy and taken a bum rap. It was getting harder to turn my back on the idea of running for office.

The Christmas holidays came and went and I thought more about it. I was officially on the department payroll until January 20 and was not going to make specific decisions until then, but the possibility was becoming attractive to me. My retirement check was $1,200 per month. This money, combined with the earnings Sharron had from her real estate business (she had left her job in the sheriff's office to work in the booming housing market), wasn't going to be enough for us, so I had to do something else, anyway. Why not be sheriff?

I told Sharron what I was thinking, saying some men at my age, fifty-four, have a mid-life crisis. To get through it, some buy convertibles, some get girl-friends. Me, I thought about going into politics.

I didn't know a thing about the political process, but if running for office was to be my decision, it was important to start understanding it. Sharron and I went to the library and checked out a book by Harry Truman. We also rent-ed the Robert Redford film, The Candidate. In Truman's book, he said the man who shakes the most hands will win the election. The Redford film showed what a run for elected office was like. It seemed like a task I could accomplish. After all, I could shake hands. I could see people. A thought began to form that maybe the forces around us had created this situation to give me the opportunity to become sheriff. It certainly seemed like the best way to finish my law enforcement career.

There was also the matter of my political affiliation. A number of years ear-lier when I was working for Sheriff Ed Stack, he asked me if I would consider switching from Republican to Democrat since he was doing it. He said it would look good if he could show internal support for the move by pointing to some of his best people that were doing the same thing. My reaction was to ask if he was sure I was a Republican. He said yes; he had checked it out with the Supervisor of Elections. I told him it really didn't matter to me - I had always voted for the person anyway, not the party - so I switched.

So there I was, a registered Democrat, about to make the first political deci-sion of my life. However, not everyone encourage me. The Broward Democratic Party Chairman John Lomelo told me that all the big guns were lining up for Brescher and that I should save my money. The die had been cast, he told me. The political machine was behind Brescher, and I'd only be a spoiler.

Word got back to me that Ed Stack thought my candidacy was a waste of time, too. He was reputed to have said that Broward County would never accept an immigrant with a Latin accent as its Sheriff.

I didn't care what Stack thought. My appeal wouldn't be to any specific ethnic group, but to all of the people of Broward County who wanted a genuine law enforcement officer as their sheriff. There had been eleven sheriffs in Broward County, including Brescher, and not one of them had a law enforcement background. They were car salesmen, insurance agents, attorneys, but not genuine law officers. The office had been used for so long as a political steppingstone that I truly believed Broward County was as tired of that as I was.

Imagine! A sheriff's Office run by someone with a police background!

If I decided to run, there first would have to be a primary against Brescher. That was all right with me; he was the guy I'd have to beat anyway. What did it matter if it was in a primary or the general election?

Brescher announced his candidacy on January 13, amid much fanfare. Governor Bob Graham took a flight in from Tallahassee, saying that even though it was unusual for him to make an early pre-primary endorsement, "Brescher was an unusual special person doing a special, effective job for the people." Even Bob Butterworth, one of the first to encourage me to run, also came down to endorse Brescher's candidacy, saying, "George, I personally believe, has done an outstanding job." I was sure that Butterworth owed the governor a favor or two for his appointment as state head of Highway Safety and Motor Vehicles. It was my introduction to the lies and lives of politicians.

Ed Stack, part of Brescher's Kitchen Cabinet was there, too, adding his two cents, as did Democratic Party Chairman Lomelo. All in all, it was a gigantic push for George Brescher. There was even some talk about the use of sheriff's office stationary to solicit Brescher campaign contributions which the sheriff denied. Clearly, though, Brescher had the meaningful support of the heads of the county and state Democratic party.

But it's not the chiefs who win the campaign. It's the soldiers. And it was the soldiers who were urging me to run. What did I owe the big guns, anyway?

The only other candidate to declare against Brescher as a Democrat was a Seminole Indian Reservation detective sergeant named Dan Goldberg. There were rumors that former Fort Lauderdale Police Chief Leo Callahan would run, too. Brescher may have been the party insider, but there was already opposition to him.

The ball was in my court. I didn't know anything about running for office, didn't have much money personally to run a campaign, and couldn't imagine asking people for money since it seemed like taking a bribe. I didn't know the first thing about giving a political speech and, frankly, had to admit my own doubts about the entire enterprise.

But Sharron had no doubts. She opened my campaign fund with her own $1,000 check. If my wife thought that much of me, I had to go for it. All of those years in law enforcement wouldn't be thrown away; if I was chief law officer, they'd have real meaning. What better way to use them than as sheriff of the county I lived in and loved.

Brescher had hundreds of people crowded into the fancy Marina Bay Club for his kick-off. A friend, Bob Gill, the owner of two Sheraton hotels in the county, agreed to let me use one of his rooms for my press conference. Sharron came along with a couple of friends, Buddy Nevins of the Fort Lauderdale Sun-Sentinel and Channel 10's Jim Reynolds, who'd been privy to the Bimini "invasion." This was going to be my first public appearance to declare and I wanted to say the right thing.

I told the small gathering that for too long, the sheriff's office had been used as a political steppingstone. I'd been in the trenches and was a professional cop. I wanted only to be sheriff, nothing else. There was no other political goal in mind; it would not be a short stop for me before going somewhere else. It was my belief that the citizens of Broward County wanted a twenty-four hour, seven-days-a-week sheriff, as did the professionals in the sheriff's office, where morale was low. The heart had been taken out of the sheriff's office and I wanted to put it back in. It was a place I loved, and I had many friends and associates who worked there with me.

I told them there was no bitterness on my part toward George Brescher. I simply felt better qualified and thought the people of this county would be better served by a law enforcement veteran. My goal was to prevent crime. It was one thing to make arrests after a crime occurs, but in that scenario there's a victim who may never get over being the target of a criminal. I wanted to cut down on the number of victims.

I told the half-dozen people standing in the room that I intended to run the campaign as I would run the sheriff's office: twenty-four hours a day, seven days a week. Let the best man win.

There were four or five hand claps from the audience. I was now in the running for sheriff.

❧

ONE OF THE FIRST THINGS WE DID WAS CHANGE SHARRON'S POLITICAL AFFILIA-tion from Republican to Democrat. Every vote was going to count and this seemed a good place to start.

A campaign manager was hired and strategy sessions held to put together public appearances, fund-raisers, contribution solicitations, and a platform of ideas. To my surprise, donations began coming in immediately from friends I'd known over the years as well as complete strangers who said they wanted a professional cop running the sheriff's office. They, too, were tired of the political maneuverings that had long been a part of this position.

This, then, became my theme: on-the-job experience. A series of quotes from various individuals I'd worked with over the years testified to my lengthy police background. These remarks served as a framework for campaign flyers and short political speeches.

The campaign was coming together. We were raising money equal to that of George Brescher's campaign. We were being called by the traditional Democratic clubs and other organizations to make speeches on an equal basis with Brescher. The support appeared widespread and my message of experience was starting to pay off.

A friend of mine had purchased a building in downtown Fort Lauderdale. He was a paint store owner who wanted to open another, similar venture at that location.

It was an old, abandoned Howard Johnson's overgrown with foliage and resided in by some of Broward County's homeless. There was a moratorium on new building and renovation at the time due to sewage problems, so my friend graciously offered the building to me for a temporary campaign head-quarters.

The goal was, as stated from the outset, a grass-roots campaign among the "soldiers" of the community. While many political candidates cater almost exclusively to the well-to-do with their $150 per plate fund-raisers, I wanted to do the opposite. For my campaign, the routine became the $10-$15 dollar fund-raisers, with fried chicken as our entree. A campaign for the people was what I wanted, and individuals who had never before thought about being involved in a political campaign were coming to these dinners.

Brescher himself had been conspicuously absent from the campaign so far, apparently content to let me try to build up whatever support I could muster, confident in having the party chiefs at his side. Dan Goldberg, the other Democratic candidate, was even considering switching to Independent status, feeling he wouldn't fare well in the September 4 Democratic primary against Brescher and me. This didn't seem like a viable option, in my opinion, since only 41,552 of the 557,909 Broward voters were Independents.

My campaign had planned a Memorial Day barbecue, a picnic at T-Y Park in Hollywood. We bought about $3,000 worth of chicken for it and we expected a large turnout of 1,000 or so people. We arrived at the park very early that holiday Monday, fired up the grills, put the chicken on, and it started to rain. The rain stayed all day, but still, some 400 people came out for the affair. Naturally, there was a substantial amount of chicken left over. A few people said the rain was a shame and that I must be disappointed at such a setback. I told them it wasn't a setback at all, but maybe the Lord made it rain that day so someone else could have the chicken. On Tuesday, the leftover chicken was distributed throughout the county to places that feed the homeless. Chicken dominated their menus for the next few days.

There was other fallout from the Memorial Day picnic. Ron Cacciatore, a friend and veteran undercover officer in the Organized Crime Division, had purchased two tickets at eight dollars a piece for the barbecue, along with several other deputies from the sheriff's office. Shortly after that Cacciatore was transferred from the OCD to an afternoon road-patrol shift in South Broward. Ed Pyers, the new commander, insisted it was Cacciatore's length of time (five years) as an undercover officer that prompted the move. Cacciatore thought otherwise, as did a number of people in the sheriff's office.

That wasn't the only transfer. Don Veliky, another member of the Organized Crime Division, had paid for and attended two of my campaign functions. He was transferred in late May to road patrol out in Lauderhill. Chris Hock, a Hallandale police officer on temporary assignment to the Organized Crime Division, also attended two functions, and was likewise removed and returned to the Hallandale police office.

These men were all on their own time, in their own cars, paying for these functions with their own money. They weren't alone at these functions: quite a few people turned out on a regular basis for the events. The reasons for transfer were vague, a smoke screen in front of the real motivation. The transfers weren't Brescher's style but likely the work of Mike Fufidio, a member of the Kitchen Cabinet. As head of BSO's Internal Affairs, Fufidio wielded a tremendous amount of power, often saying to people that if they wanted something done they should come to him. I could picture the man, short, wiry, hyperactive, systematically checking on every individual in the office to see who was a Navarro supporter. My contempt for politics continued to grow.

In July we received word of a poll taken by Brescher's people that showed him running behind me in both name recognition and the perception of being a professional lawman rather than a politician. I was overjoyed with this news. My message was being heard loud and clear. Momentum was building and a feeling of confidence was beginning to set in. Not overconfidence; simply the understanding that the campaign for the sheriff's office was proceeding as I had visualized. Some members of the media asked me if I was going to conduct my own poll. I answered, why should I? These results looked pretty good to me.

The time had come to officially file with the Office of Elections a candidate's formal intention to run for office. A week was reserved in July for this filing. My supporters urged me to be the first to do so on Monday, July 16, but for some reason, I decided to wait until Friday. To this day, I don't know what made me do that, but it seemed a lot could happen in a week and that my patience would be rewarded.

The Democratic Party was in a quandary. I had made more progress in these last few weeks than its members wished to admit. Early on, it had appeared to be a clear-cut situation. Democratic voters dominated Broward County and Brescher was the handpicked choice to keep the office Democratic. But the heads of the Fort Lauderdale Democratic Party now came to me and said they were not happy with George Brescher and intended to support me. I knew the Broward County Democratic Party didn't feel the same way, so it was beginning to get interesting. Waiting until Friday was the prudent thing to do.

On Thursday, the double-cross came down. Dismayed by lackluster county support, the Democrats urged Bob Butterworth, my former boss, to come out publicly on behalf of George Brescher. He did. At a press conference in Fort Lauderdale, Butterworth said that Governor Graham had made the right appointment nearly two years earlier when he selected Brescher to fill Butterworth's post and that he was going to do everything he could to make sure Brescher would continue as sheriff of Broward County for the next four years. I couldn't believe it. This was the same Bob Butterworth who personally told me that Brescher was tearing down everything he and I had built up over the years. The same Bob Butterworth who told me he couldn't run for the office himself but encouraged me to do it. This endorsement was a desperate act by desperate men.

At the time Brescher formally filed that Thursday, he named his campaign management team, which was composed of an attorney, Steve Josias, and three former sheriffs, Butterworth, Ed Stack, and Tom Walker. Not only did Butterworth come out and endorse Brescher, but also since he was back in Broward County (having resigned from his job in Tallahassee as Director of Highway Safety and Motor Vehicles on June 30), he was going to actively campaign for Brescher. I was hurt. I felt betrayed.

I will never understand politics. This type of backbiting endorsement by a man who is supposed to be a friend is something I could never do. Apparently, for the politician, it comes with the territory. This, to me, was rotten, even by political standards.

I did some hard thinking that day. First, as a cop: the only way I knew how to get out of an ambush was to shoot my way out. Second, as a candidate for office, I decided to call the Republican Party chairperson about the possibility of running as a Republican. She said the party would welcome me with open arms. The only candidate they had was Dan Goldberg, who had switched from Democrat to Independent to Republican, all in the last few weeks.

State statute 106 details the election laws in Florida, and I studied it carefully to be sure that a switch from Democrat to Republican would not create any difficulties for me. The wording was vague, referring to the inability to switch parties after becoming a declared candidate. I hadn't declared officially yet. But was the time of formal filing of paperwork the point at which a candidate is considered to have declared? Or was it when one opened up a campaign fund, which I'd done in January? Or did it refer to the date of the primary (September 4) or the general election (November 6)? The wording was too obscure to determine, an advantage I would have if anyone complained about the switch.

I called my attorney, who was also my campaign treasurer, telling him about my impending switch to the Republican Party. He panicked, saying it was a violation of Florida law and wanted no part of it. I told him he wasn't a part of it; the decision was all mine. To me, the wording of the statute was unclear. He said he didn't want anyone thinking that he had given me this advice, so I agreed to sign an affidavit to that effect.

I invited all of my close campaign workers to headquarters that night for a meeting. By this time, we had moved (after sewage restrictions were removed and my friend could renovate his store downtown) to a building on State Road 7 and 23rd Streets in Fort Lauderdale. I didn't tell them what the meeting was about, only that they should come if they could. Even Sharron didn't know what I was thinking.

As they gathered around, I told them there was an announcement this candidate must make. "Tomorrow, when I go to the courthouse to declare my candidacy and pay my filing fees, it will be as a Republican."

Sharron reacted first. "What! Are you sure?"

I quickly explained my reasoning. "Why limit the choice between Brescher and me to just Democrats? This move will open it up to the entire county in the general election in November. No primary. Let all the voters decide."

Most everyone felt I could remain as a Democrat and still beat Brescher in September, but not one of these fine people, who had already worked long and hard on this campaign, withdrew his or her support. We're for you, Nick, they said, not your political party.

The question did arise, though, about the contributions made so far by people to Democrat Nick Navarro. There was the possibility they would want their money back. It was fine with me if they did. I would certainly understand. However, when I called all of my largest contributors that evening, not one asked for the money back. They simply said they gave the money to me for my campaign, not to the Democratic Party, and asked if they could do anything further. It was gratifying to receive that kind of support.

The Republican Party was delighted. Dan Goldberg switched to the Clerk of Court race and a news conference was called for Friday. The deadline for filing was noon on Friday, July 20. I planned to be there around 11:30 A.M.

Friday morning, some members of the Republican Party hierarchy met me at the courthouse. I had to file several specific applications to switch from Democrat to Republican, including Sharron's so I performed that task while making my official declaration as a candidate for sheriff - as a Republican.

The administrators in the Elections Office were somewhat surprised, and there was a horde of television and other media present. Compared to the half-dozen people who attended my January press conference, this was like the cast of thousands from an old Cecil B. DeMille movie.

Word buzzed through the courthouse as the press conference was held. I made the announcement that the press was now looking at a Republican, but the people of Broward County were seeing only a law enforcement officer who wanted to serve in the county's top law enforcement office. In my speech, I said that if I was elected sheriff, the people of Broward County would see more foot patrols and community-related cooperative activities as we all had a stake in reducing crime. Crime prevention was just as important as all of the arrests we made. There would be no need for a political appointee during my tenure. I would be the Broward County Sheriff. Period. End of story.

With Republicans and some of my Democratic supporters surrounding me, I started to leave the courthouse. I caught a glimpse of George Brescher with several of his people, all in obvious wide-eyed amazement at all that had just transpired. Reporters were trying to solicit his opinion of the events, and it was clear that he hadn't expected this switch at all. He appeared to be in a state of shock.

I saw something else, too. It was the look of a man who didn't intend to let me upstage him. It was a look that said, okay, Nick. You may have won this round, but it's a long way to November and you'd better be prepared for the fight of your life because I'm not going to give up this office easily.

He was right. There was plenty of fight to come.

Six

Punch 44

THE NEWS THAT I HAD SWITCHED FROM DEMOCRAT TO REPUBLICAN WAS THE talk of the county for several days. Television stations had carried the announcement live from the courthouse. All of the local newspapers published it as a headline story. Local bigwigs from each party were interviewed, the Republicans claiming a coup, the Democrats saying it wouldn't matter one way or the other.

George Brescher was telling the press that I'd broken the law when I signed a statement during filing attesting that I had not been a candidate for nomination for any other political party for a period of six months preceding the general election.

Both sides of the argument were aired in the local journals over the next week and unless someone was out of town during this time, everyone knew that Nick Navarro had made a last-minute switch to the Republican Party.

The major differences in this campaign should have been street experience versus appointee and law enforcement versus political steppingstone. But, after my switch to the Republican party, these issues were all but forgotten. The campaign became nasty.

The mudslinging started with a late July release of an internal department audit by Brescher, the first one undergone by my Organized Crime Division. While it didn't accuse me of anything illegal, it was certainly worded to reflect poorly on my administrative capabilities. The report said we had a lot of confiscated property and money that we kept for a lengthy time before turning in. It was noted that supervision was very loose in the undercover area, with no consistency from unit to unit. The report also spoke of extravagant and uncontrolled spending.

What the report genuinely showed to me was a complete lack of understanding on Brescher's part of what undercover work is and how it is carried out. We had several operations going on at once. Sometimes the confiscated property takes a while to be processed, depending on the unit's priorities. We processed all of it; there was never a dime unaccounted for. We did make some purchases that may have seemed unusual to the average individual: jewelry, for example, for operatives to look the part of the "high roller" in undercover drug operations. All such purchases were used in taking drug dealers off the streets of Broward County.

What bothered me more about the report's release was not the inference of poor management but the timing.

It was politics, pure and simple. But the report didn't have the effect Brescher intended. If anything, I used it to demonstrate why the people of Broward County needed a professional law enforcement officer at the helm and not a lawyer turned judge, who didn't know the first thing about undercover work. But a new tone for the campaign had been established. It was going to be a political fight, and a dirty one, until the end.

I continued my non-stop campaign into August. I had done my homework and the issues seemed clear to me. My speaking had improved and the people that greeted me now at various functions knew that I was sincere about my pledge to be only the sheriff - nothing more, nothing less.

Brescher, on the other hand, was struggling. He missed a scheduled debate with me, as well as numerous other appearances. One week he was on vacation. The next week he was sick. The only people talking on Brescher's side were his campaign aides, Steve Josias and Leslie Stracher. The Sheriff quickly earned the nickname "phantom," which I used in my stump speeches.

In early September, the Federation of Public Employees, which had endorsed Brescher, filed a complaint with the Equal Employment Opportunity Commission charging that some Broward County jail guards being considered for promotion were asked in a test how they felt about Jews.

This July 24 test was a two-part promotion exam given to the 123 guards seeking to fill fourteen new sergeants' positions. Apparently, this was the first time the test had been given, and several areas of the written exam were criticized.

Brescher called a news conference to deny that he was prejudiced against anyone and state that he definitely wasn't anti-Jewish. He claimed that the charges were false, that questions regarding Jews were not asked, although he had no proof to that effect. He said that he had promoted two Jewish officers in the last year since he took office.

Strangely, it was Brescher who wouldn't let the issue die. Perhaps fearful of losing the powerful Jewish vote in the community, he continued to insist in his speeches that he was not anti-Semitic, thus calling the matter into question again when it was well over. My father used to tell me that if you're walking through a cow pasture and you find a cow pie and the sun has dried it, leave it alone. Don't pick up a stick and start stirring it, because it's going to stink again. Leave it alone and keep on going. Brescher kept stirring it up, despite assurances from everyone that the people didn't think he was prejudiced against Jews. The stink trailed him throughout those weeks.

In late September, news stories ran about the Brescher campaign being in trouble. The new local county Democratic chairman, George Platt, was quoted as saying that Brescher's campaign was not the best organized in the county and that the sheriff lacked organizational skills.

This type of criticism was surprising with five weeks to go before the election. The Broward Democratic Party, with the overwhelming majority of registered voters in the county, was often referred to as a political machine that virtually controlled area politics; to make those public statements about an office the Democrats really didn't want to lose was close to admitting defeat. One Democratic leader said it was the worst campaign he'd ever seen put together.

Ours, on the other hand, was alive and well and increasing in numbers and popularity. The ballot had been made official and I was number 44 on the list of qualified candidates. All the voters had to do to select me for sheriff was punch number 44 at the ballot booth on November 6. "Punch 44" became the final slogan of my campaign.

Destiny seemed to be on our side. The idea of Punch 44 seemed simple, but as things developed in October, there was almost no 44 to punch.

❧

O N OCTOBER 2, IT APPEARED THAT ANOTHER NAIL WAS BEING DRIVEN INTO THE campaign coffin of George Brescher. A Miami Herald article reported a probe into activities in the Broward County jail. A man my officers had arrested as a drug trafficker in 1982, Mark Holden, was apparently placed in some position of responsibility under the direction of the sheriff's detention director, Colonel Ken Collins. Holden was accused of having sexual relations with detention officer Elizabeth Hamilton, both inside and outside the jail. He had borrowed detention Sergeant Terry Saunders' car on several occasions and was being granted three- and four-day furloughs by the directors. One of these included a trip to the Florida Keys with Hamilton.

The furloughs were all part of a program called New Endeavors, which was designed to foster better relations between inmates and guards in the jail, although I'm sure a vacation in the Keys was not an intended result. Collins had kept Holden in Broward County jail, rather than send him to state prison where he had been sentenced to five years imprisonment for the drug trafficking charge. This arrangement changed after the internal investigation became public knowledge.

Holden was immediately transferred to state prison. Hamilton was sent to the main jail in Fort Lauderdale. Brescher said he didn't think furloughs were a great idea and put a stop to them. Even though the events that transpired were within the sheriff's purview, he seemed to know little about them until after the fact. He had publicly criticized my administrative capabilities, but what were his? I don't think law school teaches someone how to be a police administrator.

Two days later, a leader in the Federation of Public Employees, who had filed the complaint about the Jewish question on a promotion exam, charged that jail officials had been interfering with a ballot process to gauge whether or not the union's endorsement of Brescher should be pulled. Ballots had been distributed to the 500 sheriff's office members, and those marking their ballots were allegedly being told not to withdraw their support of Brescher or they could lose their jobs.

The reconsideration was unprecedented. Polling each member separately was also very unusual as most union endorsements are generally decided by union leaders. However, I had a lot of supporters in the sheriff's office and they weren't pleased with the endorsement given to Brescher. Losing it would be another severe blow to the Brescher campaign.

The Brescher team was desperate. Disorganization, bad press from within the party ranks, and negative news from inside the sheriff's office all were adding up to one thing: a losing effort. They had one last reckless act to play out.

On October 3, the Democratic Executive Committee of Broward County filed a lawsuit against me saying I was not qualified to run for Sheriff because I'd violated the law governing party switching by candidates. The lawsuit specified that my name be removed from the ballot.

The committee quoted the law as saying a party switch must be made six months before the election; my change to the Republican party came only four months in advance. The suit was instigated by the Brescher camp to revive an otherwise lifeless campaign.

What this lawsuit meant was that the Democrats felt Brescher couldn't win by election on November 6 and he had a better chance in court. If I was taken off the ballot, the voters would lose the right to select a sheriff since there would be no name next to number 44. Brescher would run unopposed since it was too late for the Republican Party to choose another qualified candidate with only four weeks to go.

This sent the supervisor of Elections into a frenzy. The ballots were being printed and absentee ballots were due to be mailed the following week. The lawsuit had turned the election upsidedown.

I hired some attorneys to help me fight the lawsuit. I had come too far and had spent far too many hours with the people of this county to give up now. The voters told me they wanted a sheriff free from political reins and I was determined to give them that choice.

Brescher was trying to distance himself from the suit, even though it was clear his campaign workers, manager Frank Schueler and sheriff's office employee Ralph Dean, had contacted the attorneys involved in a similar Orange County suit for specific details. Brescher was concerned that the suit could backfire on him if the Democrats lost it.

Interestingly, the Democrats had done nothing about filing a lawsuit against Dan Goldberg, who had switched from Democrat to Independent to

Republican with the same time frame. I'm sure it was because Goldberg was not considered a threat to win the Clerk of Court race in November. I was a different story.

Judge Robert Lance Andrews was to hear the case in Broward County Circuit Court in a hearing scheduled for October 9. Andrews's wife, Carole, was a member of the Broward Democratic Executive Committee. The attorneys I had retained, Linda Conahan and James Blosser, immediately wanted Andrews dismissed from the case, despite my argument that Judge Andrews had always been fair and would rule by the law, not by his wife's political affiliation.

The hearing was only a couple of days away and we were scrambling to organize my defense. The lawyers felt that my civil rights were being violated; the Democrats were rushing this suit, capitalizing on the short time frame to deny me the chance to build a suitable defense. We filed a claim in federal court on October 8 asking the court to block the state suit hearing being held the next day as it denied me a right to a fair trial.

Brescher's campaign, in the meantime, continued to stumble. A hastily called fund-raiser that was going to feature Governor Graham was canceled because there wasn't enough time to sell tickets and raise money. His campaign was short on cash. About $100,000 had been spent to date with nothing to show for it - no radio, no television, no newspaper ads. All his hopes appeared to be squarely on the lawsuit.

A decision was made by the Elections Office to mail the absentee ballots anyway and if my name was taken off by a judge, the votes I received wouldn't be counted. Fifteen thousand ballots were set to be mailed.

On October 9, U.S. District Judge Norman Roettger ruled that he had no reason, as a federal judge, to interfere with a lawsuit filed in a state court. He did tell us, however, that we could come back at a later date if we wished to seek recourse following the state's decision.

We left federal court and proceeded to state court for the scheduled hearing on the Democrats' lawsuit. My attorneys had won their argument about Judge Andrews. They asked him to excuse himself, which he did, leaving the decision in the hands of Judge Joseph Price.

Judge Price heard all of the arguments and ruled the same day. He said he felt this was clearly a case of selective enforcement against me. If the

Democrats had filed suit on July 21 or 22 right after I had changed parties, or even in early August, he would have agreed to review the appropriate law and decide accordingly, but to file the suit in October, ten weeks after the switch, leaving the Republican Party less than a month to field another candidate wasn't right. The suit was filed too late, he ruled. Democratic Party Chairman George Platt told Judge Price that he wasn't aware of the six-month rule until a short time ago, but the judge dismissed that argument, noting that Platt had previously run for office and signed the same papers I had done. My name was to be left on the ballot for the people of Broward County to decide.

I was elated. Ready to continue the hard campaigning, I charged out of the courtroom, anxious to get started again. Broward County voters could still punch 44.

&

THE DEMOCRATS WERE UPSET ABOUT THE RULING AND DETERMINED NOT TO LET it die. Two days after the ruling, word was leaked that Burton Burdick, my campaign treasurer and an attorney himself, had also served as Judge Joe Price's campaign manager in 1978, six years earlier. Judge Price responded that he had over 300 attorneys' endorsements in 1978 and he didn't make the connection between Burdick and me until after the ruling was over, but even if he knew, it would have had no bearing on his decision. Bob Butterworth claimed to be absolutely shocked by the news and Brescher's campaign questioned the judge's impartiality. Judge Price dismissed the notions completely.

The Democrats' next move was to file an appeal through the state court system in the 4th District Court of Appeals. They did so on October 12, three days after Judge Price's decision.

The speculation now arose that if an appeal was filed, it might be too late to hear it before the election. If I won the election, the Democrats' suit could, if upheld on appeal, remove me from an office I had won by ballot. Local editorials called for an end to this court fight and supported Judge Price's decision to let the voters decide.

The appeal went forward and the Democrats asked for an abbreviated schedule to get the case heard the week of October 22. The appellate court agreed to hear arguments on October 23. To put this decision in perspective, an appeal in a lawsuit usually winds its way through motions for months before a hearing is set by the appellate court. Well, it had already been an unprecedented campaign.

The appeal was taking up a substantial amount of time in addition to my regular campaigning. We worked into the early mornings, writing the lengthy brief that would be needed. It was time-consuming and mentally exhausting work, and I found myself awake and off to a campaign breakfast somewhere with barely two hours of sleep most of that week.

Our campaign, despite the lawsuit, was in full swing. A debate at the Law Center at Nova University between Brescher and me centered on the suit. Brescher claimed I broke the law and rhetorically asked how the people of Broward County could elect anyone for sheriff who was a lawbreaker. I countered by saying that I had done no such thing, that the law was poorly worded and had not accounted for the circumstances of this campaign.

October 23 came quickly for us. We had spent countless hours on the brief and we sat, weary-eyed at our table in appellate court, as we awaited the judges' decision. They had listened to forty minutes of argument and had deliberated for fifteen more. The decision was short and sweet, delivered by Judge Rosemary Barkett.

They threw me off the ballot! It happened so fast I thought I'd left the United States of America. The judge said that Joe Price ruled on the timing when he should have ruled on the law itself. Bang! Number 44 had been punched·out. While the Democrats gloated, the voters of Broward County were the losers, left with a choice of only George Brescher for sheriff on November 6.

My attorneys wanted to appeal to the Florida Supreme Court, but after the debacle I'd just witnessed, I had a bitter taste in my mouth about Florida politics.

What about federal court? Didn't Judge Roettger say we could bring our claim back to him if we didn't feel satisfied with the state's handling of the case? I sure as hell didn't feel satisfied that day.

Federal court seemed less political, more unbiased, and more likely to do what was right. This state law was confusing and, as it was being used, unconstitutional. I felt my rights had been violated and made a case for federal court.

The following day, October 24, we returned to Judge Roettger and he agreed to hear the case the next day to determine if my civil rights had been violated. My candidacy was still alive.

The Republican Party, which could have proposed another candidate as late as October 23, was backing me all the way. The absentee ballots were streaming in, with the election only two weeks away.

Judge Norman Roettger's court was our last hope. We had nowhere else to go after this, having passed up the chance to appeal at the state level. He heard the case on October 25. Whatever the decision, this would be it, our final day in court. Judge Roettger listened to testimony for five hours. He took testimony from the Supervisor of Elections, from several people in the Democratic Party, and from Republicans. The courtroom was jammed, and when the Judge issued his ruling, the place was silent.

He told the room that he didn't believe it was a judge's duty to determine election results. If the Broward County voters wanted Nick Navarro to be their Sheriff, they would tell us that on November 6. If they wanted George Brescher, then they would make their statement at that time. He said, "Nick Navarro will stay on the November 6 ballot." He then issued a preliminary injunction blocking the order from the State Fourth District Court of Appeals and said he would defer his final decision on the case until after November 6.

The courtroom was jubilant. I was confident that Judge Roettger would uphold the election results. I was exhausted, but I happily went back to the campaign trail.

The Democrats were furious. George Platt said that I would never be sheriff of Broward County. George Brescher was quoted as saying that the judge scoffed at the law and I was no hero, but quite the opposite.

The next day, October 26, the Democrats tried one last time. They appealed to the Eleventh U.S. Court of Appeals in Atlanta, contending that Judge Roettger had no authority to issue an injunction blocking the state court decision. At the same time, Florida Attorney General Jim Smith hired Bruce Rogow, the acting dean of Nova University's Law School and an authority on constitutional law, to join the cast of Democratic characters in the appeal.

That same day, a cartoon ran in the local paper, showing a marquee outside a bank building indicating the time, the temperature, and whether Navarro was on or off the ballot. today's cartoon showed "On."

The Democrats continued to try to make the best of their failed lawsuit. Brescher persisted in saying that I broke the law. I pointed out that both state and federal judges agreed that I had not. This wasn't Russia or Nazi Germany, and the voters still had a right to decide on November 6 who they wanted their sheriff to be.

On October 30, Bruce Rogow, on behalf of the Democratic Party, asked for a decision by the Federal Appeals Court before the November 6 election. The Democrats were still trying to win this one in court.

The last televised debate Brescher and I had was at the end of October, and it was particularly nasty. Clinging to his chance to be elected and rebelling against many who claimed he was a weak-kneed campaigner, Brescher selected a new issue with which to lash out at me. He accused me of accepting campaign contributions from a convicted felon.

I knew who he meant and replied that I'd accepted contributions from this person's corporations, not him personally. This person had never asked me for anything and his companies gave to a lot of political campaigns. Brescher continued to bring up the topic time and again over the course of the debate, each time his voice on edge, anger bubbling beneath the surface.

The man in question was Jim Moran, a well-known millionaire automobile dealer in South Florida. Jim is a hard-working person who does a lot for his community and for people less fortunate than himself. Back in 1981, I learned through the FBI that a group of assassins was in South Florida that had come in from South America through the Bahamas. Word had been leaked that the team, two Colombians and one Dominican, had been contracted to kill me. Sheriff Butterworth wanted me to leave town immediately. I didn't want to go, but the FBI and the DEA insisted the situation was serious and I finally agreed. Butterworth made arrangements with Jim Moran, who I didn't know personally at the time, to use Moran's Lear Jet. I called Sharron, we packed, went to the Executive Airport, and were bound for Atlanta. Jim Moran asked no questions, and demanded no payment. He was glad to help. In Atlanta, we were taken to a safe house where we resided for a few weeks until the danger was past.

When I returned to Fort Lauderdale, I called to thank Moran. He was very gracious and glad he could be of help. He then made the mistake of his life. He ran afoul of the IRS over some business expenses that were disallowed. He faced a substantial amount of back taxes and penalties, as well as a possible jail term.

When it happened, some friends of Jim's asked if I would write a letter to the judge on his behalf, detailing what he had done for me in 1981. I did. Jim then paid his debt and the situation was over. He never asked me for anything through the sheriff's office, and I never asked anything of him. Through his various enterprises, he contributed to my political campaign, but he also sent money to other federal and state candidates.

Brescher and the media seemed to think his contributions to me were more important than the money sent to anyone else. As far as I was concerned, justice had been served in Jim Moran's case and it was a closed issue. I was glad for the contributions and knew that, as before, he wouldn't expect anything in return. There was no backscratching in my campaign. The contributions I received were accepted in recognition of my qualities as a candidate, not as a part of a special interest deal that I would later make good on.

One final strange episode occurred at the end of October. A friend of mind in the DEA office in Fort Lauderdale had called me and recommended Jack Kelly as a political consultant who had experience on several major campaigns. I was an underdog, fighting my way up, and I felt Kelly could help us. I gave him $2,000 to retain him as an advisor, and suddenly he was running the campaign. He handled some publicity and certain strategies but made a mistake by boasting of his credentials to the press. He told them he was a Washington insider, apparently not thinking the media would check. They found that, not only was he not an insider, he had resigned under pressure from the Republican National Committee three years earlier. He apologized and left my campaign, having caused some damage. I should have checked his background myself, but I had no reason to doubt him.

I was near complete exhaustion. I had been operating on two to three hours of sleep per night for a month. I was coming down with the flu, but I was a driven man with only one goal in mind: win that election! Nothing would stand in my way. Not even laryngitis in the final days was going to deter me from that objective.

Endorsements from the local media were paraded out the entire week before the election. The Fort Lauderdale Sun-Sentinel recommended me, noting that the Democrats had tried and failed to take away the citizens' right to vote. They cited my experience as a career law enforcement officer and my insistence that I wanted only to be sheriff, nothing else. They gave me credit for administering a large number of people with a substantial budget in the

Organized Crime Division. They noted that Brescher had not been particularly effective on the job.

Similar endorsements followed from The Hollywood Mirror, the Hispanic Broward Billingue, the Black Fort Lauderdale West Side Gazette, The Weekly News and the local gay newspaper, showing a wide cross section of support.

Brescher received support from the Miami Herald, which called both candidates seriously flawed, having waged the dirtiest political campaign the county had seen in many years. Brescher was not given an overwhelming endorsement, as the newspaper mentioned his need to get a better handle on the major activities in his office, and though he was a man of strong personal integrity, he had consistently let the office be used as a political vehicle by the Democratic Party. The editorial board gave him its support by saying he was a better choice for the office. It was the only major media endorsement Brescher received and it can best be described as lukewarm.

One more hurdle remained before the election. The Eleventh U.S. Court of Appeals in Atlanta still had to make a decision on Judge Roettger's ruling. On November 5, the day before the election, the three-judge panel said it was a practical impossibility to decide on the constitutionality of the law before the election. They left me on the ballot and returned the entire case to Judge Roettger for his scheduled future hearings beginning November 13. The voters would be allowed to speak.

The campaign took on an added fervor that day since the courts were out of the picture until after the election. It was up to the Broward voters and I felt that some kind of a special power had guided us through this maze of legal battles. As the campaign strengthened over the last year, I felt destined to become the sheriff of Broward County. I still felt that way, even though, I was weakened by a virus and was operating strictly on whatever adrenaline my body had left to give. A poll released a couple of days earlier showed Brescher with 44 percent of the vote, compared to my 36 percent, but 20 percent were still undecided who I felt were waiting for the decision by the appeals court. It was a race down to the wire.

On election eve, I couldn't sleep. I tossed and turned, anxious for the day to begin and be over. I got up at 2:00 A.M. and went out in the hallway, trying not to disturb Sharron. It was dark, I was groggy, and our Afghan dog was sleeping in the middle of the floor. I didn't see him and tripped, falling into one of our artificial plants where one of the leaves cut my eye. It hurt like hell; I put hot cloths and eyedrops on it to try to mend it. What a way to start the day.

I went out early, stood at a busy intersection during rush hour and waved to the commuters as I held my sign while I couldn't see out of the damaged eye. Nobody could tell from their cars, though, and I had given people one last chance to think about me before they went to the polls. Tears streamed down my face as the eye throbbed. My head felt like it was going to burst from the virus. I was a human wreck. At the first opportunity I saw an eye doctor, who gave me some painkillers in eyedrop form that worked for two hours at a time. Armed with this medication, I continued my last-minute shake hands routine.

We had planned a party for our workers, about 250 or so of them, at the Riverside Hotel. We rented a room to watch the results. Once those were in, we planned to come down, thank the people who had worked faithfully for us all these months, and go home.

The results started coming in. Early returns were from the east side of town, nearest the Elections Office. It was also the Republican side of town, so I figured I'd have an early lead. I did, about 2,000 votes. Everyone with me said I had lost, that the cushion was nowhere near big enough with the Democratic west side returns still to come. This was disheartening news, but I was going to watch anyway. David beat Goliath, and I was fairly certain that I had the perfect stone aimed at the proper forehead. I still had that funny feeling about destiny.

The votes continued to come in. The lead grew to 3,000 votes, then 5,000, then up to 7,000. A lot of people out there, especially Democrats, were punching 44 on their ballots. The people in the room were starting to get excited. It was not what anyone expected after the early returns.

The lead continued to grow. All of a sudden, I was 14,000 votes ahead, 50 percent of the precincts were in, and I was being declared the winner. Outside, the noise was starting to build and we saw from our window hundreds of people streaming into the Riverside Hotel. The television announcers had told viewers where the party was being held and they wanted to be in on it. We had expected 250; we had over 2,000 people. The police had to close Las Olas Boulevard because people were all over the street. Traffic was rerouted. I could hardly believe it. It was a miracle.

Sharron told me she knew I was going to win all along but admitted she hadn't anticipated so many residents of the county joining me in the victory celebration. When it was all tallied, I had 229,032 votes (52 percent) and Brescher had 211,697 (48 percent). I thanked my supporters, who chanted "Viva Navarro!" and "Nick! Nick!" I told them that Brescher may have had the politicians and his political machine, but I had the people.

Brescher refused to concede defeat, citing the existence of 30,000 absentee ballots. He made a brief statement about Reagan coattails and disappeared from his hotel as aides had him cut his speech short. The media spent the rest of the evening looking for him.

The Democrats were bitter and still hopeful of a court victory. When counted, the absentee ballots actually increased my margin of victory slightly, so the lawsuit was their last hope. My feelings were that the people of Broward County had spoken and Judge Roettger would put a lot of faith in their decision.

Bruce Rogow, the constitutional law attorney from Nova University, stated he would argue that the state law was valid and that Judge Roettger didn't have the jurisdiction to overrule a state court. He also said Florida would fight to preserve the integrity of the state judicial system and prevent intrusions from federal courts, and he would go to the U.S. Supreme Court if he must.

My attorneys asked for a delay in oral arguments, which Judge Roettger agreed to move to December 7. He also said he would rule immediately whether he had jurisdiction to order the sheriff's race to be held, whether the election law I allegedly broke was constitutional, and whether my rights were violated by the speed of the state trial.

In the meantime, Ed Pyers resigned as head of the Organized Crime Division. I went to his going-away party and wished him well. I met briefly with George Brescher about Pyers' successor and we discussed a few names, settling on one that was mutually agreeable. Later, Brescher named Gary Ewing, who was not among the names we discussed. I suppose that was to be expected. It was still his office for two more months, so he was entitled to make his own decisions.

I worried for the next few days about the upcoming court case. That would be the end of the fight - we'd be either in or out. A group of women who met regularly at the Grapevine Pub restaurant in Fort Lauderdale told me they were praying for me, just as they had in October during the earlier court battles. I needed all the help I could get.

The other thing I worried about was my legal fees, which were at $100,000 and climbing. I had no idea how I was going to pay these fine people, not having anywhere near that kind of money.

A class action suit was filed on my behalf by a group of my supporters in U.S. District Court, arguing that the popular vote should be upheld. Again, the people behind me were terrific during all of this. I didn't want to let them down.

On December 7, Pearl Harbor Day, Judge Roettger listened carefully to everyone. Bruce Rogow brilliantly explained the constitutionality of the state law and why I shouldn't be allowed to take office. We had some incredible depositions ourselves, one especially damaging from Democratic County Commissioner Nicki Grossman. She had been summoned to a pivotal meeting in George Platt's office in early October attended by Ed Stack, Steve Josias, Bob Butterworth, and another county commissioner, Marcia Beach. They passed around copies of a proposed lawsuit against me and talked about Brescher's sputtering campaign. Getting me removed from the campaign seemed like the best strategy at that late date. No one was concerned that it would leave the Republicans without a viable candidate. They chose not to sue Dan Goldberg, who also had made a late switch to the Republican Party for Clerk of Court, since it appeared he had no chance of defeating the Democratic candidate.

Judge Roettger finally ruled. He said that he didn't know how the integrity of the legal process could be achieved by permitting voters a legitimate choice and then overturning it once that choice had been made. He felt the law was constitutional, but, in my case, had been applied selectively and unfairly. He also said the law was too vague as worded and thus infringed on my constitutional rights. I won the election and I was the legitimate sheriff.

The courthouse erupted. I was still severely under the weather and when Sharron and I emerged to a large throng of people outside the courthouse, I did my best to wave and smile, but I was dead on my feet. Television camerapersons, newspaper reporters, and Broward residents all crowded around to wish me well, asking questions as we walked. I told Sharron to go ahead and celebrate without me. All I felt like doing was going home to bed and going to sleep.

It would be years before I could appreciate the scene as described to me by someone who was there. He said that when word came out of the courthouse that I was officially the sheriff, the crowds went crazy. People who had been picketing threw their signs in air; those in cars blasted their horns repeatedly. It was as if a blanket of happiness had spread over the town - the people's choice, Nick Navarro, was going to be the sheriff.

Seven

The "Bloodbath"

THE DEMOCRATS REFUSED TO GIVE UP. AFTER JUDGE ROETTGER'S COURT decision awarded me the sheriff's office, party leaders vowed to appeal and to continue their quest to keep me from being sworn in. Not all Democrats felt the same way, which caused a rift between party heads that would take some time to mend.

The State of Florida had taken an interest in all of the court proceedings, too. Upset over Judge Roettger's ruling on December 7, State Attorney General Jim Smith was exploring a lawsuit to defend the constitutionality of the election law that had been called into question. Smith scheduled meetings with Bruce Rogow to consider appealing the judge's decision.

The Democrats continued to dig. A week after the court decision, the media released a front-page story that Judge Roettger belonged to a club that had contributed to my election campaign. The judge was a member of the African Safari Club of Florida and, according to state corporate records, was one of three club directors.

Judge Roettger didn't know the donation had been made. The club's president, a real estate salesman named Tom Edwards, confirmed the donation but also said there were twelve directors at present, not three, and the judge never participated in discussions concerning candidates and donations. He always stayed out of decisions to endorse, donate, or otherwise take a political position because of his position on the court. The club had similarly donated to other campaigns and the judge hadn't become involved in those resolutions, either.

This revelation had no effect. The threat of an appeal was there, making it look as if there was a lot of backslapping going on in my campaign. Nothing could be further from the truth. I was a cop, and I would never grant those kinds of favors.

While the Democrat's seventeen-member management committee was deciding whether to appeal Judge Roettger's decision, the state decided to watch from the sidelines. Bruce Rogow sought a clarification from Judge Roettger as to his stand that the election law was unconstitutional as it applied to me, and the judge confirmed that he intended his decision to pertain only in my specific case. Judge Roettger felt that the law was selectively used against me and therefore violated my constitutional rights. This did not mean the law could never be used again, although the judge felt that the wording should be cleared up to eliminate any doubt about its intent.

That was good enough for Bruce Rogow. His position all along was to see that the constitutionality of the law was upheld. That my case was considered an exception by the judge convinced him that appealing the case on the grounds of constitutionality wasn't necessary. Attorney General Jim Smith did not want to go further without Rogow, so the State of Florida chose to drop this line of inquiry.

George Platt tried to persuade the Democrats to do likewise. At their committee meeting, though, he was outvoted better than four-to-one as the great majority of the leadership pledged to keep up the fight. They were tiring of the press coverage of their internal deliberations and barred the public and media from this latest session. Both former Sheriff Ed Stack and soon-to-be former Sheriff George Brescher reiterated their comments publicly about me being a lawbreaker and, thus, not qualified to take office.

I received a call from U.S. Congressman Larry Smith, a Democrat, around Christmastime. He requested a meeting in his office as soon as possible. He was very businesslike and I optimistically thought that perhaps the Democrats were finally ready to bury the hatchet.

When I arrived at his office, others were waiting who apparently were also to be part of this meeting. State Senator Ken Jenne and State Representative

Fred Lipman were both there to greet me that Sunday morning. Congressman Smith sat at his desk and I sat across from him, with Jenne on my right, Lipman on my left.

Smith got right to the point. "The Democrats have decided that if you don't want them to appeal Judge Roettger's ruling and be prevented from taking office, then you should switch from the Republican Party to being Independent." He went on. "Since you have already indicated a disdain for politics, what party you represent shouldn't be a concern to you."

A slow burn flickered up my spine and I could see the only place the hatchet was going to be buried that morning was in my neck. With lips pursed, I replied, "Am I to understand that you are ordering me to change to the Independent Party?"

Smith said, "We are telling you to switch if you want this appeal dropped."

I slowly stood up. I told them, "Read my lips: fuck you! All three of you! This is the United States of America! You don't tell me which party I can belong to in this country. How dare you waste my time on a Sunday morning to come down and listen to this? You want to sue? Sue me all you want. Appeal all you want. Do what your hearts tell you to, and I will do what mine tells me. You're not going to change me. I stay as I am. This terminates our conversation, gentlemen." I turned and left.

I was as angry as I've ever been. Who do these people think they are?

The pressure didn't stop there. Carole Andrews, the wife of the judge who excused himself, at my attorney's request, because of his ties to the Democratic political leadership, told Sharron and me that we were invited to George Platt's house for breakfast. She didn't say why she was extending this invitation, but after my brief conversation with Larry Smith and company, I had my suspicions. We went to Platt's house and heard the same tired routine Smith had given me. This time I was in someone's home, so my demeanor was more respectful than it had been in Smith's office. I listened to the request from Platt and his other guests to change parties again. They presented it more nicely than Smith, saying if I chose to switch, they would persuade the Democrats to change their minds about an appeal.

"Let me be clear about this," I replied. "Nick Navarro as an Independent candidate for re-election in 1988 would hardly stand a chance against both Republican and Democratic candidates, whom both parties would be active in finding. The Democratic leadership doesn't like me now, and Republicans would like me even less if I chose to become an Independent after everything that's happened. You must realize it isn't about furthering my political career. I'm the sheriff as a Republican and it is my intention to stay that way. Thanks for your concern on my behalf, but my decision is final. Do what you have to do."

Public sentiment was clearly against the Democrats. They continued to take a beating and a number of people were calling for George Platt's resignation. The fight had gone out of Platt where I was concerned and he clearly didn't think an appeal was in the best interest of the party. Aside from that, Judge Roettger did not leave them much room to appeal. He had said this was a unique case calling for a unique ruling. The statute needed to be fixed but, with some alteration, could be perfectly acceptable for application in future cases.

On January 2, 1985, in a close committee vote, the Democrats finally decided to end the court struggles by not appealing any further. Those that still wanted to pursue the matter advocated enlisting State Attorney General Smith. If Smith took their cause up they reasoned, the state would be responsible for the Democrats' massive legal fees. George Platt pointed out that Smith was considering running for governor in two years and angering Navarro supporters would not be in his best interest. It was politics that started this mess and, in the end, it was politics that finished it.

I was relieved that it was finally over. I, too, had a substantial amount of legal fees to pay and already had a few sleepless nights wondering how to come up with the necessary dollars. The bill was now over $140,000.

My supporters came to the rescue. Led by Carl Mayhue, an effort was organized to raise money to pay off my legal debt. Mayhue was upset over the way the Democrats had come after me and felt I shouldn't shoulder the financial burden alone. Checks began to come in unsolicited and their numbers increased after publicity concerning the amount of legal debt I faced was reported in the news media. I didn't know some of the names of the people who sent money, but their generosity and words of support were overwhelming. I considered myself a lucky man and made a solemn vow that the wishes of the people of Broward County would always take precedence over mine for however long my stay in the sheriff's office turned out to be.

A country western fund-raiser at the War Memorial Auditorium at ten dollars per person brought out a crowd of well wishers. Over $70,000 alone was raised from that event, and everyone who attended enjoyed the hoedown. I will never forget the help I received in those days before, during, and after the election.

∽

I MADE SOME DECISIONS ABOUT STAFFING SOON AFTER THE ELECTION RETURNS WERE counted in early November. My acquaintance with the members of the Broward County Sheriff's Office was a lengthy one, having been in the department since 1971. The people I wanted on my team were those whose loyalty I could count on. In law enforcement, this is especially important since life-threatening situations arose on a regular basis. Also, the team concept was important to me as my officers and staff would assist in implementing a number of new programs that would benefit both law enforcement and the community alike.

I sat down and carefully evaluated what I wanted to do with the Office and who could be counted on to help achieve my goals and objectives. There were several individuals whose past work and decision making in the department were questionable and, as my swearing in on January 8 drew closer, I began to weed out the people that would not be part of the Navarro administration.

I knew that some would consider the firings to be political reprisals, but in truth, there was only one man that I let go because of his actions during the campaign: Ralph Dean. He had been a very vocal supporter of George Brescher, had obtained information from central Florida about a lawsuit concerning the sheriff's candidate who switched parties, and had made some derogatory statements about me, including questioning my ethnic background. All this led me to believe that I could not rely on his support as long as I was sheriff. On these grounds alone, I gave him his release.

My next evaluation was of the individuals at the county jail who were involved in the Mark Holden New Endeavors fiasco that had earned headline news during the campaign and embarrassment for George Brescher. After a study of the events surrounding the use of Holden, a prisoner, in performing a number of duties our officers should have been doing, I terminated another seven people, including Colonel Ken Collins, the detention director. There was nothing political here at all. These were simply sheriff's office employees who had not exercised good judgment and demonstrated a lack of understanding as to what their jobs were.

Mike Fufidio, head of Brescher's Internal Affairs division, was another of the early terminations. I had heard a lot of complaints about how he ran his department. I couldn't visualize him as one of the policy makers in my administration and knew he would not accept anything less, so he was also let go. He eventually landed a job with the FAA in the sky-marshal program.

Several employees who didn't measure up to the standards of their jobs were fired from the sheriff's office. One was a sergeant who would frequent, while on duty, one of the topless nightclubs in the county. He enjoyed having two or three girls sitting on his lap at the same time. After his employment was terminated, he felt compelled to sue both me and the sheriff's office. When we went to court, it bothered me that his wife and two small daughters sat in the courtroom, listening to stories about their husband and father who chose to spend department time in nightclubs cavorting with topless women. Whatever positive image they might have had of this man was certainly lost during this testimony. For what reason? A few extra dollars? Eventually, he lost his case.

This decision sent attorneys who had filed on behalf of other terminated employees scrambling to make deals out of court with the liability insurers who were behind the sheriff's office. The media, spurred by comments from outgoing Sheriff Brescher, called this change in command a "bloodbath," and every day new headlines appeared about the firings in the sheriff's office. My God, there were more than 1,800 employees in the office, and when the evaluations finally shook out, fewer than thirty people had been either fired or demoted - less than 2 percent! I wouldn't call that a major shake-up, let alone a bloodbath. The changes I made were, with one exception, done because of differing philosophies on law enforcement. When the current sheriff of Broward County, Ron Cochran, took over in 1993 and terminated more than 100 employees in a 3,000 employee office, the news media called it "streamlining." In 1985, my changes were dubbed a "bloodbath."

They could call it what they wanted. The employees who were fired or demoted were not ones who possessed the same outlook on the job as I held. There's much more to law enforcement than simply arresting people. I wanted the programs we implemented and the people who implement them to have a positive impact on life in the community, to give direction to kids, to make everyone proud of the area and its sheriff's office.

Most employees remained in their jobs. One of those was George Brescher's top administrative assistant, Sharon Solomon. She was extremely loyal to him (and a member of the Kitchen Cabinet), had been very active during the campaign, and now felt that since Brescher had lost, the correct protocol would be to resign. I hadn't planned on her leaving as she was well liked and a great worker. My reply to her was if she wanted to resign, she was free to do so and I'd rely on her judgment in the matter. She told me her resignation would be on my desk the day I took office.

I never received it. The day before the swearing in she called back and said she had typed her resignation but now had a problem. The tone of her voice told me right away that something was wrong. She said she'd just returned from the doctor's office and had been diagnosed with cancer. As she paused, I informed her that I didn't want her resignation, that she should stay on with us in the new administration at her current salary level. "Work the hours you can and want." I assured her, "You will always have a position here, and this office will do whatever is necessary to help you in any way." This way, I thought, she would keep her health benefits and her income; I knew she would have enough to battle through without losing those.

Sharon stayed on and continued to handle the programs she loved, the ones created to benefit children. Despite her difficult health situation, she remained tireless in her efforts on behalf of the sheriff's youth activities. She died about a year and a half after her diagnosis.

There was another individual, a sergeant, that worked part time as a cabinet maker. Among the items he built in this avocation were contraptions that were placed in X-rated video stores for peep shows. I had a philosophical problem with someone that enforced obscenity laws by day and built peep shows by night. I fired him. My attorneys told me I should hire him back. I assigned him to airport security, where he later came up for disciplinary action and was fired a second time. Broward County's current sheriff, Ron Cochran, rehired this same person again in 1993 and recently fired him (that's three times!) for cheating on a department exam. I knew I had been a good judge of that character.

Some of the individuals I demoted during this transition proved to me in due time that they deserved their higher ranking. A captain whom I'd reduced to lieutenant, Dave Yurchuck, was my choice to run the new Community Involvement Unit that was created in my first year as sheriff. He would eventually be promoted to major. Another individual, Walter Laun, who had similarly been reduced to lieutenant, was later returned to captain and then became a major. People were judged strictly on merit in my office. If they demonstrated their capability on an ongoing basis, there would always be a position available.

There were people in the office very loyal to George Brescher who were given the same opportunity to perform. A woman named Margaret Bosarge, a hard campaign worker for Sheriff Brescher, was ultimately made the head of the Records Division. Sam Price, the sheriff's office legal advisor and a loyal Brescher Democrat, was also retained. I was very confident in his ability as a lawyer. Both Bosarge and Price became very loyal to me. These were good people and very important to my administration.

The letters I received plus those printed in the editorial sections of the local newspapers showed tremendous support. Many of the writers expressed their sentiments in the following manner: "I'm overjoyed that the shackles of politics have been removed from the most important department in Broward County. We now have a professional, nonpolitical leader. He is cleaning house, something that has been needed for years. Sheriff Navarro is asking for and getting personnel that will give 100 percent of themselves, not sit and take up space because they are friends of someone in politics." I was glad that the people of Broward County understood my objectives.

I hadn't yet filled the number two spot, a key position that had been called "undersheriff" in the past but would be changed to "chief of staff." That title was more descriptive of the tasks performed on a daily basis. The person I wanted was Ed Werder, a former undersheriff in the BSO under Bob Butterworth. Werder was the police chief in the Broward County suburb of Miramar. This move, for him, would be like stepping back into his old shoes. For me, it would put an experienced officer in a vital role. It was a tough choice for Werder as he'd made a positive impact in Miramar, but the county needed him and he responded.

With Steve Bertucelli and Ed Werder filling important posts, my administration was starting to take the shape I wanted. "Veteran officers in high places" was a campaign theme of mine, and I had vowed that there would be only experience, not politics, in the Broward County Sheriff's Office. My earliest appointments confirmed how strongly I felt about this issue.

The Werder appointment was received favorably by nearly everyone. Forty years old, soft spoken, and a father of four, Werder brought a low-key approach to a role that desperately needed it. The chief of staff would be responsible for running the office when I wasn't there as well as handling much of the administrative policy making. I felt he was more than up to the task.

The swearing in was set for Tuesday, January 8, 1985, at the Parker Playhouse in Fort Lauderdale, where Sheriff Butterworth had his ceremony in 1979. The protocol was for me to be sworn in and then I would administer the oath of office to the rest of the deputies in the audience. In an effort to make it more than the usual dull routine, we asked Reverend Jim Reynolds, a master of one-liners and a sometime singer, and nine-year-old Renee Shields, who had starred in a local production of the musical Annie, to participate. Reynolds sang a song about me to the tune of "Pennies from Heaven" and little Renee sang "Tomorrow." Both were applauded warmly by the attendees.

The big surprise for me came when I entered the auditorium. The deputies in the audience gave me a standing ovation and followed that with chants of "Nick! Nick! Nick!" after I was sworn in by Judge John Ferris (another of Brescher's Kitchen Cabinet). I wanted everyone to think of the BSO as a team, and these enthusiastic reactions made me believe this message was clearly received.

With the formalities over, it was time to go to work. The Broward County Sheriff's Office has long maintained an elaborate screening process for hiring new officers, to eliminate, as much as possible, the likelihood of hiring people who would use the office for their own gain. We had very little corruption in the BSO, thanks primarily to the screening and a strong Internal Affairs department. I now wanted a consistency in police training from department to department so everyone could meet the high standards we had set. As officers, we are given the public's confidence and trust and I didn't want anyone in my administration to violate that trust.

One area that I wanted to stress was cooperation between the various law enforcement agencies throughout Broward County. It was critical that we work together effectively to keep crime to a minimum; at the same time, there must be no questions about jurisdiction and control. Our goal in the BSO, as it should be everywhere, was to apprehend criminals and, if possible, prevent crime from happening in the first place.

Almost immediately after I took office, Ron Cochran, the chief of police in Fort Lauderdale, called to ask for some help from my deputies to do beachside patrols during spring break, a traditional February-March phenomenon here in sunny South Florida. We wanted the place to be safe for the vacationing college students, and when Cochran began to explain his manpower difficulties, I simply asked him how many officers he needed. It was to be a first - city and county deputies doing patrol duty together - but why not? Law enforcement should be one big, happy family working together. Different uniforms but identical responsibilities. With an expected 500,000 students adding to our population during the five- or six-week spring break period, we wanted to be ready.

While cooperation with the Fort Lauderdale Police Department promised to be strong, other law enforcement agencies would be more difficult to work with. Some police chiefs wouldn't accept a county sheriff, no matter who the person was. Turf protection was more critical, even if the county could assist and make the chief look good.

Whenever an agency told me to stay out of its area, I knew there must be a hidden agenda. Why else would a chief try to block our deputies from working within his or her agency's territory? If any of my officers was working on a case and it led into incorporated areas of Broward County where we don't usually patrol, the investigation wasn't going to stop. My officers tracked the leads down wherever they went with the ultimate goal of apprehending the criminals. I needed reasonable assurance from other agencies that my officers would be safe in their territories. I was able to secure that support from the majority of other offices, with the city of Hallandale being the major exception.

Not being able to count on the city's cooperation, coupled with an ongoing investigation by my department concerning alleged corruption in Hallandale, I would not let my officers make any arrests or lead any raids in this town unless they were in uniform. In plain clothes, which many of my organized crime operatives wore, they could easily be a target of an "accident" in which a Hallandale officer could claim not to have realized the victim was a BSO deputy.

So our raids in Hallandale were "overt" rather than "covert." Still, there was one incident in which a uniformed Hallandale police officer drove up to the scene of a raid and pointed a gun at my deputy, who was also in uniform. This was enough for me. I arranged a meeting with the Hallandale chief of police, which he insisted must be held in a parking lot in back of a grocery store. I went warily and let the chief know, in a straightforward manner, that if my deputies were ever again subjected to harassment from any of his deputies, I would blow the lid off the Hallandale Police Department.

The corruption within this department, unusual for Broward County, was eventually exposed and the police chief indicted. After that, Hallandale settled back into a more cooperative role.

Former Sheriff Bob Butterworth had created a program during his tenure that made the city police agencies very happy. Certain individuals, selected from each of the other law enforcement agencies in Broward County, were made county deputy sheriffs and allowed to move from city to city without advising the sheriff's office of their activities. In addition, we maintained liability for any actions these unsupervised deputies took in the course of carrying out their duties.

When I took over, this program posed problems for me. I didn't want officers running around the county without notifying us of the cases they were working on. I wanted to be able to support them, if needed, or stay out of their way. This was a popular program with the cities and I knew that many of the police chiefs and the appointed deputies would not be pleased with any decision I made to revoke these deputies' authority. I didn't do anything immediately, but during spring break in 1986, my worst fears about this unsupervised system were realized.

An undercover officer from the town of Wilton Manors had arranged to accept delivery of a stolen car in a parking lot next to the Holiday Inn on the beach in Fort Lauderdale. If I had known, there was no way I would have let this occur. That kind of undercover operation does not belong on the beach at spring break where some innocent college kid could get hurt if something went wrong. But because the program was not supervised, the Wilton Manors officer did not have to check in with our office (and he didn't) and the deal was put in motion.

The criminal delivered the stolen car and the Wilton Manors officer, in plain clothes, drew his weapon to make the arrest. As it happened, a uniformed Fort Lauderdale police saw this and immediately pulled his gun and shouted at the Wilton Manors officer to drop the gun he was carrying. The Wilton Manors officer turned around to explain to the other policeman what was happening and the Fort Lauderdale cop fired five shots at the undercover deputy. Luckily, he was the worst shot on the force. As bullets sprayed everywhere, two into the pavement, two more into a tree, and a fifth round, never to be discovered, may well have ended up in the Atlantic Ocean.

While his bad aim was fortunate, any of those bullets could have hit an innocent bystander, and there were a half million extra innocent ones in Fort Lauderdale that week. Not only could a life have been lost, but also lawsuits would have followed, and the deepest pockets belonged to my office. That marked the end of the special deputies program as it existed. I would agree to deputize other agency officers in the future only if I maintained supervisory and training capability, had constant communication with the officers and controlled their operations. I wanted to know what they were doing at all times, not because I didn't think them able to perform the job but simply to avoid the type of near disaster like the spring break shoot out.

This decision didn't help my standing with the local chiefs of police. Further, some of the city agencies were contracting with the Broward County Sheriff's Office to take over their law enforcement needs. It was less expensive for them, it was more efficient to have similarly trained officers throughout the county, and it saved local taxpayers money. That combination was hard for the local mayors or city managers to pass up, but it did not make the chiefs happy. For them, being chief was the pinnacle of their careers, and a contract with BSO meant they would no longer be recognized as "chiefs." For some, their first names had been replaced with the word "chief," and to give that up was extraordinarily difficult.

There were exceptions. When we took charge of the city of Dania's police department, I made its chief the head of BSO's Crime Scene Unit. Although he had fewer people to supervise and was no longer the chief of police, he was pleased with his relatively high standing within the much larger county office and performed his job admirably.

In addition to trying to improve cooperation with local law enforcement offices, I wanted to maintain good communication with federal agencies, too. After all, I was a federal agent at one time and most of the local members of these governmental bodies knew who I was, so I figured relations would be smooth from the beginning, and they were. We set up a number of task forces that included members from many local and federal agencies, who worked together successfully, and whether it was narcotics, money laundering, gambling, or whatever, the spirit of collaboration was alive and well, a benefit for all Broward County taxpayers.

In February 1985, I received the George Washington Honor Medal from the Freedom Foundation of Valley Forge, Pennsylvania, for my efforts over the years to combat drug smuggling. It meant a lot to me, a Cuban immigrant, to collect an award bearing this country's first president's name. I truly felt part of the country I'd embraced for the last thirty-five years and I knew my father would have been proud of this latest honor. I assured everyone present that I would continue to take a stand against anyone bringing in drugs to our country and would do my best to keep this poison out of the hands of our country's children.

That same month, as if I needed reminding of the presence of drugs in South Florida, I was paid a visit by a reporter who asked me if I had any twenty-dollar bills in my pocket. I had been to the bank only that morning and proceeded to exchange my twenty for one of hers. I asked what this was all about, but she wouldn't say. She thanked me for my cooperation and advised me to read the morning paper.

The next day, my question was answered. This reporter had spent the day visiting well-known local people and acquiring their twenty dollar bills. A lab tested each of the bills for cocaine in an effort to point out how pervasive this illegal substance was in our area. Among the people who contributed twenty-dollar bills besides me were Jeb Bush, son of then-Vice President George Bush and head of the Dade County Republican Party (and a 1994 candidate to be Florida's governor); Dade County State Attorney (and now U.S. Attorney General) Janet Reno; the archbishop of Miami, Reverend Edward McCarthy; former Miss America Kylene Barker Brandon; and Jim Batten, President of Knight-Ridder newspapers, among others.

Every bill, save one, carried traces of cocaine, ranging anywhere from 0.02 microgram to 270 micrograms. They even tested a bill from the newspaper's publisher, which had 2 micrograms of cocaine, the same amount as the bill taken from Jeb Bush.

The one bill without any traces on it was mine, but this was probably because the bills came from the bank in new condition, meaning minimal circulation. There are any number of ways cocaine can find its way onto a bill, from actual inhalation of cocaine through a rolled-up bill to simply being mingled with other tainted bills. This experiment reiterated the arguments I had made about George Bush's drug task force a few years earlier: cocaine and other drugs were not being slowed down enough in our area. We had made some good progress, but we had a long way to travel yet.

The state legislature, although helpful in some ways, did not make our jobs any easier by passing new gun laws that effectively made Florida the gun capital of the country. New concealed weapons permit procedures (which were eased) and the lack of regulation involving nonconcealed weapons were sure to create problems for our state in the future.

These latest laws repealed most of the regulations concerning nonconcealed weapons and made it legal for nearly anyone to wear a sidearm down the streets of Broward County. In addition, any permanent Florida resident with no history of criminal activity, mental illness, alcoholism, or drug abuse could obtain a concealed weapons permit by simply paying a fee, filing an application with the Florida Department of State, and attending a brief gun safety class.

This was scary. With thousands of Floridians likely to arm themselves "against criminals," what would it take for someone to decide to use a handgun? Someone cuts someone else off in traffic and the dispute is settled - Dodge City style. Accidental shootings from the misuse of guns was another likelihood, and children playing with a gun they don't believe carries any danger to them could certainly result in youth fatalities. There had to be a better way to strike a balance between the safety of society at large and an individual's right to own a weapon.

In response, we shored up security at the Broward County Courthouse early in 1985. As much as I disliked the idea of a police force presence in a public building, we had little choice but to set up a twenty-member Courthouse Security Unit to monitor individuals and respond to any judge's request for help when a courtroom turned unruly. The deputies wore civilian clothes to make it more difficult for a person bringing a weapon into the courthouse to identify who might be a cop.

My first year as sheriff found me doing much reorganization to make our daily operations more efficient and reduce the probability of something going wrong. A $720,000 computer purchased in 1982 was collecting dust when I took office. Some computer specialists were brought in and able to get the machine functioning to track crimes and furnish other data. Road patrols were strengthened to tie our officers more directly to the community so residents could meet them and know who their local officers were. Our office also had only a four page hurricane response plan that essentially instructed officers to report to their regular posts with sandwiches and a thermos. We expanded this plan to nearly eighty pages by detailing specifically the actions each officer was expected to take to assist the community in getting back on its feet after a hurricane strikes.

The biggest accomplishment, though, was the increased cooperation among all the agencies in the county. Bob Butterworth, now the mayor of Sunrise, a community in west Broward County, admitted that the relationship between his police agency and ours was much better. The sheriff's office was helping local agencies on a regular basis and participating in task forces that previous sheriffs had declined to join. This was what I wanted, officers helping and working with other officers successfully.

The Broward sheriff's election of 1984 was not quite out of everyone's mind yet. Early in the 1985 legislative session, State Senator Ken Jenne, one of those who had been present in Larry Smith's office when he told me to become an Independent if I wanted the Democrats' suit against me dropped, introduced legislation to clarify the election rules. His proposal would require a would-be candidate to state that he or she had been a registered member of a specific political party, and no other, for a period of six months prior to the general election. The legislation was affectionately nicknamed "The Navarro Bill."

What finally emerged in the subsequent Campaign Reform Act was that any candidate, upon opening a campaign account and naming a treasurer, must stay with the party he or she belongs to at the time of the account opening. In passing this law, legislators felt this would end the last-minute switching that had been popular in recent elections.

Whatever the motivation, this new statute was perfectly explicit and would have affected my decision last year. Had this been the wording then, I would have run against George Brescher in the Democratic primary, but fate dictated a different scenario. The rest, as they say, is history.

Eight

Neighborhood 2000

ITH THE ELECTION BEHIND ME AND THE TRANSITION MADE FROM THE Brescher to Navarro administration, I wanted to get on with the job of law enforcement. I wanted to clean up neighborhoods, get more involved with local citizens, encourage more local residents to help us, work with the youth of the county to give them a better idea of law enforcement, and get them involved with projects or clubs in their spare time and divert their thoughts from any potentially illegal activities. Unless we opened up communication between us and the people of Broward County and help everyone understand that we were all on the same side, we were not going to make this community a better and safer place to live.

An article was published in U.S. News and World Report in August 1993 that made it sound as if community-oriented policing was a new idea. It wasn't. In 1985, a handful of agencies around the country knew this was to be the wave of the future and were testing certain aspects of it. I called our overall program "Neighborhood 2000," as this was my vision of how law enforcement could function most effectively in the future.

My first change was to get our police officers closer to their patrol zones. In the course of any given day, in addition to criminal investigations, there are reports to be written and routine patrols to conduct. I wanted the maximum use of routine patrol time. Instead of randomly driving through their sectors, the officers were advised to get out of the car, stop and greet people, converse with them, let folks see the name on the badge. This would make the officers better acquainted with the area and hopefully would create more affinity between patrol officers and neighborhood residents. The better known an officer was, the more the people could trust this person and vice versa. Trusting residents are more likely to tip off an officer to any crimes or, better yet, to potential crimes not yet committed.

When I was a Metro Dade cop back in 1959, I knew all of the locals within my beat and it helped me (and them) tremendously. I wanted to get back to that kind of policing in Broward County in 1985 and beyond. Otherwise, we were simply a reactionary force, going from call to call, where the sight of a police officer creates an element of fear as people wonder what's happening. When people see an officer because they are victims of a crime or reporting one, it gives them a skewed view of law enforcement and causes a discontent since the act has already occurred.

I gave my deputies a directive: get out of the car and see the people you're protecting. Be a part of the community, not apart from it.

In addition to more foot patrols, bicycle patrols were also established. Patrolling the beat on a bicycle also gave an officer the opportunity to visit with area residents. In addition, an officer could go places on a bicycle no car would be able to traverse. On a bike, an officer is aware of more sights and sounds and can detect problems earlier than if riding in a patrol car. Also, it was more likely that residents would approach a police officer on a bicycle than one in a patrol car. We instituted a training program for BSO deputies that included bicycle safety and conditioning. One has to be in shape to ride a bike. We wanted to erase the image of officers sitting in a donut shop, putting on weight by the minute.

Other cities within Broward County expressed an interest in the bicycle patrols and we helped to train them, too. The program was modeled after Seattle's five-year-old bicycle unit and was adapted for us by Deputy Phil Ordono, with much of the training done by Deputy Pat Presley. We were starting to become a part of Broward County again.

Community Oriented Police Enforcement (COPE) became our agency's byword. As part of this, we started several programs to literally clean up our neighborhoods. Under "Operation Community Pride," we made attempts to clean up blighted areas, particularly those affected by high crime. Deputies cleared away trash, abandoned cars, appliances, and other unsightly debris that can damage the image of otherwise good-looking communities and render them unsafe. Even prisoners participated in the cleanup. A work crew consisted of ten inmates, sentenced for misdemeanor crimes, working eight-hour shifts on cleanup projects. It was felt that there would be numerous benefits, from cleaner neighborhoods to fresh air, exercise, and the idea of an eight-hour work shift for criminals who would eventually be returned to the public sector.

As part of this cleanup program, deputies were assigned to work closely with the Building and Zoning Commissions to achieve beautification of neighborhoods through strict enforcement of zoning laws. I firmly believed that crime would be reduced as residents experienced a cleaner, more attractive environment in which they could take pride and would be less likely to destroy.

Other programs went right to the heart of community-oriented policing. A talking computer purchased with confiscated funds from a drug dealer was activated to help check on elderly shut-ins. We asked for any elderly shut-ins, sick or handicapped individuals, to register with the BSO. The computer dialed them every morning to see if they were at home or needed any assistance. If a resident was not at home, the computer would then dial a neighbor to ask him or her to check on the shut-in. If the neighbor couldn't be reached, a deputy assigned to that sector would check on the well-being of the elderly individual. I wanted to avoid situations where a person lay in the house or apartment for a couple of days before anyone knew there was trouble. Now, when the computer called, if the person could answer the phone and press a number other than one (the signal that all is okay), help would be sent immediately. We hoped to avoid any unnecessary deaths this way. Several local city agencies also used this concept and it fit in with our community policing activities.

We also utilized handicapped local citizens to help us patrol handicapped parking spaces. We gave them a forty-hour training course on writing citations, dealing with angry motorists, and testifying in court. We gave them uniforms and assigned them to various Broward County areas, especially where the numbers of violations were high. Prospective volunteers were screened, as we didn't want anyone with a personal vendetta given a citation pad. In one three-month period, the volunteers gave out 264 warnings and imposed fines totaling $73,360.

A short time later we extended the community policing concept further in a program called Problem-Oriented Policing (POP). A deputy was assigned full time to an apartment building or a housing complex that had become run-down and/or crime infested. One such example was the Kingston Square Apartments, a 176-unit complex just northwest of Fort Lauderdale ruled by gun-toting drug dealers and prostitutes. Nearly 12 percent of all the calls we received for the entire northwest area was from this complex, with incidents ranging from kidnapping and shooting to drug dealing and domestic violence. The deputy assigned there was welcomed by most residents. One said she was tired of sleeping on the floor every night with her two children but did it for safety's sake because of the nightly gunfire. The deputy began meeting residents and becoming acquainted with them. As part of the program, we helped the owner arrange for a low-interest federal loan for renovations.

Community policing and crime prevention begin with our youth, and it was critical that we concentrated a major portion of our efforts on them. The gap between police officers and our youth had been widening since the 1960s, and it was going to take time to close it up. During the crucial years, when children are attending middle and high schools, I wanted to develop a positive attitude on their part toward the police. To do so, I began a program to place deputies in schools as school resource officers. It would create better communication between the community's youth and the officer and could eventually change youthful perceptions of the cop as an enemy not to be trusted. Before long, the children might view the policeman or policewoman as a confidant, giving the police an opportunity to help them.

I didn't anticipate the angry tide of reaction to this idea. The thought of placing officers in schools brought to mind, for some, the image of storm troopers patrolling the corridors - the opposite image of what we wished to convey. I felt these criticisms were invalid. With more than twenty-five years in law enforcement, I had spent a significant amount of time in schools and found the kids to be naturally curious about what the police did and desirous of learning more about our work.

Finally, I convinced the school board and the county commission to put a couple of selected officers in specified schools on a trial basis. I chose these officers carefully, looking for ones with a natural affinity for teaching or counseling and those that enjoyed being around children.

Each school resource officer spent his or her full shift at an assigned school to create a good rapport with the children and encourage them to come to the officer if they had a problem. There was a tendency on the part of many school employees to not fully address the problems brought to their attention by students because they didn't want to make the school look bad. Since nothing happened after communicating with a school employee, the kids stopped going to them.

My orders to our resource officers were to listen and evaluate everything carefully and not to sweep anything under the rug. They were there to help the youths. They created so much confidence that some students began advising the officers of upcoming truancy days planned by other students. Truancy rates plunged dramatically in those schools, much to the surprise of the school board. Officers counseled the students on drug and other substance abuse. I wanted the kids to trust the officers and develop some respect for the career of law enforcement and the judicial system.

Some resource officers went beyond the written job description. One policeman, Deputy Bruce Stern, assigned as a resource officer to Lauderhill Middle School, learned of the unexpected death of one of his students due to leukemia. He offered the family his help in getting through the ordeal of losing a child. He found the family was living in near poverty, without the money for a funeral for their child. Stern went to a local bank and established a benefit fund in the child's name and attended his local Fraternal Order of Police (FOP) meeting that evening. After explaining the situation, the FOP voted to donate $500 to the fund to get it started. It wasn't long before the needed funds were raised.

This was an example of what I was trying to accomplish. I didn't want our officers viewed as only authority figures. I wanted them to be seen as compassionate, caring friends on whom all Broward citizens could rely.

The school board and county commission rethought their position on the school resource offices and voted to expand the program to the entire county. In 1986, our county was recognized as having the top program in the state. (There were fifty-seven other such arrangements around the state of Florida.) The school board, county and BSO split the resource officer's salary in thirds, except for the time school is not in session. It was one of our best successes.

Not only was the well-being of the community important in law enforcement, but so was that of the police officers. In the first year after taking office, I set up a Psychological Services Unit, headed by Deputy John LaPointe and intervention specialist Marie Irwin. They were called upon to help counsel officers on the death of a fellow police officer. Of course, any number of stress-inducing situations could be faced during the daily course of law enforcement, and it was important to minimize them as much as possible. As a deputy, LaPointe knew what the officers went through every day, what it was like on the job, and for this reason I sensed fellow officers would trust him to empathize with them.

I set their office up in a private building so there was no obvious way to know who was seeking psychological assistance and who wasn't. I wanted everyone to feel they could get assistance without worry of recognition or retribution. This was a positive to me, not a negative, and I thought the entire community would benefit as a result.

This unit was also looking for cases of "burnout," usually found in long-time law enforcement professionals who wanted to do things their way and not necessarily "by the book." Detecting this problem was especially important since we most often paired up a rookie or inexperienced cop with a veteran officer. The last thing we needed the vet telling the new kid was "Forget everything you learned at the police academy, I'm going to teach you what really goes on in the streets and how we handle it." I didn't want that. The basics learned in the police academy stay with an officer throughout his or her career. These fundamentals mold, shape, and give an officer proper direction in law enforcement. This "early detection" system we put in place to catch burnout cases was able to salvage some officers who otherwise would have been kicked out of law enforcement or worse. This was another program in which we trained other law enforcement agencies in Florida and around the country.

Sharron was instrumental in creating a couple of other programs in this vein called Spouses of Law Officers (SOLO) or Partners of Law Officers (POLO). The objective of these programs was to help nonaffiliated police partners (family members or significant others not employed in law enforcement jobs) understand more of what their partner did. It was not hard to find an officer divorced or on a second or third marriage. By conducting regular monthly programs on a variety of topics related to the officers' work, we created a better understanding of the job and what it entails. This philosophy spread to every activity we held and was not limited to employees but extended to their families, too. We were trying to develop an unprecedented cohesiveness among the members and extended family of the Broward County Sheriff's Office.

For this reason, I had no problem with family members employed within the BSO, as long as they were not in a direct supervisory capacity to each other. Nothing improves understanding of the job better than when both spouses or partners are part of it. We had some excellent family "teams" in the BSO, including the Callahan family and Ed Werder and his wife (who worked in the detention department), both of whom were among my top associates. The media criticized our office continually for "nepotism," but we employed outstanding officers who coincidentally were related by birth or marriage.

Many of our programs were made possible by unsolicited "grants" from drug dealers. Our Confiscated Funds program in Florida help pay for virtually all of the equipment upgrading and some of the programs we used to help fight crime. I will always be grateful for all of these donations from drug dealers. They were in the drug business for one reason – to make money and accumulate riches. They just didn't know that when they were arrested, tried, convicted, sentenced, and packed off to jail, they would bestow this wealth to the cause of bringing down more of their fellow criminals.

We confiscated money, cars, yachts, jets, homes, gold chains – you name it – and if I could have taken the gold out of their teeth, I would have done it. In so doing, we were able to bring the BSO's technology out of the dark ages and into the late twentieth century.

We purchased helicopters with these funds to assist in drug raids, law enforcement, and emergency situations. We bought a new fingerprint system called AFIS (Automated Fingerprint Identification System), a revolutionary program that matched the fingerprints of a suspect within a minute to those on file anywhere in the country. Prior to AFIS, we mailed the prints to Tallahassee, Florida's capital, and waited or sent someone through the time-consuming and laborious process of examining prints by sight and looking for a match. The system cost $500,000 and was completely paid for with confiscated funds. Another $150,000 went into a laser process to identify whether any latent prints occupied a surface. Without this equipment, we might miss a slight fingerprint that could identify or incriminate a perpetrator.

We also purchased a computer that could reproduce a color photograph of a suspect based on a physical description. The computer searches for similar characteristics among the criminals on file to see if a match is possible. Called X-imaging, it was, once again, through the benevolence of drug dealers that we owned this machine.

The use of DNA in criminal identification was in its infancy at this time and, using confiscated funds, I sent our technicians to Washington, D.C., to train with the FBI in this area. We purchased crime lab equipment suitable for DNA testing, including a specialized microscope. We were one of the first offices in Florida to successfully use this type of crime scene data.

We also used confiscated funds to create a Drug Court in Broward County. It was likewise called the "Court of Second Chance" and gave drug addicts an opportunity to clean up their acts, kick their habits, and work their way back to being productive members of the community. The only way to help these addicts was to arrest them, put them through drug court, and place them in rehabilitative programs as directed by the court. These individuals couldn't afford the $3,000 to $5,000 necessary to go through treatment programs in the community, so for many, this was the only viable option. It helped a lot of people get back on their feet who otherwise might not have survived their own personal nightmares. The program cost $1 million in confiscated funds and if it saved only one human being, it was worth it - but it saved many more than that.

After taking office in January 1985, I honestly thought I had left politics behind, which only proved once again how naive I was in this arena. It seemed like every program I proposed was scrutinized by every official in the county and every reporter who wanted to write a story about the nonpolitician who was politicizing the Broward County Sheriff's Office. Advice streamed in from all corners, usually saying that the program I was promoting wasn't politically palatable or might hurt my reelection chances.

Who cared? The only question I ever asked myself was, will it help someone? Will it create a better environment in which to live? If so, then I wanted to do it. Politics couldn't be allowed to enter the equation, if it did, the human element was taken out of the decision. As police officers, we had the chance to improve the quality of life for the people we served. This was the primary objective of all of the BSO programs I introduced.

As these programs were implemented, the reputation of the office rose dramatically to the point where law enforcement agencies all over the country and, indeed, all over the world wanted to learn how it was done in Broward County. We started the Organized Crime Center to teach representatives from other agencies about our methods of law enforcement. The State Department had more frequent requests from other countries to train in Broward County than for any other similar educational program. I hired a director and secretary to help fulfill these requests, but all other costs were paid for by attendees of the classes.

Everyone benefited from this association with other agencies, including us. We trained members of Israel's Mossad, for example, and in turn called on their help during Operation Desert Shield/Desert Storm outside Kuwait. We have a substantial Jewish population in Broward County and we took lessons from the Mossad in terrorist prevention in case of any attacks in Florida.

Law enforcement officials from Europe, South America, the Middle East, Asia, and various island communities came here for training. We held classes on subjects such as underwater investigations, which were attended by police officers from around the globe. We taught these courses to our officers as well. It was a program that made good officers even better.

Our Community Involvement Department had grown from seven to twenty-two people. These were law enforcement officers working in tandem with educators and individuals with strong backgrounds in working with children, adolescents, and the elderly. This unit developed awareness programs for senior citizens, visiting them and showing them how best to avoid being victims of crime. A lot of criminals preyed on older Americans and we were especially sensitive to that. We also conducted drug and alcohol awareness programs in elementary and high schools and at PTA meetings.

Our children's programs were ones in which we took great pride. The hamburger chain Wendy's donated a robot we called Deputy Wendy who was transported from school to school to give kids tips on bicycle and traffic safety, drug abuse, and staying away from strangers. The manufacturer of the robot told us that children would remember Wendy's lessons five to seven times better than if they had been related by an adult. The youths' reactions seemed to support that assessment. It was a popular program with them from the start and continued to help us break down the barriers between kids and the police.

Another youth program that we had was the Sheriff's Explorers. This program included about fifty kids between fourteen and twenty-one years old who expressed an interest in learning about law enforcement and who performed community service projects with our deputies, often raising money for a variety of worthy causes.

I also assigned a full-time deputy to work only on missing children cases. This officer, Jeff Georgevich, had a tremendous success rate in the two and a half years he worked in this unit. It was his suggestion to make it a full-time position and he put everything he had into the job. For those parents whose children were missing, Jeff Georgevich often was the only hope they had and he frequently delivered, locating the youth and returning the child back to his or her home. He died of a heart attack in 1987, just after bringing another case to a successful conclusion.

Youth programs are at the forefront of community policing. So many kids have large amounts of idle time between the end of the school day and the time their parents come home for the evening - time that I wanted to see used in a positive way. We established the Police Athletic Leagues whereby we arranged to pick up kids after school and take them to a baseball field or basketball court.

There is a mistaken impression about law enforcement officers that I wanted to see corrected. We feel no joy in putting a teenager in a jail cell, only emptiness and frustration that somehow this could have been avoided. I wanted the BSO to be as active in keeping people, especially children, out of jail as we were in arresting criminals. To me, prevention is a bigger priority than simply filling up jails with offenders. It's much harder to accomplish, but it's well worth the effort. The whole objective of community policing and Neighborhood 2000 was to detect problems early and solve them before they reached the violation stage.

These programs we implemented all served a fundamental purpose: to unite Broward County in its fight to reduce crime and make this the greatest place in the country to live. Law enforcement and crime prevention are a critical part of that goal, and efforts in areas other than just making arrests became the foundation of the Broward County Sheriff's Office, then and well into the future.

Nine

Tent-Gate

BARNUM AND BAILEY MADE A CAREER OUT OF PUTTING UP BIG TENTS AND FILL-ing them with people. I did the same thing and it nearly shortened my term as sheriff of Broward County.

When I took office in January 1985, Broward County was already faced with a jail overcrowding problem. When former Sheriff George Brescher departed, he left me about 1,050 inmates and a federal lawsuit that had been filed on their behalf in 1976 against then Sheriff Ed Stack. The lawsuit had not yet been resolved and had been passed from Stack to Bob Butterworth to George Brescher and now to me. Because of the lawsuit, Federal Judge William Hoeveler had imposed an inmate limit of 1,170, which didn't leave me much room for further arrests. In actuality, only 1,104 beds were available for our inmates.

Help was on the way, though, in the form of an 840-bed jail facility set to open in late July, six months away. What we had when I took office was a jail that was part of the courthouse that had a limit fixed by Judge Hoeveler at 360 and another facility in Pompano Beach that could handle 744 inmates. But the state of Florida had different ways of measuring living space and felt that only 160 should be held at the main jail at the courthouse and 526 in the Pompano Beach cells. Because of the construction of the new facility, the state had agreed in December to give Broward County some leeway since we were working to remedy the problem.

Memories are short in the political arena and in March 1985, an official from the state Department of Corrections came into my office with an order ,from his department saying I had ten days to find other beds for 431 Broward County prisoners or I had to release them.

I told this state official exactly what he could do: turn around and get his ass out of my office. The last thing I intended to do was to release criminals into the county streets on this guy's word. I advised him that if he wanted these prisoners released, he could get a judicial order telling me to let them go.

We really had no other place to put these prisoners. I was abiding by Judge Hoeveler's 1,170 limit, but that's all I could do. At the time of the state inspection, we had 1,163 prisoners, of which 70 were charged with murder, 70 with armed robbery, and 54 with rape or sexual battery. A total of 643 of the prisoners were being held without bail, and another 124 had bails set at $10,000 or higher. I did not want felons returning to the streets of Broward County anytime soon.

Our county was not singled out in this matter. The state had sued thirteen other counties because of what state officials termed "prison overcrowding and conditions." We were close to being the fourteenth. Not only was a federal lawsuit pending, but also the state was involved.

I encouraged the county commission to budget immediately for another facility to be built, since we would lose 500 of the old beds once the new jail opened, to comply with the new state mandate. There was land in a couple of different sites that was perfect for this purpose.

The main jail in the courthouse had presented difficulties before. It had antiquated facilities, where noise traveled some distance. When the inmates found the need to protest conditions, the banging of tin cups on cell bars or walls created a racket that disturbed the rest of the courthouse, from offices to judges' chambers. The more prisoners we housed, the louder the disturbance.

I had more than just an inmate limit to worry about. While we couldn't exceed 1,170 prisoners at this time without risking daily fines, certain segregated inmate caps also had to be met: a certain number of female prisoners, juvenile prisoners, and violent crime offenders. If we exceeded any of these limits, daily fines were also imposed, even if we were under the overall cap. Our lack of jail space was nearly dictating who we could arrest.

Ironically the federal government was also contributing to our prison populations through a program called FIST, the Fugitive Investigative Strike Team. Its objective was to make a concerted effort to round up long-standing fugitives from justice. Combined with our own vigilant attempts to reduce crime in the streets, our prison ranks began to swell past the 1,170 federal limit. We faced continual fines, but I thought the people of Broward County would be better served by paying the assessments than leaving these people on the streets.

As July neared, what began as a $20 million building project in 1979 and was already close to $50 million. Fortunately, construction of the new facility was finally coming to an end. The attorney representing the inmates in their nine-year-old lawsuit asked Judge Hoeveler to require the county to meet the caps by the first week in August. (As of June 15, we had 1,330 inmates, 160 over the limit.) The judge agreed that the jail needed to be operational by then.

The new jail was far different from the facilities I was used to seeing. Each prisoner would have a private cell with his or her own bed, desk, toilet, and sink. There was a common area for each grouping of 24 inmates that had dining tables, telephone, color television, and board games. Apparently, we had decided to reward crime these days. This facility was far better for many of them than any place they'd ever lived.

The new jail also offered a staffed infirmary, a library, a barber shop, and a huge outdoor recreation area in the middle of the complex. The laundry room was capable of handling up to 300 pounds of bedding and jail uniforms and a kitchen was ready to prepare 3,500 meals a day.

At the end of July, I asked some of our public officials to join me for a night's stay at the jail to give them an insider's view of what an inmate goes through. The press dubbed it "Nick's Pajama Party," but I really wanted people like Judge Hoeveler and our public defenders, county commissioners, and legislators to remember this jail experience when they addressed prison issues in the future. The media was also invited to see that this place was not the "New River Hilton" as some of them had called it.

Despite the opening of the new jail, space continued to be at a premium. By year end, we had over 1,600 inmates, the substantial majority of whom were awaiting trial. County commissioners appealed to Chief Judge Miette Burnstein to do something to relieve the court backlog and decrease the numbers of prisoners, but the judge felt the legal system was doing all it could to move individuals through it. Our real tourist season was beginning and criminal populations always seem to swell during this time. I wasn't about to give a Christmas present to the citizens of Broward County by releasing felons on the street. My officers would continue to perform and make the appropriate arrests as they'd always done.

Late in 1985, we bid for and acquired the Broward County Stockade, a ninety-bed facility that would help us increase the number of prisoners we could hold at any one time. Takeover was slated for February 1, 1986.

The courts kept up the pressure. Judge Hoeveler ordered the release of 284 inmates unless we found other facilities for them. Some were transferred to the state prison. Some were designated for the new stockade. Despite the county commission's protests, the legal system had processed 500 more cases in 1985 than in the year before. The jails, though, were bursting at the seams.

It was a constant battle. I eventually compared the square footage of the single cells in the new jail to that of a Holiday Inn room with double beds. Our single cells were larger. I brought a bill to the state legislature in Tallahassee to "double bunk" the cells to increase our capacity in the new jail. This would mean two inmates sharing a desk, toilet, and sink. State Representative Peter Weinstein helped push the bill through. Judge Hoeveler went along with the double bunking and raised the limit on prisoners. By November 1987, it had been elevated to 2,426. The county had also refurbished the original main jail cells and re-opened them, which added more than 200 beds to the Pompano facility. We were working on the problem but were still paying fines, incurred since August 1986, for exceeding our limits.

There was room next to the North Broward complex in Pompano Beach to put up a tent. This was no ordinary tent, but a 60-by-100-foot version that had been used (according to the person who rented it to me) by Donald Trump for a party with some Palm Beach socialites. If it was good enough for Donald Trump, I figured, why not for inmates? The prisoner population was now at 2,789 and our cap was at 2,650.

County Commissioner Ed Kennedy had given his blessing to the tent solution. He encouraged us to try it, saying it would probably be tested by the courts, but it was better than trying to allocate millions of dollars more to further building of jail space. I leased this tent for $3,000 per month and set it up on a concrete basketball court west of the Pompano Beach facility. The next step was to rent portable toilets and borrow cots from Homestead Air Force base. The tent could hold no more than 100 prisoners, but I vowed to keep putting up tents as long as we were keeping criminals off the streets. Besides, it was better than current conditions in the gymnasium, where inmates had to share one bathroom and sleep on the floor.

The track record on using tents in this state wasn't good. Ones that were tried in 1987 were removed when prison inspectors likened conditions inside to those in Third World countries. I felt we had done all we could to make this tent habitable. It would only be used to house non-violent criminals until space opened up inside the complex for them.

Enter Will Willis, Pompano Beach's chief building inspector, who publicly said on Wednesday, July 13, 1988, the week the tent went up, that a building permit was never filed for it and wouldn't have been granted anyway because the South Florida building code prohibits institutions from using tents for sleeping purposes. The Department of Corrections officials echoed Willis's sentiments, saying they would not approve of a tent, either. Willis advised us that he would be inspecting the tent, after which he would prepare a report and proceed from there. I said that no other alternative was readily available to me, that drug sweeps would continue, and that nothing short of a court order would close my tent.

A couple of inmates spoke out publicly in favor of the tent. They both preferred to be outside, in the fresh air, but that didn't stop the inmates' attorney, Chris Cloney, from filing a motion with the federal court that the tent be declared illegal.

Judge Hoeveler agreed, calling it unconstitutional and cruel and unusual punishment. He ordered me to return the thirty inmates in the tent back to the building where they would sleep on the floor, which, apparently, is not cruel and unusual punishment. To my knowledge, the eighth amendment to our Constitution does not say anything about housing, but I am not a judge. The media used the opportunity to take a shot at me, saying the whole thing was a political charade used for publicity since I was up for re-election that year.

Judge Hoeveler, who had always been a gentleman and the type of individual one wants on the bench, finally agreed to turn the case over to the state Department of Corrections. If the department approved it, with modifications to improve living conditions, then he would approve it, the judge ruled.

However, there was the sticky matter of getting approval from Pompano Beach, whose officials continued to insist that if prisoners slept in the tent overnight, it would violate city ordinances. The state Department of Corrections would not approve it if the city didn't, so I was back to square one.

Public sentiment was in favor of the tents. Letters to local newspapers and interviews on the evening news brought out a lot of support for this temporary solution. A number of military veterans came forward to say they had slept in tents during far worse conditions while serving their country, not breaking its laws.

We did everything we could to make the tent more habitable. We added running water and more netting for improved ventilation. Nothing was acceptable. City and state officials were apologetic, but they couldn't approve a tent for housing inmates. Judge Hoeveler's order would stand.

The government didn't like the tent. The media didn't like it, but the people I served did like it. While newspapers claimed I was grandstanding with large drug sweeps to help my re-election campaign, a group of 150 citizens marched through a troubled neighborhood in North Broward, vowing to reclaim the area from drug dealers and users. They encouraged me to continue my arrests. These were the people that elected me so I felt more determined not to change our battle plans against the criminal element.

By the end of July, the prison ranks had ballooned to more than 3,000 inmates. I proposed other housing possibilities to the county commission. The first was construction of a portable jail complex next to the county stockade that could put up 392 prisoners. The second was to build a mammoth 4,000-bed facility in Southwest Broward. The third option was to acquire a warehouse that could be converted to a dormitory for the inmates. Adding to the stockade seemed the most feasible to them.

We continued to use the tent occasionally for processing purposes when arrests were first made. Florida Governor Bob Martinez, who had accompanied my deputies on some July drug raids, liked the tent idea, too. The media had, by now, labeled the affair "Tent-Gate."

Our final stop was with the Board of Rules and Appeals, where we argued that the tent be considered an "alternate type of construction" to circumvent the building codes. But the board voted to reject the idea and the tents were pulled down.

For the time being.

∿

T HE SITUATION DIDN'T GET MUCH BETTER OVER THE LATTER HALF OF 1988. WE were close to receiving the dubious honor of being among the top ten counties in the United States for inmate populations. While our prison numbers had now increased to over 3,000, our cap remained at 2,650. We still didn't have much in the way of additional bed space.

The county had approved the revamped stockade idea, but the haste of the project led to difficulties in design. Although the facility was due to open on February 20, 1989, problems with storage areas, the kitchen, security, and inmate processing remained to be resolved. Fitting these items into what was already built was becoming an engineering nightmare.

In January 1989, the pot finally boiled over. Joe Robbie Stadium, on the Dade-Broward County line, was hosting Super Bowl XXIII at the end of the month. There would certainly be the usual criminals who turned out for such events, preying on the people who flocked to South Florida to be involved with the country's biggest football game. To make matters worse, a Miami police officer had shot and killed a black suspect, and the local black population rioted in the Dade community of Overtown. Bad feelings were running deep over this shooting incident and I fully expected some troubles in Broward County as a result.

Meanwhile, jail inmates were sleeping wherever they could, some next to toilet bowls used by other inmates. I feared for major problems between the inmates and my prison staffers, but I had no way to ease the tension.

So, I floated the tent idea again.

I went to see County Administrator Les Hester about temporarily setting up a tent during Super Bowl week. He wasn't enthusiastic but was glad I had asked him first. He actually had no objection to the tent as long as it was truly a temporary fix. Word leaked to the media, however, and the news was published two weeks before I'd planned to raise the tent. As sheriff, I am only in charge of the inmates; the county handles the issue of shelter.

I had initially intended to use the tent for processing the inmates. I had Judge Hoeveler's blessing on that. I put it up on the same site as the one used last July, but after a week of arrests, I was nearly 650 inmates over the cap the judge had imposed. There was, literally, no where else to put people. It was decision time.

This was a tough corner to be in. More space was being built, but at our arrest rate, we would be over whatever new cap was imposed before too long. The county was reluctant to spend more money on jail space, leaving me with inmate overcrowding problems and leaving the taxpayers $800,000 in the red because of fines. I had to do something dramatic to make everyone understand how potentially dangerous this situation could become. I knew the people of this county thought the tents were a good idea, far preferable to releasing criminals back out into the streets.

Sometimes one needs to put oneself in the line of fire. I'd been out in front a few times in my life and felt that this situation called for it again. Judge Hoeveler did not want the tents used to house prisoners, but I had nowhere else to put them. I made my decision with no intention of offending the court or the judge, both of whom I held in high esteem. But I did what I thought to be right. My cause was higher. The tent was raised.

On Friday, January 27, I transferred fifty-eight prisoners to the tent to be kept there on a temporary basis. It was a violation of the agreement to use it only for processing inmates, but I couldn't let these prisoners stand up all night, so we put them on cots in the tent. This was January and the climate was much more conducive for this purpose than it had been the past July. I filed a motion in court that day to give us latitude to use the tent temporarily to house the prisoners. I was also negotiating for a building that could be used as an emergency shelter for about 300 inmates that would grant relief at least until the stockade expansion was finished. But since nothing was progressing on that front, I had turned once again to the tents.

The situation came to a head fast. The question arose, how could I, a man sworn to uphold the law, defy a court order? Well, I'd filed a motion to get a temporary reprieve to house the prisoners in the tent and hadn't heard anything yet. I knew I was violating the agreement made to use it only for processing, but I really had no choice. This was a last-ditch effort to keep criminals off the streets and a riot from breaking out in prison. If the members of the press didn't like it, they could try to have me arrested and put in jail. I'll add to the numbers already there.

The media, of course, probably relished the idea of me languishing in jail and published my comments in the newspapers. Judge Hoeveler was not amused. The press caught up with him on a Sunday and told him I was willing to go to jail to keep the tent; the judge said that could be arranged. He advised he would look into issuing a show-cause order on Monday, January 31, that would call for me to come before the judge to explain my actions or be held in contempt of court.

Timing is, as they say, everything. I had a scheduled trip to Los Angeles that had been planned weeks ago to meet with the producers of the new television series COPS, which featured my office and was set to make its world premiere shortly. I was leaving the next day for California and didn't intend to alter those plans. I didn't feel I had violated the court order from last July. That order was for the July tent. This was a different tent, erected under different circumstances. If a new court order was issued to apply now, I would abide by it. In the meantime, we were facing Judge Hoeveler's warning from earlier that month to release one prisoner for every new one arrested - a situation I found intolerable. But we were now more than 700 prisoners over the limit, and using the new tent was all we could do, pending arrangements to use the vacant building we were trying to obtain.

The judge called an emergency contempt hearing on Monday, January 31, but I was already Los Angeles-bound. He allowed a postponement until I returned from the west coast but said his July order was still valid for this tent and his ruling stood. He ordered the prisoners out of the tent and into the facility. That Monday, we had 3,387 inmates, 737 over capacity. The judge felt I had exceeded my authority and was being selective about which court orders I obeyed. I thought he was being unfair, but I would have my opportunity to talk with the judge. Another hearing was scheduled for Tuesday, February 7.

A lot was publicized over the next few days while I was out of town. One columnist compared me to the Sheriff of Nottingham in terms of power. People blitzed the media with letters, many saying they had no problem with their tax money being used to pay the $1,000 daily fine for being over the federally imposed inmate limit, as long as the criminals stayed off the streets. The limit was obviously insensitive to what was truly happening in Broward County as we continued our crusade to give the streets back to the people.

Judge Hoeveler received his share of mail, too. One woman wrote, "Were you ever in the Service? Our men spent many hours in pup tents, eating out of mess hall tents, going to the bathroom in open fields, and defending the rights of people to walk, work, and play freely without having to worry about some miserable creep stabbing, stealing from, or killing them as they go about their normal, everyday living."

There were many more letters like that one and I sincerely appreciated the public support I received. I was in a corner and the only people that backed me were the ones that elected me. It made me want to continue to do my job with the same diligence for the next four years. I would follow the will of the community.

As Sharron and I headed to Judge Hoeveler's hearing on February 7, we drove past a boy scout campout in Holiday Park. A jamboree was going on and the scouts were all voluntarily sleeping in tents. There I was, going to court where, quite possibly, a judge could throw my behind in jail for putting criminals in tents to sleep. The world was turning upside down, I thought.

The hearing lasted two and a half hours. I explained to the judge that I didn't think last year's court order applied to this year's tent. If it did, I was wrong and would freely admit it and apologize. Federal prosecutors and the inmates' attorney, Chris Cloney, were hoping for my head on a platter. They argued that I should be jailed, that ignorance of a court order is not a defense.

Judge Hoeveler and I had always worked well together in the past and he believed that I was not holding the law in contempt but, in fact, was doing the opposite in prosecuting violators to the fullest extent. He forgave my action but made it clear that the court order applied indefinitely and that he, Judge William Hoeveler, was the ultimate authority on what is acceptable and what isn't with regard to prison shelter. The gallery in the courtroom burst into applause, the attorneys looked dejected, and the judge felt we understood each other. He wanted, and rightly so, to preserve the integrity of the court. He agreed again to let me use the tents for processing.

The judge added that he wanted to visit the jails himself on Friday to see the conditions and to meet with the county commission to settle this matter. This would give him an opportunity to observe what I saw every day.

On the day of the hearing, a huge advertisement had been take out by a number of Broward County citizens that began by saying, "Florida's solution to overcrowded prisons is to release criminals early. Sheriff Nick Navarro's answer is to confine lawbreakers in temporary, inexpensive facilities. Which

Yours truly at 16. (Eat your heart out, Elvis!)

At age 7 with a couple of friends. (I'm the tall one.)

In Yokohama, Japan for some R & R. 1952.

Sharing a laugh with my special friend, John Candy.

My wife, Sharron, with Geraldo. (The husband is always the last to know.)

Visiting an orphanage while on R & R in Tokyo, Japan. 1952.

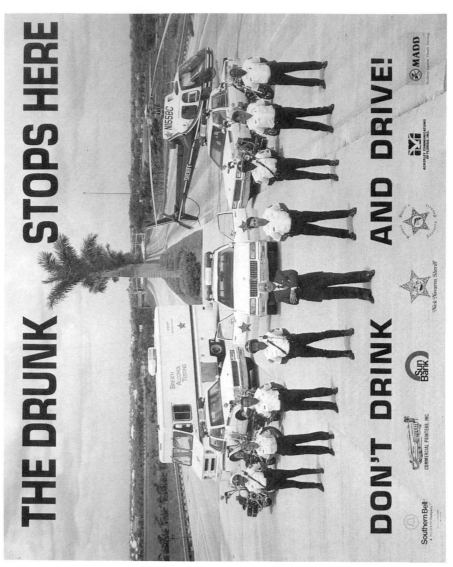

So many fools on the roads. So many innocent people killed or hurt.

A meeting with a good man and a great President.

James Brady and his wife, Sarah. Two wonderful people.

President George Bush. He has all my respect and admiration.

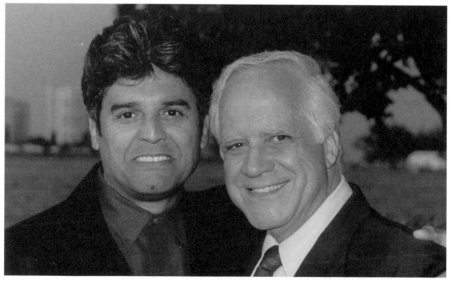

A good friend, Erik Estrada.

Enjoying a laugh with Ivana Trump.

Barbara Bush. A wonderful lady.

Playing with our best friends, Zorba and Bambi, in our backyard overlooking the river.

1988 re-election swearing-in ceremony. Florida Governor Bob Martinez, Sharron, and myself.

idea makes more sense?" During that day's hearing, the Judge stressed that this wasn't the issue at all; the issue was whether or not I had openly and knowingly defied a court order. He felt assured that I had not, and now it was time to move toward solutions.

The judge reviewed the jail situation and inspected the stockade expansion, which was moving rapidly toward completion. He agreed to consider raising the inmate cap once the stockade was finished.

The stockade opened at the end of February and Judge Hoeveler made good on his promise. He raised the inmate cap to 3,049. At the time, we had 3,004 in our various prison facilities.

Even as we were making the major drug sweeps over the past few months, I was confident that, eventually, the prison population would begin to decline. Word would ultimately get out that Broward County is not the place to commit a crime. The criminals would go elsewhere or they would stop committing crimes. After 1989, that forecast began to pan out and the number of arrests started to decrease. We wouldn't likely be faced with the same overcrowding difficulties again as criminals learned that Broward County was not the place to get caught.

I felt strongly about the tents, though, and worked to have them approved by the state legislature as alternative housing in an overcrowded, emergency situation. The legislature passed a bill on May 30, 1990, letting Broward and nine other counties use tents to house inmates to relieve overcrowding situations. The House approved it 110-0; the Senate, 35-0. At the time of passage, we were 262 inmates under the new cap and had no need to procure a tent, but I knew if I needed one, I could use it without problems the next time. If a major crime wave erupted in Broward County, we would be ready, willing, and able to arrest all comers.

My office continued to work to improve jail conditions. Education and substance abuse programs were very progressive in our institutions. In 1990, 109 of our inmates earned high school diplomas, hopefully lessening the odds that they would be repeat offenders and taking up space in our jails.

Ten

Courting Disaster

O N TUESDAY, JULY 28, 1987, CLYDE MELVIN, A THIRTY-YEAR EMPLOYEE AS A security guard at a paper plant, prepared for his court date that morning in the Florida Panhandle town of Port Saint Joe. Most of the town's 5,000 or so residents were just getting their mornings started as Melvin sat in his pickup truck in front of the Gulf County Courthouse building. In his possession were two weapons: a .357 Magnum and a .22 caliber derringer.

The Gulf County Courthouse was not equipped with metal detectors. In all likelihood, the bailiff at Melvin's hearing would not be armed. Since Clyde Melvin's appearance before Circuit Judge W. L. Bailey concerned his compliance with a recent divorce order, his wife, Inez, was also expected to be present. In Port Saint Joe, this was not the type of court business where an armed deputy was necessary.

It was all routine. That is, until the sixty-two-year-old Melvin pulled out a gun and started firing. The attorney representing Inez Melvin, a Vietnam veteran named Tom Ingles, attempted to disarm Melvin and was shot. Judge Bailey ducked inside a nearby doorway, but Melvin fired right through it, killing him. As he chased his wife, Inez, another woman, Peggy White Paulk, a relative of Inez's and a witness in the proceedings, was coming up a stairway. Melvin saw her, fired a fatal bullet, and continued on.

Inez Melvin made it to the roof before she was cornered by her ex-husband. He yelled at her that she was paying now for running around on him. She shouted back that she never ran around on him in her life, then she began to pray. The court hearing had been called to bring her ex-husband into compliance with the $350 a month alimony settlement that had been reached. Instead of the money, she took a bullet to the head as Clyde Melvin continued his tirade.

Gulf County Sheriff Al Harrison was watching the action from the ground and, too late to prevent Melvin from shooting his ex-wife, fired and hit Melvin in the neck, ending the killing spree. Inez Melvin was taken to Gulf Pines Hospital. Clyde Melvin was captured and secured and taken back down through the courthouse, past the bodies of his victims.

The morning terror was over but would not be soon forgotten. The Port Saint Joe incident would reverberate throughout the state over the next several days as judicial fears about courthouse security reached new heights.

∾

SECURITY AT OUR OWN BROWARD COUNTY COURTHOUSE IN DOWNTOWN FORT Lauderdale had been an issue for the last dozen years, the debate increased in intensity over the last three years. Back in July 1984, a new security system was ready to be installed. It included metal detectors at four first floor doors as well as hand scanners. The equipment was never shipped and work was postponed. By the time the equipment was ready and a two-year plan to implement all of the changes had been agreed on by a panel of judges, circuit and county court judges decided to delay installation until the courthouse lobby had undergone extensive renovation.

In January 1985, when I began my term as sheriff, it was obvious that we needed to have a security team assigned to the courthouse. We had a twenty-member unit, consisting of six deputies and twelve Community Service Aides (CSA) under the direction of Lieutenant Hank Faucette and Sergeant Ian Griffiths. The deputies had the essential task of security and I directed them to wear civilian clothes, making it more difficult for a potential violator to identify an officer. The CSAs reported building maintenance problems, issued parking citations, and answered general information questions posed by the public. Entry to the courthouse was sealed at 11:00 P.M. and any entrants could gain access only by being buzzed in by a security officer. Renovations to the first floor had not yet begun, so the metal detectors were still months away from being installed. The county commission, which authorizes expenditures in this regard, had never felt the same sense of urgency that the judicial branch of our local government did. The judges have always feared that some-one could hurt them in their courtrooms. Let's face it, the people that come before them each day were not the best members of our society, and some of them were genuinely dangerous.

Buttons were installed near the judges' benches, which a judge could press as a signal for help if the need arose, but this was a Band-Aid approach to fix-ing the problem. Metal detectors and hand scanners were a very expensive but far more effective way of trying to keep the courthouse "clean" from weapons.

Security problems were further complicated by the presence of more than just courtrooms in the courthouse building. The state attorney's office was there as well as the public defender's. By law, those employed there were allowed to carry guns. In addition, investigators employed were also licensed to carry guns. Some judges themselves carried their own weapons. Police offi-cers went in and out of the courthouse to testify at hearings or to visit the state attorney's office and they, naturally, carried weapons.

With all of these individuals who had a legal and lawful reason to carry a gun into the courtroom, the chances of rendering conditions totally sterile within the building were virtually impossible. The more guns in the court-house, the more likely a scenario could develop where someone legally carry-ing a gun could be overpowered and the gun taken away. Merely screening everyone else wouldn't guarantee anything; if someone wanted, he or she could attempt to obtain a gun once inside the building.

My idea was to have total security: absolutely no guns for anyone except for deputies assigned to protect the judges and handle courthouse security. This would be the optimum situation - as sterile an area as could possibly be achieved. I proposed to Chief Judge Miette Burnstein that no one be allowed to bring a weapon in to the courthouse. The day we put this mandate into effect, we would conduct a sweep of the courthouse building and eliminate all weapons from the premises. After that we'd have as close to total security as we could have, using the metal detectors and hand scanners.

This plan wasn't popular with the judges. They didn't want to give up their weapons. Ditto for the state attorney's and public defender's investigators and the police chiefs whose officers would be going in and out of the courthouse. As plans go, this one had zero support.

Once overruled, I proposed Plan B: thirty-six officers assigned to courthouse security, a contract with a private security firm to install magnetometers and x-ray machines for detection purposes, and a special training program for officers to do proper search measures. One shouldn't just throw people up against the wall and pat them down; there were other more subtle methods of spotting a weapon. The judges approved Plan B, which would cost nearly $2 million, but security was critical and no one wanted the judges to be in any more danger than they were. The county granted the budget increase request and everything was set in motion in mid-1987. I sent the officers, new and veteran, to police school for special training; I planned on pairing the rookies with the seasoned pros once they graduated. The security contract was awarded to Wackenhut. The machines were ordered for installation at the entrances, and closed-circuit television monitors were to be installed. Improvements would be made to alarm systems for both judges and their secretaries. A bridge linking the parking garage the judges use and the courthouse would be constructed, and a separate elevator would be arranged for the judges. We expected everything to be in place by November 1987.

Chief Judge Miette Burnstein had taken me to task earlier in the year over the seniority system of assigning bailiffs in the courthouse. She wanted specific bailiff assignments. She didn't just ask me about this, she sent an order via certified mail. Judge Burnstein had long bemoaned the slowness of effecting better security procedures at the courthouse. In this instance, she moved to take over the supervision of the bailiffs, something she said was her right as chief judge, according to an obscure 1972 state law.

She was already displeased with the Broward County Sheriff's Office's "slow" response in providing heightened security measures when the Port Saint Joe courtroom exploded in violence. Her reaction, or, quite possibly, overreaction, to this occurrence, dictated her next move.

I had just sent a letter to the judges letting them know about increasing the number of deputies and that we had an implementation date of September 21 for the new metal detectors and scanners. That same day, I received an order from Judge Burnstein telling me to have thirty-five certified deputies in the courtroom by Monday, August 3, to patrol the halls and check visitors from 7:00 A.M. to 7:00 P.M. daily until all of the other measures were in place. I was to do this or face a contempt-of-court charge and possible jail time.

I appreciated her concern. We all shared it. No one in our office wanted the judges to be in any danger. But I was moving as fast as possible on this issue and I didn't know if I could have everybody trained and ready by Monday. Her letter insisted that we use hand-held scanners, but we didn't have any. She actually used the word "sanctions" in her letter. In short, comply with my request, Sheriff Navarro, or prepare to be jailed.

The county commission felt that Judge Burnstein had overreacted and responded that the commissioners didn't want untrained deputies in the courthouse simply to rapidly increase their number. The issue concerned more than costs, although it would add about $500,000 to my budget for the fiscal year, which would end in September. It was about proper security, plans for which had been set in motion already and agreed to by all parties. Now, a member of one branch of government was dictating to another what to do, regardless of plans already underway.

I contacted Bruce Rogow, the attorney the state of Florida had employed to test the constitutionality of my political party switch back in 1984, and asked him about the constitutionality of this order. While Rogow agreed that the judge had overreacted to the Port Saint Joe incident, I had no choice but to comply with the order. So be it.

The court order had been signed on Wednesday, July 29. By Friday, July 31, I was still running around trying to meet her demands. The judge and I had not talked, but reporters shuffled between our offices looking for quotes. Things were said that shouldn't have reached anyone else's ears, but we were both touchy about the way courthouse security was being handled. I had been asked continually about the court order since it had been issued and finally suggested a more appropriate use for it, except the paper was too coarse. I'm sure Judge Burnstein didn't share my sentiments.

In the meantime, I scrambled. Between the time the order was issued and Monday morning, August 3, I could come up with only two hand-held metal detectors. No x-ray machines. No magnetometers. I had called the U.S. Marshal's office; Port Everglades (Customs); the Fort Lauderdale, Miami and

West Palm Beach airports; and every private security firm in South Florida. We could have x-ray machines shipped to us, but they would take two weeks to arrive, well past my Monday deadline. Two hand-held detectors. That was it.

Bruce Rogow filed a petition with the Fourth District Court of Appeals to have the order repealed, but by Sunday night, we still hadn't received a ruling. I had the judge's court order enlarged and copied and posted around the courthouse, advising everyone of the requirement for tightened security and apologizing for any inconvenience this might cause. Deputies were pulled from other assignments to work the security detail. I decided the only way to operate Monday morning would be to close all but one door, the type of security Judge Burnstein required.

I felt I had done my best to meet the unconditional terms outlined in the court order. The judge had spent the weekend telling reporters that I was an officer of the court, according to Florida statutes, and in her role as presiding judge, she had the power to dictate to me how courthouse security was to be handled. The real problem with that was the judge had no clue how to put together an acceptable security program. She also reiterated her stance that she would take over the bailiffs' assignments, but she was going to have to fight me and their union on that issue, which was obviously still unresolved.

On Sunday, I tried to think of everything possible that we could do to increase security. I ordered that everyone be searched, including the judges. I tried to estimate the delay that this would cause in addition to using only one door, but I had forgotten about the jurors. Every Monday, hundreds of extra people show up at the courthouse to perform their civic duty as jurors. Of all days to begin a new, hastily formulated security plan, Monday was not a good choice. I contacted Court Administrator Carol Ortman and said she had better call as many judges and court officials as possible to warn them of what would likely be a long delay entering the courthouse Monday morning.

Monday, August 3. The Florida heat and humidity was present in all its unbearableness. Lines of employees and jurors stretched around the block outside of the courthouse's single entrance. The line simply got longer as the morning hours went by and the heat intensified. Two people fainted and had to be treated for overexposure to the sun. Judges waited in line like everyone else, and, without exception, were late for court trials due to start at 9:00 A.M. That wasn't especially critical, since all the other parties involved in the various cases were late, too. It was a total disaster.

As sheriff, I took the brunt of the verbal heat about the long lines and delays. People outside waiting complained. People who had arrived early and were inside echoed these sentiments. Judge Franza ordered my deputies to leave and not come back, which they refused to do, and the courtroom was never cleaner as far as weapons were concerned than on that Monday. We'd "swept" the place Sunday night and confiscated all the weapons in the building. Now, except for the security deputies, no one had a weapon inside.

Judges Franza and Burnstein were furious. Judge Franza said we (the sheriff's office) were worse than having no security at all. He removed my deputies from their jobs and replaced them with officers from the Fort Lauderdale police department. He criticized me and my handling of the entire affair, but at least one judge made the best of it. Judge Mel Grossman, husband of County Commissioner Nicki Grossman, was holding his hearing on the sidewalk outside the courthouse with the appropriate parties. Judge Burnstein emerged to say that I was attempting to blackmail her into foregoing her order by making a farce out of it, with one door and ridiculous delays getting people and officials into the courthouse building. Newspaper editorials on Tuesday called me either arrogant or incompetent. Judge Franza ordered me to appear at the contempt-of-court hearing on Tuesday morning.

I thought most of the criticism was unfair. Judge Burnstein's order was pretty explicit about my being sanctioned and possibly jailed if I didn't have a safe and secure courtroom by the crack of dawn on Monday, August 3. I did my best to round up equipment to make the process faster, but with only two hand-held scanners, searches were going to take time, and how else could one improve security without access to high technology? I could have handled the situation better, and there was no need to talk about Judge Burnstein to the press the way I did. Still, I went to great lengths to avoid a contempt-of-court charge. Even though I felt I had done my best to comply with the order, Judge Franza was calling me to a hearing. "As the Courtroom Turns" rolled along. By Tuesday, we'd worked out an arrangement to continue handling security along with some private security employees. We managed to get our hands on three metal detectors and one x-ray machine, so we could open three entrances instead of one. Instead of hour delays, the longest it took to get into the courthouse was about ten minutes. One of the judges, Susan Lebow, came prepared to wait as long as she had to, in more comfortable attire. She told us she didn't mind the wait if it ensured extra security. Others didn't see it that way.

One man's pen kept setting off the metal detector and he refused to remove it from his pocket. He got in a shoving match with a deputy and ended up being arrested for disorderly conduct. An attorney filed a lawsuit against me saying that the searches were unconstitutional and violated his and every other citizen's rights.

I had not received a written order from Judge Franza asking me to appear at his court hearing Tuesday morning. I went to a breakfast meeting in Plantation instead, a commitment I had made some time ago. When I left the meeting, I was served with an order asking me to appear, within twenty minutes, in the judge's courtroom.

Well, I was not about to attend a hearing before I consulted with an attorney. I called my attorneys immediately, who rushed down to the courtroom to advise the judge they were representing me and that I would not be there. Judge Franza was upset but proceeded anyway. One of my attorneys, David Bogenshutz later said that the proceeding made little sense and that most people would be outraged at the way the sheriff was being treated if they were in the same position. Judge Franza issued a warrant for my arrest. The order called for Governor Bob Martinez to have me incarcerated. Credibility on all sides of this matter was slipping rapidly.

Governor Martinez issued a statement saying that he hoped that two responsible elected officials would be able to work out their disagreement. The newspaper headlines raged, "Arrest Sheriff, Broward Judge Asks." What a mess! Judge Franza refused to rescind the arrest order and said he would talk only to me about it inside his courtroom. There seemed to be no other alternative. I felt that the judge's authority needed to be preserved, which could be done only if I went to court and apologized.

So I did. Tempers had cooled significantly since the day before. Neither the judge nor I wanted an argument on Wednesday, so it took only a few minutes to settle the matter. I told the judge that I had done everything within my power to comply with Judge Burnstein's order, which explicitly called for the use of hand-held scanners and threatened sanctions if I didn't follow the order to the letter. My compliance created chaos on Monday morning for which I apologized. Wackenhut was able to help obtain more useful security equipment for Tuesday, and security checks were operating relatively smoothly.

Judge Franza appeared to be satisfied by this explanation. "There are quite a few people out there who like you," he said. "Be a good Nick, not a God, Nick." He also urged me to iron out my differences with Judge Burnstein. I told him I would and said that security would improve further as time passed, more equipment came in, more deputies were properly trained, and procedures became routine. As far as I was concerned, the situation was resolved. I apologized to the people of Broward County for my part in the affair. Certainly I could have handled it better, although I didn't think what I did would create major disruptions.

Governor Martinez was glad the security issue was finished and we could all go back to work fighting criminals. I'm sure he was secretly pleased that I had stayed out of jail. I know I was.

Judge Burnstein's reaction was to say that Judge Franza retained jurisdiction of the case and would hold me accountable if the judges believed the security measures at the courthouse were lax. She denied that she was trying to tell me how to do my job, but it was clear she would continue to wrest control of courthouse security through Judge Franza.

No other county in Florida reacted like ours did to the Port Saint Joe incident. Not Dade, where arguably the threat was even greater. Not Palm Beach, not anywhere. Only one judge responded with an excitability that bordered on hysteria. But beyond the rhetoric and the newspaper headlines, we were all friends before the "Great Courthouse Security War" and would be still, long after everyone had dismissed it from their minds. A number of cases that were canceled on Monday when the courthouse was virtually shut down had to be rescheduled and attempts made to comply with the "speedy trial" language contained within the Florida law.

A local citizen wrote to one of the South Florida newspapers saying that he was surprised that judges felt their lives were more precious than anyone else's. While more deputies were pulled off the streets to comply with the extra security ordered by the judges, the citizens of Broward County were left with a little less protection than before. I had tried to point this out to the judges myself, which is why we were training people specifically for this purpose, but my argument fell on deaf ears. The letter writer also reminded the judges that neither Presidents Lincoln, Garfield, McKinley nor Kennedy was killed inside a courthouse.

The judges eventually decided that the police can and should be armed and gave that order on August 12.

On September 1, the committee, appointed by the county commission, recommended that police officers, state investigators, judges, and anyone else legally licensed to carry a firearm be permitted to do so. I was not pleased with this recommendation, since it would definitely hamper security measures. We had collected over 300 weapons in the previous three weeks, all pieces that would have otherwise been carried inside the courthouse prior to implementation of the new stricter procedures. Judge Burnstein agreed, saying she was glad these weapons were confiscated and was not eager to lift the restrictive methods being used by my deputies. She did, however, want judges to be able to carry their weapons and pointed out a state law recently passed that permitted judges to bring weapons inside courtrooms. She also said she didn't mind if police officers were allowed to carry their weapons in, feeling it would enhance security, not lessen it. "No problem," I replied. "If you want bazookas in the courthouse, you'll have bazookas. If you want tanks, you'll have tanks. Just tell me what you want. Earlier this year, it was no weapons at all."

Judge Burnstein replied by saying her earlier decision was a mistake. I told her I would comply with whatever her wishes were and whatever the commission decided. I wasn't necessarily going to applaud it as sound security, but I would follow their directives.

On September 8, the agreement was worked out: judges and law enforcement officials could carry weapons. The order also gave the security officers the discretion of letting in firefighters, paramedics, and other emergency workers without weapons screening. Judge Burnstein herself had received a couple of death threats in the past two weeks, although she downplayed them, saying she had received one or two a year since she became a judge eleven years ago.

The security plan wasn't ideal, but had been reached by a consensus compromise, so at least everyone was in some form of agreement. The courthouse wasn't a totally secure area, but the orders were clear and I followed them.

The courthouse security issue didn't exactly die. Within a short time three county court judges refused to go through the metal detectors, saying it could be injurious to their health, especially since they were of child-bearing age. The three magistrates, June L. Johnson, Susan Lebow, and Linda Pratt, appealed to County Court Administrative Judge Larry Seidlin, and he asked me to exempt the nineteen county court judges from having to pass through the machines like everyone else. I could see this was going to be the first of many exceptions requested as time went on.

A few weeks after that infamous August day, I attended a breakfast with about 150 other business leaders, presided over by Lieutenant Governor Bobby Brantley. All attending were asked to briefly introduce themselves to the audience. When it came to my turn, I stood up and said, "Nick Navarro, director of security at the courthouse."

In a 1987 year-in-review column, a local writer penned a poem that contained the following stanza:

His war with Miette was one Nick had to win,

That's why, at the courthouse, you couldn't get in.

The lines were so long people started to faint.

On that day we learned our Nick was no saint.

Eleven

Crackdown

RACK: A CONCENTRATED DERIVATIVE OF COCAINE, IN ROCK FORM. METHOD of absorption: Smoked, absorbing rapidly through the lungs to the brain in seconds. Effects: An intense rush then a powerful crash that creates an immediate need for a second hit. Stages to addiction: (1) Stimulation, (2) depression, (3) sleeplessness, (4) paranoia, (5) delusions. Average time to addiction: Within six weeks, 15-20 times faster than regular powdered cocaine. Medical results: Lung damage similar to emphysema, increased heart rate, a form of schizophrenia related to the brain craving the drug, a sensation of bugs crawling over the skin, loss of appetite leading to serious weight loss and malnutrition.

Crack cocaine made its debut on the streets of America in 1985. I don't believe it was mere coincidence that this was the year I took office as sheriff of Broward County. I felt as if this was my big test in narcotics policing; everything up until then was only practice. I'd had some success at interdiction with other drugs, but crack was going to be the biggest challenge yet for me, for my fellow officers and associates, for the people of this country.

This drug tests us as a society in every way, and until we can virtually eliminate it from our shores, we will continue to struggle with crime in the United States.

Cocaine was once the preferred drug of the wealthy, but as the American market became glutted with the white powder, the price for a kilogram dropped in half. When criminals figured out how to change its form from a powder to a solid, to be sold for as little as $10 per rock, virtually everyone had financial access to this addictive drug. With that access came a new wave of criminals.

For someone who smokes five rocks in one day, which is a small dosage, the cost at $10 per rock, seven days a week, is $350 weekly. Most of the people using this drug do not have that kind of money. If they are unable to earn this type of income, then they steal - any type of goods they can resell. Fences don't pay these people top dollar, so roughly $700 in goods or more must be acquired each week to bring in the amount of dollars necessary to feed a small habit. If a thousand individuals are trying to pick up $700 per week in stolen goods, the result is a crime wave.

The increase in the number of felony arrests after I took office illustrates this. The typical spin-off crimes like burglary, armed robbery, and automobile break-ins went up 30 percent overall in 1985 and then another 50 percent more in 1986. Conservatively, 60 percent of our entire sheriff's office's time was spent, directly or indirectly, on the illicit drug trade. In excess of 70 percent of those arrested for non-drug-related crimes tested positive for recent drug usage. One out of every six Florida youths admitted, in 1984, to having used cocaine. Sixty-four percent of all youth arrests were due to the use or abuse of drugs or alcohol. The same number, 64 percent, of all homicides are related to drug and alcohol abuse.

Quite simply, crack took over Broward County for a period of time in 1985 and 1986. People didn't know their neighbors. Bars appeared on the windows of homes. If you drove through the streets, you'd ordinarily find them deserted except for the dealers. No one wanted to go out on the street. Everyone was afraid to leave their homes.

Addicts trying to move stolen property often passed up pawn shops and headed straight to "crack houses" or "rock houses" to trade stolen jewelry, televisions, radar detectors, or whatever they had for a small $10 rock of cocaine. Their desperation reached such a high level they turned to crime in their own neighborhoods, pouncing on friends' houses in order to feed their habits.

The Broward courtrooms began filling up as arrests were made, jamming an already overbooked schedule. Jail space was at a premium as cells overflowed with crack-addicted criminals. There was an epidemic on our streets, more far-reaching than the plagues of medieval times. We were a county in crisis and the Broward County Sheriff's Office reacted as quickly as it could.

In 1984, Governor Bob Graham established an anti-drug program, aimed primarily at Florida youth, called Project Free Way. In 1985, after I took office, Broward became one of the first counties in the state to embrace this program and to implement it locally. Community-oriented, it was primarily an educational program to increase public, especially youth, awareness of drugs (and alcohol) and to coordinate treatment and rehabilitation for those that had come under drugs' influences.

At the BSO, we set up an entire spectrum of programs that focused on this issue. Interdiction, enforcement, education, treatment, and rehabilitation were all various phases of trying to rein in the problem. We knew we were dealing with more than just the large drug dealers now. Crack cocaine made dealers (and users) of even small-time hoods. Our goal was to go after everyone involved, from the end-user up through the ranks to the leaders of the cartels, who were making a fortune off of other people's troubles. I had no use for anyone on that ladder and was bound and determined to take crack completely out of Broward County.

On Monday, we arrested the owner of a chain of shoe repair stores who had been running a cocaine operation out of their back rooms for years.

On Tuesday, one search warrant for a restaurant turned up fourteen kilograms of cocaine and resulted in the arrests of four men without any prior arrests, let alone convictions.

On Wednesday, we raided a home and arrested a husband and wife when we found nearly a pound of cocaine contained in a doughnut bag jammed into a crawl space of a bedroom closet. The home was equipped with two-way and shortwave radios that were tuned to locations in Colombia, South America.

On Thursday, we arrested two individuals who confessed to shipping around forty-five pounds of cocaine to Texas every month.

On Friday, we seized 963 pounds of cocaine from a fishing boat cruising toward Broward County's Hillsboro Inlet.

Broward was, literally, a battlefield where the war on drugs was being fought. We had undercover officers everywhere disguised as sellers, buyers and high

rollers - whatever it took to make an effective presence and send these criminals out of the county or off to jail. Our officers spent thousands of extra hours
following even the smallest lead in this quest.

It took time for our tactics to turn things around. Dealers controlled the
neighborhoods for a time. Crack sales added a lot of addicts to their rosters of
customers - people who turned to crime themselves to feed their habits. If we
could eliminate the dealers and treat the addicts and users, we would go a long
way toward solving the problem.

Thus, our strategy was divided into in four phases:

1. Identify the drug dealer.
2. Arrest the drug dealer.
3. Convict and remove the drug dealer from the street.
4. Replace the drug dealer with an undercover cop pretending
    to be a dealer.

Phase one was the easiest; a good cop could spot a dealer without much
difficulty. In Fort Lauderdale, the western part of the city contained the highest concentration, even though the dealers were spreading out around the
county. We began in this saturated area first and then moved on to other parts
of the county.

Arresting the drug dealers was somewhat more difficult, but we developed
a number of methods to make arrests that would result in convictions. Posing
as buyers, we began slowly removing drug dealers from their favorite spots on
the streets.

Obtaining convictions was never easy. Our laws over the years had been
relaxed with regard to drugs. In the late sixties, someone could be sent to jail
for possession of marijuana. By 1985, only major dealers with a couple of prior
arrests earned any sizable length of time behind bars. Therefore, many of the
criminals we took off the street ended up back on it almost before we could
process the paperwork. We weren't just fighting an infinite number of offenders, but we also had to deal with the same ones over and over again.

The fourth and final phase in this enforcement process was to replace the
drug dealers with our own undercover police officers. We found some willing
participants who would, essentially, stand around and wait for users to
approach them to buy drugs. Our officers had some of the seized contraband
with them and were ready to sell the crack and then arrest the user on the spot.

Removal of the user/addict was also important because it took a different type of criminal off the street; these were the people who were breaking into homes and cars to steal what they could to sell or trade for crack. If we could put them away, get them help in a treatment program, and hopefully cure them, we would make even larger inroads against crime. Dealers could be replaced, but if we began curing the users, demand would drop and the supply would follow.

What this four-part law enforcement program was intended to do was to create fear. We wanted the drug dealers to be concerned that every buyer they conversed with could be an undercover cop. We wanted the users to believe that anyone who was willing to sell them drugs could be a police officer. We wanted these violators to know that they weren't welcome in Broward County. If they came within our borders, they did so at their own peril. It was a gamble so risky it wouldn't be worth the chance.

So we went to work, and a curious thing happened. A number of the neighborhoods where, in the past, it had been made clear that police officers weren't welcome, suddenly were demanding greater police protection. "Beef up patrols" was their cry, a sentiment far removed from that expressed a couple of years earlier when there was concern we were concentrating on their areas out of some misguided sense of justice.

Drugs were nothing new in poor neighborhoods. Heroin was around in the 1940s, marijuana in the 1950's, LSD and mescaline in the 1960's and cocaine in the 1970s, but crack changed the rules of the game since it was a substance even people of modest or low means could afford. It opened up a wider market for the dealers and these communities suffered as a result. Pushers hung out on street corners, selling crack to motorists cruising by. The dealers often had grade-school kids on their payroll to keep an eye out for police. Drugs were no longer something that was being done inside corporate boardrooms or in communes. They were in our homes, in our next-door neighbor's house, down the block, up the street, and through the entire area. The invasion was essentially a bloodless coup and now these citizens wanted to turn away the barbarians.

We responded. In the first couple of years after crack turned up on our streets, we made the following progress:

~ In northwest Fort Lauderdale, more than 300 buyers and sellers were arrested.

~ In unincorporated Roosevelt Gardens near Fort Lauderdale, another 300 or so buyers and sellers were detained.

~ On a street corner in Deerfield Beach, more than 40 buyers and sellers were rounded up within a two-week period.

~ In South Broward and West Hollywood, the amount of arrests on narcotics violations doubled since the previous year.

~ In southwest Pompano Beach, undercover BSO officers, posing as drug dealers, arrested more than 20 buyers in less than a week.

~ Special drug task forces were set up in virtually every community consisting of officers and residents working together to effect arrests, educate the young about the problems associated with drugs and addictions, and find suitable treatment for the addicted.

In March 1986, our agency scheduled National Drug Week for the first seven days of the month and we went after the illicit drug trade full force. Two dealers ready to trade two kilograms of cocaine for $61,000 were arrested in a rented hotel room as they attempted the transaction with two of our undercover operatives. As the dealers were arrested, one of the detectives said, "This is National Drug week, man, where's your red ribbon?"

But were we making progress? The role models the kids in school were seeing were dope dealers and users. A Florida survey that showed 78 percent of crack users to be under age twenty-five seemed to bear this out. We arrested the dealers, but then the kids saw those same offenders back on the street.

As our local jail population multiplied, we conducted Operation Crackdown in August 1986. Coordinating with several other local law enforcement agencies, we "hit" six street corners well-known as the essential hub of crack activity. In so doing, we made 196 arrests on various drug-related charges. We seized more than 300 rocks of cocaine, $3,000 in cash, and twelve cars including a Cadillac and Corvette. One of the dealers we arrested in the sweep was a guy we'd put away for heroin trafficking a few years earlier who was apparently trying his hand at crack. When confronted by deputies, he swallowed six rocks and needed his stomach pumped at Broward General Medical Center - we added tampering with evidence to his charges.

For Operation Crackdown, we utilized members of the media, who were allowed to ride with us and witness arrests, filming and reporting as they went. We wanted the people of the community to know what we were doing on their behalf. I could say that we were trying to scare violators with reports of arrests, but most of those people didn't bother to watch television anyway.

The next day we served search warrants on forty-three suspected crack houses, which resulted in thirty-seven arrests and the seizure of 300 cocaine rocks, 45 small bags of marijuana, a few hundred dollars in cash, a couple of guns, and fifteen cars. Many of these houses had ceased operations after the publicity generated by day one of Crackdown.

After the dust settled, we ended up with about forty possession arrests. The balance of the offenses were misdemeanors, mostly charges against lookouts for loitering.

We had effectively sent a message to the drug community that no one was safe from our enforcement. If you were dealing or using drugs, sooner or later you would come to the attention of the Broward County Sheriff's Office.

Later that month, I found myself in a bizarre situation at the Thunderbird Swap Shop, a gigantic flea market in West Fort Lauderdale. A man representing the Great South Florida Contraband company was selling fake drug kits, which consisted of a "cocaine kilo" (a bag of baking powder), a package of fake hundred-dollar bills, a bogus passport, and a short straw. The package was labeled "Take Home A Real Florida Souvenir," all at the retail price of $6.95. The seller was telling people to use the pack to get apprehended and then sue for false arrest. I realize we live in a free enterprise system, but it was ridiculous - even sick - to make money on something that was strangling our communities. The owner of the Swap Shop, Preston Henn, asked us to evict the man, which we did. Some people will try to make a buck from anything.

Arrests continued their upward climb throughout the balance of 1986 and into 1987. We realized the crack cocaine problem was not going to go away easily, despite some progress on our part in slowing it down. It was time for Operation Crackdown II.

The first "crackdown" in August 1986 netted far more misdemeanor than felony arrests and we wanted to improve on that with a two-day sweep at the end of June 1987. As we did a year earlier, we invited members of the press to accompany us and televise the results in an effort to further publicize our vigilance against this highly addictive drug. On Monday, we arrested dealers as they hawked their wares on street corners, executed search warrants, arrested the occupants of drug houses where activity had been increasing, and performed "reverse stings" in which our undercover cops posed as pushers and arrested buyers that solicited them for crack purchases.

Over fifty arrests were made, down significantly from a year ago, but the charges brought were primarily felonies. This time, we had aimed at specific areas that we had observed to be high activity areas, rather than perform a broad sweep, a tactic that was criticized the previous year for a lack of "quality" arrests.

This year, we honed our arrest style, perfected the paperwork flow to move cases along as quickly as possible, and improved the communication with other city police departments concerning our presence in their areas. We had started the operation at 8:30 A.M. during what we liked to call "drive time," since many crack users make their purchases on the way to work in the morning.

The second day of Crackdown II netted the same amount of arrests as day one and included mostly felony charges. It was amazing to me that despite all of the publicity on television and in the newspapers concerning the crackdown on Monday, with the promise of still more to come on Tuesday, people were out on the street dealing and buying anyway. It illustrates that crack is so addictive, someone will break the law, even though the chances of arrest are high, simply to get one's hands on the substance.

Day two saw one tragedy. The last search warrant, served on Tuesday evening, was to a man named Arnold Miller, a fifty-one-year-old Fort Lauderdale mobile home resident who had been observed selling crack in the days leading up to the sweep. Several officers approached the door and knocked, while others waited outside on the sidewalk in the event there was trouble. One of the officers saw Miller look out at them through the window next to the front door and moments later observed a handgun in Miller's possession as the suspect made his way to the door. Officers opened fire and Miller was hit before he could discharge his gun. Taken to the hospital where a search turned up five rocks of crack in his pocket and more than $200 in cash, he died a couple of hours later.

According to the SWAT team members at the scene, they warned Miller to drop his weapon after announcing that they were there on a raid. Four of the officers had taken shots at the suspect. They were put on administrative leave without pay until a homicide team could verify their accounts.

Overall, officers participating in this second sweep made 119 felony arrests; confiscated nineteen cars, two pick-up trucks, and a motorcycle; and seized more than $8,000, which was put in the Drug Confiscation Fund. We'd also timed this effort to occur at the beginning of the summer school break, hoping the message "stay away from crack" would make an impression and force some of the youths to pursue other, more legal activities over the hot summer months.

But South Florida continued to be a haven for the drug trade. In August, two officers stopped next to a recreational vehicle that was sidelined in the emergency lane of Interstate 95. It was apparently deserted as no one responded to the deputies' knocks and shouts. One deputy looked in to see if someone was asleep, or worse, and saw a pile of padlocked duffel bags. The other deputy found a note under the windshield wipers: "Gone to get tow truck."

Since RVs were the smugglers' vehicle of choice and duffel bags the common mode of transportation for narcotics, the deputies alerted our narcotics investigators and me. We drove to the site and staked out the vehicle for over an hour, but the occupants did not return. We then forced open the lock and opened the duffels to reveal about 526 kilos of cocaine, unwrapped, from Colombia, worth a street value of $105 million.

The crack problem didn't affect only the dealers and the users. One early eveying in January 1988, choir practice was about to begin at a local Baptist church. One of its members, a sixty-six-year-old woman, was getting ready to attend. She walked to her couch and sat down to visit with her grandchildren for a few moments before departing. Suddenly, shots rang out, shattering the quiet of the early evening and scaring the wits out of the grandmother. A bullet ripped through her bedroom window and traveled all the way into the living room where she and the children sat. Thuds sounded in rapid succession as more slugs peppered her house. The shooting continued down the block, as other neighbors sprawled on their floors, praying they would be spared.

Miraculously, everyone was. The incident had started as a drive-by shooting that began on another block and moved up the street, as the occupants of a black Chrysler LeBaron convertible continued to fire at houses all the while. The grandmother was helped to her feet by her grandchildren, and they searched each other quickly for wounds. There were none.

This neighborhood was like many others in Broward County, a calm and peaceful tract that had turned into a stage of violence for crack dealers and users. I sent deputies to town, homeowner, and church meetings to explain how we could help if the citizens would assist us. A local citizen can spot something out of the ordinary in his or her neighborhood long before a major problem develops, and our narcotics team and other drug-related task forces can respond in a prompt manner.

Crackdown III was conducted in March 1988. Again using sweeps, search warrants, and reverse stings, we were able to arrest 110 people, all but 8 of them on felony charges, including a Baptist preacher from Saint Petersburg who was in town to speak at a local church and decided to buy some crack in northwest Fort Lauderdale. We also picked up an ex-Pompano Beach police officer and drug counselor who was riding his bike in the Fort Lauderdale area and stopped to buy three rocks of cocaine. He had been a good police officer before resigning in 1985, but he told us after his arrest that he was simply hooked on crack and unable to break the habit.

We confiscated more than thirty weapons in the sweep, including semi-automatic machine pistols, sawed-off shotguns, and revolvers, further evidence of the danger drugs bring to a community. Cash and vehicles were also seized during this successful law enforcement effort. I vowed to keep doing these crackdowns for as long as it took to give the streets back to the citizens of Broward County.

In July 1988, we decided on a month-long crack attack on the violators within our county's borders. In a joint effort among church and community groups, Crime Stoppers, and several police agencies, including the DEA, this effort to take as much crack off the streets as possible, along with its criminals, was our way of continuing to fight the battle on the homefront. Governor Martinez asked to participate in the drug sweeps, which would be a daily occurrence throughout the month. We vowed no let up, no safe haven, no break from the threat - if you dealt drugs in Broward County you were making the mistake of your life.

The governor, equipped with a bullet-proof vest, witnessed the storming of a drug dealer's home and then joined in a chase of a suspected drug buyer through the streets of Broward County. At the drugs dealer's home, only nine people and some plastic bags with cocaine residue were found - no cocaine powder or rocks and no drug dealer. The suspect's mother was there and she said that she'd heard rumors that her son was dealing but that he didn't do it inside the house. The woman and other occupants were in mourning for her husband, the suspect's father, who had passed away earlier in the day, a fact we didn't know before the raid.

The chase was a different story. A man had stopped his car to buy some crack and when he realized the sellers were deputies disguised in a reverse sting, he panicked and floored the accelerator pedal in a desperate attempt to escape. He cut off a woman in a red Toyota, drove through traffic the wrong way, and forced an unmarked sheriff's car into a stop sign as the van carrying the governor and me continued in pursuit. The man was finally trapped by officers a few more blocks down the road. The governor observed that drugs are not a victimless crime as the buyer had endangered several dozen motorists and pedestrians while trying to elude police.

The raids conducted that July emphasized the frustration of dealing with the cocaine problem. In one house occupied by a half dozen people, all denying that they were doing anything wrong, officers found cocaine in a bedroom, hundreds of dollars enclosed in a plastic bag, a beeper, a razor blade, and a "Saturday night special." In an ashtray, three cocaine rocks sat on a package of food stamps. At the end of the day, it was a quick trip to the grocery store to buy food with stamps and a pass by the neighborhood dealer to buy crack with cold cash. Some days, the war was more wearying than others.

By then, we were having an effect. A dealer standing with a group of friends no longer tried to flag down potential customers driving by in their vehicles. The dealer waited for the driver to make the first move and preceded any conversation with the question, "Are you a cop?" By August, we were averaging six arrests a day. The word was out on the South Florida streets: If you're dealing, stay the hell out of Broward County.

One had to do things that were different and innovative to make a dent in the cocaine crime wave. We gutted the inside of a confiscated van, installed a camera that could view outside, and placed a couple of officers in the back. We painted the vehicle and labeled it "Nick's Trash Pick-Up." Operation "Trojan Horse" was about to begin.

The drivers of the van, undercover officers, went in search of dealers willing to sell them drugs. The camera videotaped any transaction and the dealer was arrested. Although the van had a distinct look, it wasn't the typical cop vehicle, undercover or otherwise. The dealers had a difficult time catching on to this sting, and as a result, "Trojan Horse" pulled a substantial number of them off the street.

Bob Freeman, who was a lieutenant in our office in charge of the juvenile gang unit, had been a cameraman for traveling reporter and talk show host Geraldo Rivera. When Rivera decided to do a special for television on the subject of drugs, "The Doping of America," Freeman steered him to our department, advising that we were the agency most likely to cooperate with the media. And because we had operations going on every day, it was likely that reels and reels of footage could be shot within a week's time, just on our routine assignments.

I'm not sure what I expected, but Rivera turned out to be a gracious, down-to-earth individual who was serious about his work and respectful of what we needed to accomplish as law officers. We first took him on an undercover situation, disguising him in a beard, wig, and dark glasses. In soliciting the dealer, the suspect looked straight at the television personality and said, "You know, you look a lot like Geraldo Rivera." Fortunately, no one panicked and the moment passed without any true recognition from the dealer, Nelson Scott. Later, Rivera would testify in court like everyone else involved in the case.

In February 1989, at a meeting of the Florida Sheriff's Association, the number one complaint was voiced - the basic inability of law enforcement to stem the rising tide of crime associated with crack cocaine. From Dade County to the Florida Panhandle, the question was the same: What can we do together to beat back the crack invasion? All agreed we had to act, but how and with what methods?

I proposed a plan for all communities where resources for the entire state would be pooled (some counties could afford to help others) and officers from every section of the state identically trained to fight the problem. I offered our Broward training facilities and our trainers for this program. Since my experience in this area was more extensive than any other sheriff's, I was appointed chairperson. I told my fellow officers that I would create a plan outlining a joint statewide crackdown to be implemented in mid-summer 1989.

Before leaving the conference, the specifics began to formulate in my mind. Within ten days, my proposal was formally written. Dividing the state into six regions (Panhandle, Jacksonville, East Central Florida, West Central Florida, Southwest Florida, Southeast Florida), we appointed one member to oversee each region and coordinate the overall program with me. We requested some funding for this special program, including an "800" line for intelligence gathering.

When we launched the plan in the summer of 1989, all of the Florida sheriffs were part of it. Operation Rock-Pile netted more than 2,000 arrests and a multitude of weaponry and vehicles, along with a substantial amount of cash, which would be spread around for use as part of the confiscated funds program. By any standard, Operation Rock-Pile was a success, and in Broward we had made a lot of progress since our first Operation Crackdown.

Other states began to take an interest in what we were doing and we eventually set up a tri-state sweep, using officers from Georgia and South Carolina along with our Florida-based troopers. Deputies were assigned to different states, although they wore their department uniforms. It drove the criminals crazy, when, for example, a Broward County deputy arrested a drug dealer in Macon, Georgia. It made the violators look over their shoulders even more, as they never knew who or where the danger to their enterprise would come from.

On one of our three-state sweeps, we arrested over 13,000 drug dealers. Even the media complimented this effort. I would have loved to see a nationwide, one-day sweep. This would have sent a major message to drug dealers everywhere that their activities are destined to become extinct. The only way to get a true foothold in the war against drugs was to have cooperation, from agency to agency, from state to state, but there is too much provincialism, further complicated by varying state laws. The dream of the "Just Say No" solution is just that - a dream.

Innovations like the Trojan Horse method and exchanging officers from other states to keep the criminals off balance are ideas that were successful in waging the day-to-day battles in the war against drugs. We were also conducting searches at major transportation arenas such as airports, train stations, and bus terminals with the same kind of success I had back in the late 1970s as head of airport security. Some people, especially criminals and defense attorneys, didn't care much for these tactics and fought them all the way to the United States Supreme Court.

Another innovation that initially fascinated people was the Broward County crack lab that we set up when our own crack supplies, confiscated in our arrests, were running low and we needed the substance to continue to run our successful reverse stings. When we made an arrest, the crack taken at the scene was tested, marked, and saved as evidence for future legal proceedings. The more arrests we made, the more crack was tied up in court cases, with some of the legal entanglements taking months to unravel. That crack, once earmarked for evidence, could not be used in our reverse stings.

These sting operations were arresting the buyers, hopefully while they were still in he curable stage, when rehabilitation could help them kick the habit before it caused them to steal or kill to obtain the drug. The pushers were important, but reducing the demand for the drug and saving someone from addiction and more jail time was equally critical.

While the rocks were needed as evidence, we had a lot of confiscated pure cocaine powder that was destined for destruction. After continued pleas from Steve Bertucelli of our Organized Crime Division, for more rocks to "arm" our undercover cops with, I talked with our sheriff's office chemist, Randy Hilliard, about the possibility of making our own rocks from the cocaine powder.

Hilliard was immediately enthused with the idea since in the process of manufacturing the rocks, he could mark each one with a small, almost undetectable identifying tag, which would indicate that the crack confiscated during an arrest had been made in our own laboratory, thus avoiding the costly process of testing it again for verification purposes.

I checked with the state attorney's office to see if extracting some of the cocaine hydrochloride to convert it to crack would violate any laws. All we were doing was changing the molecular structure of powder we already had in our possession. John Pennie, the director of our sheriff's lab, told the media in an interview that making crack was sort of like making fudge - without the cookbook. The whole process of manufacturing takes about ninety minutes, with another day needed for crystallization.

We received the go-ahead from the state attorney's office and double-checked with the DEA, then Hilliard set up his lab.

The first batch of rocks was made in February 1989. Hilliard received a kilo of cocaine (2.2 pounds) from the powder we were ready to destroy a couple of weeks earlier. The rocks that resulted were sealed in separate, glassine bags. As long as the bag remained sealed during the "transaction" and arrest, it could be marked as evidence without additional testing.

Every conceivable effort was made to ensure that the crack we made did not fall into the wrong hands. It was used exclusively for reverse stings and only in controlled environments.

Defense attorneys were incensed. They cited my latest idea as an extreme violation of civil rights and morally unethical. These were the same people who would do or say almost anything to get their clients off, guilty or not. Any technicality, no matter how marginal, was exploited if it meant their clients could go free. Apparently they didn't operate under the same moral constraints that apply to the rest of us.

While I expected some criticism of our new operation, the media avalanche was completely unexpected. I was invited on the Today Show to debate an attorney about the merits of our crack lab. I defended my tactics. In the first three months of 1989, we had made 2,300 drug-related arrests. That tied up a significant amount of crack that we couldn't use for reverse stings. Powder that we already possessed was being converted into crack for use in law enforcement. It wasn't any different than if we'd simply used the powdered cocaine itself to conduct the stings; we simply changed the form of it.

The majority of court cases in which our crack was used were successful. One case was appealed to the Fourth District Court of Appeals, and the guilty verdict was upheld.

USA Today featured a story about the BSO on the front page. I couldn't understand all the attention. The crack lab was intended to be used only until our temporary shortage of the drug was relieved. I saw no reason to continue the practice once our supply was sufficient to continue our vigilance against crack.

The publicity generated eventually hurt the operation. Cases featuring our rocks were constantly appealed, generally to no avail, until one finally went to the Fourth District Court of Appeals, which reversed the lower court's guilty verdict, citing the fact that the sheriff's department manufactured the drug used to make the arrest. At the time of this decision, we had already stopped manufacturing the drug since we had a sufficient quantity to work with.

The media seemed to "go with the flow." From the early praises we received for innovation, the rhetoric turned to the unconstitutional and immoral manner in which we were operating against the people in our society. The fact was, we were getting the buyers and the dealers off the street and driving them indoors.

This complicated our efforts a little as search warrants were necessary and more police work had to be done to effect an arrest indoors, but we were still bringing in the criminals. If one life was spared as a result, it was well worth it.

The crack lab was soon rendered obsolete. Carl Hiassen, columnist for the Miami Herald, wrote another in a long series of articles critical of our department, saying that manufacturing crack simply illustrated "the misguided, haphazard state of the so-called war on drugs." The fact that Hiassen's brother-in-law was a high-ranking Broward County Democratic commissioner probably had very little to do with his continued attacks on our office. Judges influenced by the media started to "piss backwards," changing their minds on the legality of it all, and simply ordered the crack lab closed down. Since its usefulness was long over, it didn't set back our efforts.

In September 1989, President George Bush delivered a twenty-minute speech to the American public about the need to unite against drugs, saying that the will of the entire country could do far more than any amount of money poured into a program. Still, he did put up $2.2 billion to be used in a comprehensive strategy to divest the country of illicit drugs.

Among the components of his program were more money for local law enforcement; more prisons; more drug prevention and education programs; money to help Peru, Bolivia, and Colombia fight drug lords; more treatment programs; and greater border interdiction emphasis.

The president was right about one thing: it takes more than money to win the drug war. Community involvement was the key that drove the long-term success of our efforts. While we had been getting good local cooperation, more was needed, and more consistency in the vigilance by all residents was our best chance to make a difference in the war's outcome. The enemy wasn't in Colombia or Peru or Southeast Asia. It was right here. We were the ones causing the problem.

Arrests and interdiction continued on a regular, coordinated basis. In June 1990, the search of a warehouse revealed 2,600 pounds of cocaine packaged in forty-one burlap bags and plastic sacks. An anonymous tip had told us of this location, advising us that there had been a lot of pre-dawn activity at this site. This seemed to be not only a local distribution center, but also a regional, and quite possibly, national distribution point.

The record number of arrests we had been making caused one of our local judges to lose his composure. In his chambers, donning his robe for the day's hearings, Judge Robert S. Zack was alarmed to hear that his court calendar was again chock-full because of another of our sting sweeps the night before. According to astonished onlookers, Zack lashed out at me, using very derogatory language toward me.

One expects judges to be always in control, but as events have shown, we are asking them to be superhuman in that regard. We all "lose" it at one time or another and make judgments, decisions, or statements we would like to take back a moment later. I prefer to think that the judge, in this case, was simply reacting to the newest parade line of dope peddlers, users, burglars, and so forth that he would have to see all day long.

In our arrests, we continued to work our way up the chain of command in the underworld. While we often pulled in the rank-and-file members of a drug organization, the bigger fish were always harder to catch. One distribution group that we had followed for a couple of years before we had enough evidence to move in was located in Dania, a town in eastern Broward County. A real estate operation called the "McCutcheon Organization" had been working for ten years in the county and eluding police through their money and connections. Ivory L. McCutcheon, the group's leader, was a well-respected businessman who had built a drug empire, distributing over 1,000 kilos of cocaine over the past six years. He had numerous businesses and we had informants placed in a number of them. The boss himself was observed to be in on several of the larger drug transactions. It was a good feeling to put one of the major players away.

The crack war goes on. It has taken more lives in our country than any war, including the American Civil War. Law enforcement can do only so much. Reinforcement must come from each and every family. Spending more time together instead of in front of the television set is a good place to start. The family support circle can help a member in need, but you'll know someone needs help only if you take the time to find out.

We are in danger of losing almost an entire generation of youth in this fight. I don't want to see that happen. We can't deal with our children and their problems by saying "Get out of the house," for when they do, they often end up in one of our public facilities, alive or dead. We need to convince our kids to reject drugs as an outlet, but we can't let them struggle with this issue alone. If we take an active role, we can cut off the need for drugs and reduce the demand for those who will gladly make a buck from someone else's misery.

Together, we can all decimate this problem.

Twelve

Re-Election

O N DECEMBER 15, 1987, POLICE AND FIRE DEPARTMENTS WERE ASKED TO respond to an explosion that had set a building on fire in the North Broward County area. Shortly after they arrived on the scene, it became clear that this structure had been severely damaged. The establishment was called the VIP Men's Club, and as arson experts combed through the smoldering wreckage, evidence of a firebomb was uncovered.

The VIP Men's Club was a men's nightclub and believed to be a front for a prostitution ring, although not enough evidence was ever available to build a case. The club would not reopen, but the investigation of the incident would point directly to one of the candidates for the office of Broward County Sheriff in 1988.

It's probably one of the only campaigns that started with an actual explosion. However, given my dubious ability to achieve the same result with some of the issues I touched, it was definitely an omen.

There was a substantial amount of encouragement among the citizens of Broward County for me to run for another term. Having been tied up with the affairs of the past four years, I hadn't given it much thought. Four years was long enough to forget the pains associated with my first campaign and the Democrats' tactics. At the end of four years, the citizens of Broward County could see some positive results.

Clearly I had made some mistakes in judgment. Run-ins with judges over tents for inmates to help ease overcrowding and the circus over courthouse security were episodes that I regretted, even though I felt strongly about my position in each matter. While I may have made some wrong decisions, the people of Broward County knew that indecision was not one of my character traits. Judging from the mail my office received and the letters written to local newspapers, the majority of my decisions were well received. Community support was evident, so I decided to run again.

Once I had made the decision to seek re-election, an early-bird campaign account was opened. Contributions immediately began to come in. Looking back on it, this reaction from Broward residents gave me an extraordinary boost in confidence that people wanted us to continue what we started. All of these monies came in without solicitation, and they came from people of all party affiliations, another factor that encouraged me. The sheriff position should not be a political position; the objective of the position is to fight crime, not worry about who was going to be offended. These people hadn't elected Nick Navarro, Republican, back in 1984, they had elected Nick Navarro, period.

A poll was published toward the end of 1987, surveying only Democrats, that found that 50 percent of those asked had a favorable viewpoint of the job I was doing. 18 percent held an unfavorable view, and the rest were either neutral or not informed enough to respond. This news, from the opposite party, pleased me as the work we were doing went beyond political boundaries, and the residents of the county seemed to sense this.

The media did not see it this way at all. Convinced I was some political power-monger, there were repeated attempts to paint me as something other than the head of a law enforcement agency. News reports pointed to the increase in personnel and budget, but much of this came from contractual arrangements the county made with small city police departments to place their agencies under ours to consolidate efforts and be more efficient, financially as well as from an enforcement standpoint. The more towns that were added to my budget, the larger my power-base, according to those in political power and those that reported the news.

What they refused to accept is that I wished only to be sheriff and achieve success at stopping crime in our county. Every move I made, every decision, every strategy was analyzed and reviewed to ascertain the political motive involved; when none was apparent, one was invented out of pure frustration.

Further confounding these critics was the amount of money that was sent into the early-bird campaign account before any active campaigning was done. There were weekly updates on this fund in the local South Florida newspapers. Reporters searched everywhere for examples of favors handed out in return for campaign contributions. Again, there were none to be found.

Exasperated, the media dredged up the Jim Moran story again, pointing out that a couple of his corporations had made contributions to this re-election campaign, similar to what happened in the 1984 campaign. But Jim Moran did not make a personal contribution nor did he call me or contact me in any way about the corporate money donated to my fund. There was no reason. He wouldn't ask for a favor and I wouldn't grant one anyway.

By October, the campaign fund was larger than the amount I had raised during the entire 1984 effort. The headlines continued.

Despite the financial head start, at least one person didn't hold out much hope for my re-election chances. Psychic Marie Fresca predicted in the Broward News that I would lose the 1988 election because of the "great deal of adverse publicity" that was "starting to penetrate," costing me a loss of power and strategy. She went on to say that she had recently met me and considered me to be an honorable man, dedicated to my job. She reminded people not to forget my accomplishments when they went to the polls. I didn't know what her prediction track record was, but even though psychics went on the Tonight Show and predicted the end of the world, we were still walking around on terra firma.

By January 1988, the Democrats were trying to select my opponent. They had been criticized openly for what some believed to be an obvious yielding of this election as a result of the substantial amounts of campaign money I had accumulated before the first candidate had declared for office.

Their first choice seemed to be Kelly Hancock, the State Attorney's office chief homicide prosecutor. Broward Democratic Party Chairman George Platt had held a couple of conversations with Hancock, who had refused to speculate on whether he would run. Hancock had convicted a number of the criminals we had arrested and was one of the county's most successful prosecutors. He seemed to be more interested in being a judge than a sheriff, and I doubted he would run.

The first Democratic candidate to declare was Walter Ramsdell, a former chief of police in Lauderhill, a town now under contract with the Broward County Sheriff's Office. Ramsdell had been affiliated with a BSO Organized Crime Division task force; in fact, he'd headed it. However, he seemed primarily a figurehead, leaving most of the command duties in this task force to his second in charge, Ralph Finno, from the Fort Lauderdale Police Department. Ramsdell used to go into his office and lock the door, presumably to study task force documents, yet he made few decisions. I didn't view him as being very competent and after my election 1984, Ramsdell was one of the few people I let go. He was running a private investigation and security firm when he entered officially as a Democratic candidate. The fact that the Democrats were still actively seeking another candidate showed the amount of faith they had in Ramsdell. But they also had little faith in me in 1984, a mistake that continued to haunt them as a new election campaign neared.

The media was pushing for the Broward County Sheriff's Office to be made an appointed position, a policy I felt would be a tragic mistake. Dade County is the only county in Florida with an appointed sheriff, and it was arguably the area with the worst crime problem. Instead, the office could be non-partisan but still elected. That way, voters could simply choose the person with the higher qualifications, not vote based on the party the candidate belonged. This seemed a better strategy to me. The Broward County Commission met and decided to leave the process alone. The sheriff would continue to be an elected position and party affiliations were allowed.

In February, the number two man on Walter Ramsdell's Organized Crime Division task force, Ralph Finno, threw his hat into the Democratic ring. Finno had been on the Fort Lauderdale Police Department for twenty-seven years before retiring in 1986 to run for the Broward County Commission against incumbent Nicki Grossman. He was a Republican then and was overmatched against the popular Grossman, to whom he lost the election handily. Finno had switched parties, from Republican to Democrat in December 1987, and opened up a campaign account a month later, well ahead of the now less vague six-month requirement about party switching clarified three years earlier by the "Navarro bill."

When Finno declared, he said that I would hurt the cause of police throughout the county by revoking the rights of municipal police outside their boundaries. Finno also said I had let politics permeate my office, contrary to my promise to keep politics out of the sheriff's department. I'm not sure what politics he meant, but he was entitled to his opinion. He had switched to the Democratic party because there were substantially more registered Democrats then Republicans in the county, a fact that never bothered me in 1984 and seemed even less important now.

I had originally met Ralph Finno at about the same time as I'd met Walter Ramsdell. They had both been assigned to an OCD task force put together by Sheriff Ed Stack and some other chiefs, who each agreed to contribute one or two members to it. Ramsdell was selected to head it with Finno chosen as the number two man. This task force on anti-racketeering wasn't very effective and, as mentioned, Finno seemed more in charge of it than Ramsdell.

In 1984, some Republican Party officials approached then Fort Lauderdale Chief Leo Callahan about promoting Finno to captain. Callahan refused. When I switched parties to Republican, these same Republican bigwigs had opposed backing me. I was never sure why they were opposed to me specifically, but I always wondered if they hoped Finno would be the ideal Republican candidate at some point in the future. I subsequently forgot about the confrontation, Leo Callahan stepped down from the Fort Lauderdale chief's position and took a job with me in the sheriff's office, and his replacement in Fort Lauderdale, Ron Cochran, eventually gave Finno his promotion.

That Finno and Ramsdell, former task force partners more than a decade ago, were both running for the Democratic nomination for sheriff was unusual enough, but there was an even more bizarre twist of fate than people would imagine. Following the firebombing of the VIP Men's Club in North Broward County last December, the resulting investigation had turned up Ralph Finno's name, along with his brother Anthony's. They had been involved in a power struggle over the club and retained as partners the preceding March by the club manager, Michael McNaboe, to bounce out a couple of other owners. After this successful purge, the Finnos became more involved with the club, taking an active role in managing the operation. This is not usually the type of affiliation an ex-cop of Finno's stature has and the deeper the investigation of the club went, the more likely it seemed that there was some illegal activity going on that the Finnos were undoubtedly aware of.

I was in a peculiar position. I had been kept informed of the progress of this investigation in my role as sheriff, but since Finno had declared his candidacy, I needed to take a "hands off" approach to the ongoing police work. I advised Steve Bertucelli, my head of the Organized Crime Division, to get some third-party help in this matter. By engaging either or, preferably, both the state attorney's office and the Florida Department of Law Enforcement (FDLE - formerly the FBLE), no accusations that my office was deliberately investigating my political opponents could be made. This had the makings of another strange election.

A week later I had my first Republican opponent; one of my former employees, Jim Howard, entered the race. He happened to announce his candidacy on the same day we were staging publicity to drum up attendance for the annual "Pig Bowl" football game between our sheriffs and county lawyers, which raised dollars for youth charity events. In the past, Geraldo Rivera, among other local celebrities, had helped to raise a lot of cash for these worthwhile programs.

When I pulled up to the courthouse, Jim Howard was on the steps with Ron Cochran, now the former Fort Lauderdale police chief, and Howard was apparently giving his candidacy speech. I emerged from a 1928 Franklin touring car, wearing a top hat and waving a gun - a la Eliot Ness and the Untouchables. I grabbed a microphone, as planned, and began to promote the game.

Howard, too, entered the race carrying some past baggage. He had told people that he had been a cop in New York City, but this turned out to be false. He knew somebody in the sheriff's office, who was able to help secure Howard's appointment by Butterworth. He had been promoted, also during Butterworth's tenure, to the position of commander, and put in charge of the Crime Stoppers program, which rewards anonymous tipsters with cash in exchange for information about a crime.

Since he hadn't been a New York City police officer, Howard had to go through the police academy before he could be hired by the Broward County Sheriff's Office. After my election to sheriff in 1984, I reviewed Howard's file and demoted him from commander to sergeant, a position more in line with his true length of experience. All reports about the Crime Stoppers program and Howard's running of it seemed positive enough, so I let him remain in charge of it.

In 1986, charges against Howard were filed through the Internal Affairs division. Among the complaints was the mishandling of Crime Stoppers funds.

In one instance, a credit card firm wanted the Crime Stoppers unit to produce a program for television about credit card fraud in the hope of soliciting anonymous tips about such activity. Several companies involved in the promotion of the program offered $3,500 as a donation to Crime Stoppers in exchange for producing the television report, but Howard reputedly asked for a car equipped with a mobile phone instead.

The second case involved a refrigerator bought by the sheriff's office from Sears and installed on Jim Howard's boat. At the time this information surfaced, Howard had sold the boat and the new owner said that while the boat had come with a refrigerator, he had sold the appliance already.

Howard submitted to a polygraph test and failed. He was suspended with pay, pending further investigation. It certainly looked as if some violations may have occurred, but I wanted the investigation to be complete before making any decisions.

The community leaders of the Crime Stoppers program were concerned that anything surfacing about Jim Howard's conduct may reflect poorly on what had been a successful program. If Howard was allowed to resign, they argued, the integrity of Crime Stoppers would be preserved. I agreed with the resignation request, which I received shortly thereafter from Howard. Perhaps I should have pursued the matter further, but there seemed nothing to gain from more investigation.

More interesting to me now was Ron Cochran's presence in the race. Cochran, who had earlier stated that he would run for sheriff, had signed on to be Jim Howard's campaign manager. In his statements, Cochran reiterated his stand that the position of Broward's sheriff should be appointed, as Dade County's and a number of the other non-county police departments' were. I responded immediately, saying that making the office an appointed one would give the people no say in who would clean up their streets of crime and that the office would continue to be a political steppingstone.

This had become an interesting group of opponents. Ramsdell and Howard, former BSO employees, and Finno and Cochran, former cronies in the Fort Lauderdale office. It was a group of men who knew each other reasonably well. Cochran, who had some disparaging remarks to say about me, had established a rift between us after my hiring of Leo Callahan. Callahan and Cochran did not get along at all and Callahan's association with me finished my relationship with Cochran, although we had started off well when Cochran was assigned deputies by me to help him with spring break in 1985. The old nemesis of interdepartmental cooperation - difficult personal relationships - had intensified turf problems so much that Cochran decided to take an active role in the 1988 campaign against me.

Cochran had resigned his post as Fort Lauderdale's chief in 1986. He was supposed setting up his own business after he returned from a lengthy trip to Ireland, but it never came to fruition. He eventually applied for the job as police chief in another Broward community, Plantation, a far cry from his Fort Lauderdale position, but he didn't get the job. The chief of security for the Broward School Board had passed away and the job was given to one of my lieutenants, but a county commissioner, a friend of Cochran's, encouraged the school board to reopen the files and give Cochran the job instead. This was exactly what happened - politics as usual.

Local Republican Party members seemed to be split over which candidate they should support. Jo Smith, the Republican Party chairperson, resigned her post as chair. She and a couple of other party officials had decided that I was not a true Republican with a sincere conservative philosophy and thus decided to back Jim Howard. They were upset that I wouldn't put the word "Republican" on my campaign signs.

I was never sure what a "true Republican" was, but my apparent lack of political identity didn't bother me any more than having the backing of some Republicans who showed support simply because I was a member of their party. My political leanings were immaterial to my job. We enforced legal statutes, not political philosophies. If this upset some Republicans, fine. In the end, the ones I answered to were the citizens of the county, not the local party honchos.

I had backed Republican Governor Bob Martinez in his 1986 run for the office because I thought he was the best man for the job. Truthfully, Martinez was not a straight-line Republican, either. After his election, his appointments included both Republicans and Democrats; he simply selected people he felt were qualified to do the job. This was in sharp contrast to his predecessor, Bob Graham, now in the U.S. Senate, whose appointments were almost strictly along Democratic party lines. It seemed to me that Bob Martinez was doing the right thing, and I continued to support him.

The Democrats, with Ramsdell and Finno, added more candidates to their September primary. Jim Deckinger, another deputy from the Broward County Sheriff's Office, resigned to make a run at my job. His spouse, Linda, was a sergeant in the Davie police department, a Broward town that was independent from the BSO. He was another surprise candidate. He'd been only an average officer. His wife had urged him to run and he took up the challenge. More power to him!

Also joining the Democratic field was retired correctional officer Gil Gesuldi. The name under which he filed to run was "Mr. G." His wife also worked for us in one of our detention centers. Mr. G was a twenty-two-year Marine veteran and had spent eighteen years serving as an officer in the state prison system. He was an imposing figure, six feet tall, about 200 pounds, with a number of missing teeth. He was a refreshing opposite to the typical candidate.

He told me later that he decided to run after seeing me on the eleven o'clock news one evening. At the time he told his wife that he could beat me in an election. She dared him to run. In the morning he didn't remember accepting her dare, but she insisted he had.

The other individual who decided to run in the Democratic primary was Howard Fox, a Davie patrolman I didn't know. That brought the total number of Democrats in the race to five: Ramsdell, Finno, Deckinger, Gesuldi, and Fox. Only Jim Howard and I had filed as Republicans.

Howard, by this time, was an angry candidate. With all of the drug busts and other arrests the Broward County Sheriff's Office was making, my office and my face were on the television news several times a week. Howard demanded equal network time, but the local stations told him the BSO was news and they would continue to report on it whether he liked it or not. To make matters worse for Howard, Governor Martinez, concerned with the crack cocaine problem throughout the state and in particular South Florida, asked if he could come down and see what we were doing to clean up the streets. He arrived and accompanied our operatives on a couple of drug raids. Martinez and I, on a bust together were on the local news shows, but it was never publicity for publicity's sake. When Martinez made the suggestion about coming down, I didn't make the connection between the governor's visit and a free television opportunity. No matter what the news media and other politicians believed, this wasn't part of my thought process, then or ever.

Howard was also upset because I declined to debate him. Actually, Ron Cochran issued the debate challenge, but I was too busy running the sheriff's office to accommodate them. Cochran had indicated that the editorial boards of the local newspapers would organize and moderate the debate, but he hadn't bothered to check with them first. They knew nothing of it and didn't seem too interested themselves at that early date.

Naturally, as the primaries neared, revelations about the candidates started to surface. My slate was fairly clean and I had a record in the sheriff's office to point to and be proud of. As I was able to do to some degree four years earlier, I stood on my past record. The most significant problem the BSO had was the lack of jail space. The tents were only a temporary situation and more building was being done, but having a new jail was going to expand my budget and cost taxpayers dollars. The citizens I spoke with, however, seemed to feel this was a good trade-off.

The other candidates weren't as lucky as I was. Jim Howard's polygraph failure was made public along with the news about the missing refrigerator and his resignation from Crime Stoppers. Howard claimed the entire Internal Affairs investigation was a sham. Since the probe was initiated by calls from outside the department, there wasn't much for me to add to the story.

At the same time, information emerged regarding Jim Deckinger's record as a police officer, which showed a suspension for sleeping on duty, two written reprimands, some negative job reviews, and an accusation of harassment. Deckinger's biggest problem, according to his superiors that wrote his reviews, was his need to be motivated on a consistent basis. His commanding officers often felt that Deckinger had lost his enthusiasm for the job.

Ralph Finno floated some rumors that my deputies were pressuring his supporters, by telling them that my office would hire a couple of them in exchange for switching their loyalty to me. Reporters combed my office trying to substantiate the story. They even interviewed my personnel director, Ann Lee, trying to find out how many political appointments I'd made while in office. Her reply: "None." Try as they might, there was nothing for them to find. A letter to a local newspaper summed it up best by saying the criticism of the budget was unfounded and this taxpayer would gladly pay fifty-one cents of every property tax dollar for fighting crime rather than pay even one cent for the community commission to build road projects like the Sawgrass Expressway, a new road artery running east to west across the county.

It was inevitable that Ralph Finno's involvement with the burned-out VIP Men's Club would eventually make news. After all, he was the target of an investigation being spearheaded by the FDLE. Finno naturally downplayed it, saying my office was fabricating evidence to discredit his campaign. In truth, we didn't know the real extent of the Finno brothers' involvement with the club yet and were still working to verify a story about Finno extorting the VIP Men's Club's manager to take over the club.

Walter Ramsdell had to deal with a 1980 grand jury report about illegal operations within the jail in the town of Lauderhill while he was chief of police. Some inmates were given access to liquor, women, drugs, and weapons - incidents Ramsdell blamed on his subordinates. Lauderhill contracted with the Broward County Sheriff's Office in 1982, ending Ramsdell's reign as chief.

Mr. G didn't have any of these skeletons in his closet but had to constantly answer the question about whether he was qualified to run a large law enforcement agency. But this was a far easier question for him to deal with than the ones being put to the other candidates.

It was an interesting group of candidates, to say the least, even though they were all unqualified to run the sheriff's office.

As the September 6 primary drew closer, the local newspaper published their endorsements. The Miami Herald, on August 24, selected me as its Republican choice and Ralph Finno as its Democratic recommendation. My endorsement was a decidedly lukewarm one and it probably bothered the editorial staff to write it. They tried to downplay it by suggesting that the office should be an appointed one in the future.

It was shortly after these endorsements that word of the Finno investigation caught the ear of the media. Articles filled the papers for the next couple of days about the ongoing investigation, something I hated to see because the case wasn't closed yet. This revelation would only make it more difficult to accumulate evidence. That Finno was a target of an investigation caused some embarrassment for the Herald, which changed its endorsement a week later to Finno's old partner on the anti-racketeering task force, Walter Ramsdell.

The Fort Lauderdale News, which had the benefit of knowing about the Finno investigation at the time of its endorsement, gave me the Republican nod, saying that my strengths far outweighed my shortcomings. Their editorial board chose not to recommend a Democratic candidate, saying that Broward voters were poorly served by the quality of Democrats running for sheriff.

Finno tried to put his campaign on firmer ground by publicly stating that he was seeking a grand jury investigation into whether I had broken a campaign law that prohibits candidates from spreading lies about other candidates. It seemed a desperate move, given that I had not instigated either the investigation or the publicity about it, but Finno really had no choice.

When primary day, September 6, was over, Finno was the top vote-getter among the four Democrats (Fox having dropped out). He received 43 percent of the vote to Jim Deckinger's 29 percent, followed by Ramsdell with 22 percent and Mr. G with 6 percent. Since Finno didn't get 50 percent of the vote, there would be a runoff on October 4 between him and the second place finisher, Jim Deckinger. Finno seemed pleased that voters had, in his words, "ignored the character assassination that had been taking place from the Broward sheriff's office."

My primary was more clear-cut. I outpolled Jim Howard by more than two to one, picking up 67 percent of the vote. This seemed to be a message from Broward's citizens that I was doing the job they wanted me to do. It was a very satisfying result.

Jim Deckinger felt buoyed by the primary results, which gave him another crack at Ralph Finno. He immediately emphasized that as a result of the investigation into Finno, the only Democratic choice for office with a chance to beat me in November was himself. He was counting on tactic and the hope that the large number of Democratic voters in the county would agree with him.

Both Deckinger and Finno had their work cut out for them as almost immediately after the primary, a group calling themselves "Democrats for Navarro" announced a fund-raiser on my behalf. It was a similar group that helped me gain success against Democrat George Brescher in 1984 and I welcomed them to my "non-political" campaign.

While I continued to focus on my record rather than personalities, the Democratic opponents exchanged barbs throughout September as they positioned for the October runoff. A virtual smear campaign developed as they denigrated each other's character, qualifications, and integrity with repeated attacks. Deckinger implied that Finno might soon be indicted and challenged the loyalty of anyone who had switched parties. Finno responded with Deckinger's record of suspensions, harassment charges, and poor work performance reviews. In Davie, at a Democratic club meeting, both candidates were loudly booed by the audience when they resorted to personal attacks. I didn't know who would win, but wondered how much of either candidate would be left to run against me in November. I wasn't overconfident, but the lack of a quality candidate was bothering the Democratic party.

On the Saturday before the runoff election, I helped organize an anti-crack march to a known crack house where we had made over fifty arrests in the past few weeks. At the conclusion of the march, the place would be bulldozed, providing one less refuge for criminals selling their wares. It was not a political event - no campaign signs or bumper stickers - just an awareness march to demonstrate to the neighborhoods that the sheriff's office was continuing to take action against drugs and would keep doing so no matter who the sheriff was. When I arrived where the rally was to begin, greeting me in the parking lot were ten cars sporting campaign signs for Ralph Finno that apparently planned to drive along the route. This was ridiculous! The message of the march was supposed to be anti-crack, not a political message to Broward County residents. The demolition of the crack house was postponed until after the runoff. I saw no reason to participate in the march while surrounded by political campaign signs.

On Tuesday, October 4, Jim Deckinger surprised Finno and a host of political analysts when he outpolled the Fort Lauderdale police veteran by 2,700 votes. Finno was upset and took shots everywhere - at the media, at my office, and at Democratic party leaders who refused to openly support him even though he had garnered 43 percent of the vote in the primary election. Finno claimed that since he was now defeated and no longer a threat to the sheriff, the investigation into his dealings with the VIP Men's Club would simply disappear. I had purposely stayed out of the police work on his case but doubted that Finno was anywhere near from being cleared.

The Democrats had decided that Jim Deckinger would be my opponent on election day in November. He immediately challenged me to a debate, but after seeing the circus atmosphere surrounding the Finno-Deckinger campaign and the sleaze tactics employed by both men, I wanted nothing to do with that type of political campaigning. I decided to keep spreading the word about my office's accomplishments and let Deckinger debate my record instead.

Democrats, by in large, were not happy with the choice they had. During October, I spoke frequently to the same Democratic clubs that were the focus of my 1984 campaign. Trying to emphasize that the sheriff's office's responsibility was law enforcement, I told these citizens that the political affiliation of a criminal had no bearing on any investigation. Republicans did not receive preferential treatment nor were political appointments made in my office.

County Commissioner Nicki Grossman, a Democrat, spoke out on my behalf, underscoring this message. She said there was an obligation on the part of all residents to look at the qualifications of each candidate, not merely his or her political party. In 1984, she went on, the citizens clearly stated they wanted a professional law enforcement officer at the head of the Broward County Sheriff's Office. That's what Broward got, and there was no reason to believe that I wasn't the right choice then or now.

I certainly appreciated her comments and was pleased with the number of public crossovers by Democrats to support my candidacy. Deckinger said he was talking to all of the Jim Howard Republicans about coming over to his side to counter this pro-Navarro movement.

George Platt, the Democratic Party chairman who instigated and pushed the 1984 lawsuit against me, surfaced briefly that October to decry the number of Democrats that were openly supporting me in the sheriff's race. According to Platt, it was a slap in the face to the members of the Democratic Executive Committee that this was happening.

As the election neared, I received another lukewarm endorsement from the Miami Herald, whose editors, by this time, must have been getting tired of coming out for anyone in the Broward Sheriff's race. The Fort Lauderdale Sun-Sentinel was somewhat more effusive.

Money continued to be contributed to my campaign and the local papers and Deckinger made an issue of the amount as it neared $500,000. There seemed to be weekly updates on the amount of dollars in my campaign account and each new record amount drew headlines. Both the media and Deckinger assumed that favors would be given in exchange for this money, but they were still confusing me with the typical politician. I sincerely believe that since everyone knew my stubborn stance on keeping the job of sheriff non-political these financial contributions merely reflected the success of our office and that the individuals who gave us money just wanted us to keep doing the job we had pledged to do.

The biggest obstacle to overcome in this campaign was not Jim Deckinger, but vandalism that systematically destroyed my campaign signs and culminated with a tire iron thrown through the plate glass window of my re-election headquarters. Still, volunteers continued to stream in to work on my campaign, something for which I will be forever grateful.

The voters came out on Tuesday, November 8 and gave me 62 percent of the vote. This was more than anyone in the media had predicted because of the belief that a large anti-Navarro contingent would vote for Jim Deckinger. The vote tallies crossed all party lines and affiliations, confirming what I had been hearing from the average citizen: we were doing the job, providing security for them and making Broward County a better and safer place to live.

As for Jim Deckinger, he was out of work. He had resigned from his deputy sheriff position with the Broward County Sheriff's Office to run for office and, given his mediocre record, wasn't likely to be eligible for rehire with my office. He told the press he would look for a job elsewhere in law enforcement.

Governor Bob Martinez swore me in during a January ceremony held at the Sunrise Musical Theater. In turn, I swore in 1,500 deputies for four more years in the Broward County Sheriff's Office.

Shortly afterward, I endorsed, along with the majority of other county sheriffs in Florida, a measure to make all sheriff elections in the state non-partisan. I thought it important to remove the political tags and simply run on law enforcement qualifications. Included in the draft bill are minimum standards a candidate would need to meet to be eligible to run. This makes more sense than the current process in which a used car salesman can be elected to the office if he chooses to campaign and garners the most votes. It is also a far better solution than making the office appointed, guaranteed to bring politics into the position. Hopefully, our legislators will agree.

That should have been the conclusion of the 1988 election. But there was one more chapter to be played out, with Ralph Finno and his brother, Anthony, taking center stage.

Thirteen

The Blood Brothers

O N A STORMY SPRING EVENING IN 1989, I WAS IN MY OFFICE HELPING TO develop a traffic routing strategy for the next morning's rush hour - a cave-in had occured as a result of construction along Interstate 95. Traffic had been a mess anyway because of the road work but the storm and its aftermath would wreak havoc with commuters the following day unless we came up with an effective plan.

The phone rang and I wondered, What now?

It was an old friend from the Florida Department of Law Enforcement in South Florida.

"Nick," he said, "I want you to come down to the office. I have something you should definitely see."

"Oh, man," I groaned. "Have you looked outside? This has to be the worst night of the year."

"This is important, Nick."

"I don't suppose it could wait until tomorrow, could it?"

"Sorry, Nick. I wouldn't have called you if it was something that could wait a day."

I knew that, but was hoping for a last-second reprieve to avoid the drive through the rain. After a call to Sharron to tell her not to hold dinner, I set out for the FDLE's offices, wondering what could have prompted this call. A few minutes after I arrived, I understood the need for me to be there.

The FDLE, in cooperation with our office, had been working on the bombing of the VIP Men's Club for several months. It had been this investigation that diminished the hopes of Ralph Finno in his bid to unseat me from the sheriff's office. A lot of evidence had been uncovered linking Finno and his brother, Anthony, to some illegal activities. Our Organized Crime Division asked the FDLE for help to avoid the case being labeled as a political tool to oust Finno from the sheriff's race.

As part of the probe, the FDLE had been doing surveillance on Ralph Finno. While this was going on, the Finno brothers had approached two individuals with ties to organized crime about some illegal enterprises. The two men were also informants for the FDLE and they reported the conversation immediately, especially since part of the package the Finnos were requesting was a contract on my life.

A contract on my life?

The Finnos thought these two men were part of the Genovese crime family. The Finnos, in essence, wanted to become part of the family and give the family a share of the earnings from some loansharking activities the Finnos were running.

I could hardly believe it. Ralph Finno, with twenty-seven years in law enforcement, wanted to join the mob? "Are you sure about this?" I asked.

"You won't believe it, Nick, but we've got it on videotape. That's why we called you to come down and see it."

"A videotape?" I was astonished. But there it was in black and white. Unfortunately for the Finnos, the two gangsters they had contacted were trying to work out a plea bargain deal with FDLE and doing some informant work as a result. They knew the mother lode when they saw it and went straight to the state agency after the Finnos contacted them.

The Finnos' plot was incredible. After I was "eliminated" by some means, Ralph Finno would use his influence to secure the appointment to replace me as sheriff. Then the mob would have the run of the county under his jurisdiction, with gambling houses, prostitution rings, all under the eyes of the sheriff's office. All he needed to do was to get rid of a minor problem: me.

The videotape showed everything. There they were, Ralph and Anthony Finno, discussing my demise and Ralph's ascension to the position of Broward's sheriff. It was like being dropped into the middle of a television mini-series.

The FDLE officers said they would continue to encourage the two informants to meet with the Finnos regularly and continue videotaping. I asked them to work closely with Steve Bertucelli, my OCD head. For now, I intended to keep staying out of this inquiry. Obviously, these informants weren't going to set up a contract on my life, but who knew if the Finnos had approached bonafide underworld contacts who would agree to their request in a heartbeat? I asked if I could tell my wife, Sharron, as this was something she needed to know. They agreed, but beyond her, no one else was to know. I thanked them for their concern and left.

As I drove home, I thought about Ralph Finno and his career and wondered what brought him to this point in his life. I remembered that when he was on the anti-racketeering task force I heard rumors about a few things he had done, but there was no proof and taking gossip as gospel was not my method of operation. In light of this new information however, one had to wonder how much of the gossip was true back then.

A few years before he retired from the force, Ralph Finno had been accused of notifying a restaurant owner and personal friend of an impending raid on his establishment by the State Beverage Department. No tangible proof was found and the charge was dismissed by the department's Internal Affairs division.

I also recalled the time subtle pressure was put on Fort Lauderdale Police Chief Leo Callahan to promote Finno to captain, a suggestion Callahan didn't act on, but that his successor, Ron Cochran, the 1988 campaign manager for Jim Howard, did.

In another situation, an individual who was jailed and bragged about killing over 300 people in South Florida - boasts that could never be substantiated - was eventually released on parole. Later, one of our officers found the man carrying a weapon, a serious problem for a convicted felon. He was sentenced to fifteen years in jail for that violation. The gun was traced back to Ralph Finno, who claimed it had been stolen.

What did all of these items add up to? It seemed that Ralph Finno, walked a tightrope between cops and criminals. Maybe it was something more sinister than that. In any case, why was he trying to win his way to a mob connection by going to two lowlife informants?

The Finno surveillance continued. The FDLE and OCD felt it was warranted based on the events surrounding the VIP Men's Club and its firebombing in December 1987.

The co-manager of the VIP Men's Club, Michael McNaboe, was convinced that Anthony Finno was an organized crime figure whose brother, Ralph, had lots of political connections. McNaboe and a Colombian were the original 50/50 partners in the club, which they opened back in 1979. During the mid-1980s, McNaboe received a threat that unless the VIP Men's Club started making payments to a certain organized crime organization, the place wouldn't be open long. McNaboe told this to a friend, Joseph "Boca Joe" Fofone, who, along with a man named Joe Diamond, bought out the Colombian partner's interest and said the extortionists would not be returning to collect any payments.

McNaboe moved to Marco Island in 1986, but Fofone and Diamond were not paying him his half of the VIP Men's Club revenues and he returned in 1987 to put things straight. The new partners wouldn't pay McNaboe, nor would they buy out his half-interest or sell their own. McNaboe was in a tight spot.

He was introduced to Anthony Finno, who implied that he was part of the mob, having been inducted into the "family" by John Gotti, the Gambino crime family boss in New York. McNaboe asked for help as he couldn't push Fofone or Diamond out by himself. Tony Finno agreed to help.

Ralph and Tony Finno had a meeting with the accountant who handled the club's records, according to McNaboe, and the brothers demanded to see all the statements for the VIP Men's Club. When the accountant, Robert Hall, refused, Ralph Finno pulled out a gold badge and threatened to have Hall, Fofone and Diamond jailed unless Hall came up with the records.

This occurred in March 1987, after Finno had left the Fort Lauderdale police force, which means he was impersonating a police officer. At this point, Tony Finno pulled back the leather jacket he was wearing to reveal a gun he had tucked into his waistband. The accountant gave up the records.

The Finnos closed the club for eight days. On the ninth, the club reopened with new locks on the doors and new muscle at the front, including a couple of guys named Big Moe and Fat Sal, according to McNaboe. Tony Finno had taken over the club's books. Hall, Fofone, and Diamond were out of the club business, although Diamond would shortly be arraigned on a past drug trafficking charge and thus had other things to keep his attention.

The club generally employed about fifteen women, who would accompany male club members back to any one of five rooms, each furnished with a bed and dresser, for half-hour and hour sessions. At one point, McNaboe would testify, Tony gave Ralph some of the club's money to go in back with one of the women. This was interesting because, during the campaign, Finno claimed he had never been inside the club.

The first three weeks after the club reopened, profits exceeded $18,000, but Michael McNaboe found himself back in a familiar situation: not being paid his half of the profits. He discovered that the club had new incorporation papers that made Tony Finno's girlfriend, Debbie Jordan, the president of SOCH, Inc., which now was the corporate owner of the club. McNaboe had never agreed to this. The Finnos, who appeared to be running the club, had not paid a dime for their apparent share, let alone McNaboe's. When McNaboe complained, Tony threatened him with a gun and said his friends from New York wanted to dump McNaboe in the Everglades.

It might have been the end for McNaboe in the fall of 1987 except for an odd twist of fate. He received a call from Boca Joe Fofone to see if he was interested in getting his club back. Angry at the Finnos, McNaboe agreed. Overnight, locks were changed and the Finnos apparently shut out. But Ralph, hearing from his new manager that the locks had been changed, called the sheriff's office, which closed the place down for the weekend and told the various parties to work it out by Monday.

On Monday, the VIP Men's Club was still under the Finnos' control. McNaboe continued to threaten exposure, he said, and even went as far as having his attorney write a letter to the Finnos' attorney about suing to reclaim his stake in the club. A week after that letter was sent, McNaboe was beaten severely and left unconscious in a Fort Lauderdale parking lot - one of three beatings he claimed to have received. This one sent him to the hospital.

Not long after that, the VIP Men's Club was fire bombed out of existence, and our Organized Crime Division began its investigation, which came to light in August 1988 after the Miami Herald endorsed Ralph Finno in the Democratic primary. All along, Ralph denied everything, saying the investigation was Nick Navarro's way of taking him out of the race for sheriff. It looked as if Ralph had actually taken himself out.

The prostitution ring at the VIP Men's Club had been covered up by members paying with credit cards: the charges showed up on their monthly statements as purchases from a West Broward candy store owned by Anthony Finno. The club even got a call from a woman once wanting to know what her husband could have bought for $70 in a candy store.

After deciding to throw his hat in the ring for sheriff, Ralph Finno had instructed VIP Men's Club employees to say nothing of his connection there. Several of these people were more than willing to testify to that effect.

Now Ralph and Tony Finno were meeting regularly with the two FDLE informants, urging them to talk to the Genovese crime family about the Finnos running their Broward County operations for them. Boasting of a fruitful loan sharking business, the FDLE decided to test the Finnos' involvement in this kind of illegal activity. This was tricky because the FDLE had to use people that had never come in contact with the Finnos.

FDLE agents set up three loansharking arrangements totaling $20,000 and spread them around Dade, Broward, and Palm Beach Counties so as not to arouse suspicion. In one of the staged deals, FDLE agent George Villardi met Tony Finno in June 1989 to ask for money to help pay for his daughter's wedding. The Finnos agreed to the loan at 260 percent interest.

Villardi then brought another agent to the Finnos to secure a similar loan. Tony Finno agreed, but he pulled out his gun to emphasize that the man must pay back the money or else he would be killed. Tony recorded Villardi's license number and gave it to his brother. Ralph then called a friend in the Fort Lauderdale police department, to ask him to run an identification check on it. The officer agreed, which was an outright violation of any department's procedures. The agents had expected the move and the license was already "covered." It checked out to the Finnos' satisfaction. They made the loan and collected seven weekly payments of between $250 and $500.

The meetings with the FDLE informants took an even more bizarre turn. Having already discussed taking out a contract on me, the Finnos wanted to go through an initiation ceremony into the Mafia family and asked if the informants could accommodate them. They wanted to be sure it was done right, that the ritual would include a sharing of blood that they believed to be an integral part of any induction into a mob family. The informants agreed to set it up.

The blood oath rite was not something that organized crime families practiced, to my knowledge. It was, however, the type of thing one might see in a movie or read in a book, and that must have been where the Finnos became taken with this notion.

At the next meeting, the blood oath took place. Ralph Finno greeted the informants with a Sicilian kiss. The informants wanted to be sure the Finnos understood there was no going back after this. "It's not a part-time job," one of them said.

"I understand that," Ralph replied, "I'm doing this of my own volition. I am my own person." Ralph had brought with him a gun he said he had taken off some "scum bag" years ago and that it was absolutely untraceable. Ralph's understanding at the time was that the gun was needed for a job in New York and part of his initiation into the "family" was to provide a suitable weapon for the occasion.

Tony went a little further. Using a knife that the informants told Finno he would be stabbed in the heart with if he ever betrayed the family, they attempted to cut Tony's finger, but the blade was too dull to do the job. At that point, the resourceful Tony produced his own knife and cut each person's fingers. As they all held their fingers together, Tony Finno said, "The main thing is done."

Sometimes, Ralph Finno discussed doing away with me and securing his appointment to the sheriff's office. He didn't care how it was done, he only wanted to be informed so he could be out of town on the day it happened. At other times, he tried to advance a few ideas to accomplish the same thing politically without having to "whack" me. He also warned that my protégés in the sheriff's office would never rest until they found out what had happened to the sheriff, should some incident occur.

By August 1989, the FDLE and local prosecutors thought they had enough evidence to make arrests. They set up one last sting in which the Finnos thought they were each meeting individuals regarding loansharking deals. Ralph Finno was arrested quietly in a Pompano Beach parking lot, while Tony Finno was taken into custody by several officers who surrounded him with guns in Fort Lauderdale. FDLE agents also arrested Jean Tremblay, the Finnos' strong-arm man who had delivered personal blows to Michael McNaboe during the VIP Men's Club fiasco. This was Thursday, August 10, 1989.

Both brothers looked stunned at their arrests as they were led off to jail.

The media had a field day. The following day, one paper even emblazoned across its front page, "Navarro Jails '88 Opponent." Sharron and I both felt better with those people locked up.

After the Finnos had been captured, information started to trickle out about Ralph's police past, details that didn't emerge, interestingly enough, during the election campaign. Current Fort Lauderdale Police Chief Joe Gerwens said that he and then chief Ron Cochran forced Finno into retirement in 1986 because of his association with some "questionable" people who had documented criminal pasts.

Tony's past also reared its head. When bragging to McNaboe two years earlier about being connected with John Gotti, Finno was nearly beaten up by some of Gotti's associates in the parking lot of his Margate (another Broward County town) office, where he worked as the city's chief electrical inspector. Apparently that episode convinced him he needed to find another way to actually break into the "family" other than just saying he was in.

A total of 17 different counts were levied, including keeping a house of prostitution, loansharking, firearm possession during commission of a felony, aggravated assault, and impersonating a police officer. Tremblay, on parole for a manslaughter conviction in Massachusetts, was arrested in that state and charged with several counts, including aggravated assault.

The Fort Lauderdale police officer who ran the license plate for Ralph, was suspended. The agents who brought Ralph in told jailers he might be suicidal so a watch was placed on his cell. The *Miami Herald* used the opportunity to push again for the sheriff's office to be an appointed position, which was exactly what Finno wanted: an appointment to fill my vacant seat after I was "fed to the fishes."

Ralph had certainly lost his touch when he was forced to retire in 1986 after twenty-seven years in police work. He had sat through about twenty hours of videotaping and never noticed a camera. Still, he had retained enough sense to never make any overt death threats to me on camera. He walked a fine line, but his words weren't damning enough to add conspiracy to commit murder to his laundry list of counts. He participated in an initiation ceremony where he and Tony both bit into a bullet that would be used on them if they ever betrayed the "family." Real life is always stranger than fiction.

The following Wednesday, all three men were arraigned in Broward circuit court. Judge Leroy Moe reviewed the tape evidence and listened as Ralph Finno explained that this was all part of a reverse con game that he and his brother had been playing with the two FDLE informants. The judge denied bond for Tony Finno and Jean Tremblay, but he put off for a day his decision about Ralph. The next day, Judge Moe had decided to deny bond for Ralph, too, saying he would rather err on the side of safety (in this case, mine and Sharron's) and thus Ralph would be jailed until the trial began. Once the bond was denied, the city of Margate formally fired Tony from his job as chief electrical inspector.

The main job of the Finnos' defense attorneys would be to attack the credibility of the two FDLE informants. After all, the informants were pleading guilty themselves to a federal wire fraud charge involving the theft, from several people, of over $1 million. The attorneys claimed the Finnos knew it was a con but played along to get back the money they had given to these two men.

In September, the Finnos' attorney claimed their clients were being treated unfairly by being placed in solitary confinement. With Ralph Finno, solitary was the safest thing to do, as a twenty-seven year police veteran is sure to know a few people behind bars that would like to get their hands on him. I'm not sure why Tony was initially confined that way, but a judge ordered him held in protective custody instead of solitary, where he would have some contact with other inmates. The attorneys also filed an appeal with the Fourth District Court of Appeals to have the "no bond" decision of Judge Leroy Moe reversed. I didn't think they had a chance. I was wrong.

On Monday, November 6, the Finnos were both released on a temporary basis and given fourteen days to raise a $250,000 bond. This was incredibly unusual as bond is generally raised while the person is still behind bars. A defendant without bond must be tried within ninety days of arrest unless the defendant agrees that more time is needed to prepare a defense. The prosecution, in this case, should have been ready by November 8 to go to trial, but once the fourteen-day grace period was put into effect, the trial was moved to March 4, 1990.

I was not happy to see Ralph and Tony Finno put back onto the streets and their trial postponed until the next year. Something stunk here, but I couldn't figure out what. I was and will always be an outsider when it comes to the closed-door deals made on certain cases. I didn't frequent the establishments that the high-powered attorneys and judges did and was not privy to a lot of information. I merely made arrests and tried to make cases that could be successfully prosecuted. Somehow, some way, a deal had been made and the Finnos were released.

The Finnos used their property holdings to meet the bond. Sharron and I were provided with twenty-four hour security in the event the Finnos tried to have anything done while out on bond, as they were convinced I was the one that had set them up. By November 19, the protection seemed unnecessary and was discontinued.

In December, Jean Tremblay decided to testify against the Finnos when he found out they were laying a lot of the blame on him. He would testify in exchange for a five-year state prison sentence with a five-year probation period to follow. Tremblay acknowledged he was not a "good guy," but he was concerned that the Finnos would somehow be released at his expense.

Tremblay was a part owner in a nightclub called Harbour Lights and the Finnos had tried to force their way into that enterprise much as they did to Michael McNaboe and the VIP Men's Club. Unsuccessful, they arranged for Tremblay to be picked up on drug trafficking charges. They bragged about this episode on tape with the FDLE informants and when Tremblay saw this, decided to turn on his former employers. "They set me up on the charge," he said, "to get control of my nightclub."

The March 1990 trial ended with Judge Daniel Futch declaring a mistrial over the FDLE informants' testimony and their grainy videotapes. Judge Futch then withdrew himself from consideration for any new trial. Two other possible judges also withdrew - one because he knew Ralph Finno, the other because he was too busy with other cases. In October 1990, the prosecution rewrote the indictment, breaking it down into two trials: one for loansharking and one for muscling into a house of prostitution operation. This effectively removed the informants and the videotape from the trial altogether, a point defense attorneys immediately seized upon. The longer this went on, the lower the likelihood of conviction.

The indictments were brought and trials rescheduled. Before any further trials were held, however, one of the FDLE informants was indicted for wire fraud and securities violations. Defense attorneys moved to dismiss the case, but the judge, Thomas Coker, who came out of retirement to hear the case when no other judge could be found, declined to do that. He was inclined to consider evidence, however, that the informants entrapped the Finnos illegally.

In 1992, prosecutors then opted to indict the Finnos for possession of a silencer, for which they had reasonably good videotape evidence. It was an effort to keep the case alive, nearly five years after the bombing of the VIP Men's Club. The other cases had fizzled and the silencer indictment, which carries a fifteen-year minimum sentence in federal court, was the last charge pending. The Finnos posted $50,000 bonds to avoid jail time and were released quickly.

This case has still not been brought to court. The Finnos are still walking around, although the publicity surrounding the trial has certainly taken its toll. The case has gone through many twists and turns and the FDLE informants were discredited by the defense attorneys. The chances of getting convictions drop with the passing of each day. Tremblay's worst fears have been realized. He is the fall guy and the Finnos, so far, are free.

The media considered the whole affair another example of my grandstanding to attract publicity. I have news for them. There are many ways one can attract attention, but having my name bandied about under a death threat is not one I would choose.

I will always feel that the Finnos were serious about their idea to have me removed from office, by whatever means, and Ralph placed in the sheriff's office with Broward County at the beck and call of the mob.

Fourteen

Guarding The President

FOLLOWING MY RE-ELECTION IN NOVEMBER 1988, I WAS BOTH ELATED AND humbled by the plurality I'd received from the citizens of Broward County. While still riding that high, I received a call from Washington, D.C., placed by the head of security for President-elect George Bush's inauguration committee, asking if I would like to be part of the security team for that momentous event. The committee members were asking only one sheriff nationwide, and I was their first choice.

In a law enforcement career, there really isn't anything equivalent to the Super Bowl. One gets satisfaction from successfully putting a big-time crook behind bars, but since all arrests are significant to me, there isn't a specific case I can point to and say "this is the big one."

National security is another matter. The inauguration of the president of the United States, the leader of the free world, which involves visiting dignitaries from around the globe and for whom security is critical, is the one chance to utilize all of one's law enforcement ability and instincts as well as the opportunity to work side by side with a number of highly qualified and distinguished officers from a variety of agencies around the country. This may not be the Super Bowl, but it certainly could be called an "All-Star Game" for police officers.

It was an honor to be asked and one I gladly accepted. As a boy in Cuba, the United States always had a special meaning to me, and my father's stories about the country to our north intrigued me enough to make me want to move here and become a citizen. I remembered my first days here nearly forty years earlier and how glad I was to have finally arrived to be part of the United States of America. The presidency of this country is an office of the utmost respect, and having the chance to be a witness to and have a role in an inauguration ceremony gave me a tremendous feeling of patriotism for my adopted country. This would be an assignment to cherish for the rest of my days.

My wife, Sharron, shared my enthusiasm about the upcoming trip north. We bought her a ticket to go with mine and prepared to leave on Sunday, January 15 for a week in the cooler climate of the nation's capital.

I was no stranger to Washington, D.C., but this was a special week inside the Beltway. It was a time to celebrate, a time to rejoice in the democracy that America is all about. The specific honor was for one person, the president, but in a sense we were all honoring ourselves. The parties, festivals, and balls held that week were all testimonials to freedom.

I was assigned to one of several security teams. The Secret Service had the lead role, as its members are the president's own security team. All of the armed forces of our country were represented as were twenty or so federal agencies, the Washington Metropolitan Police Department, and local agencies represented by other individuals like myself. Members of the Boston Police Department were also there, but I think their presence was more honorary than for security purposes since they were the first police agency to endorse George Bush during his election bid. It was ironic that the honor went to Boston's finest, especially since Bush's opponent was the governor of Massachusetts, Michael Dukakis.

In an old army barracks that was converted into our "War Room," all the security planning and coordination took place. We were all issued badges giving us security clearance to certain areas. My badge let me travel almost anywhere around the city. I also secured one for Sharron to give her access to various events. She asked for clearance to Dan Quayle's room, but I refused. In fact, I wasn't sure I could get into Dan Quayle's hotel room.

While Sharron attended the multitude of events, I reported for security duty. The Secret Service had the entire week broken down into different categories of work. Assorted functions needed security, and well-known attendees arriving from around the globe required protection. The parade route on inauguration day was especially important as it appeared President-elect Bush would be walking a portion of it - something that hadn't been done since Jimmy Carter did it in January 1977. Finally, we had to secure the area where the swearing-in ceremony would take place.

Everything was mapped out for us in detail and we ran through our assignments and the security checklists over and over again. We reviewed the parade route from every angle and examined every piece of ground around the area that would house the stage for the oath of office and the president's speech. Every imaginable element of security was analyzed, discussed, designed, redesigned, deployed, stretched, and compressed - all to ensure the safety of every participant. Because of the number of people who would be in close proximity to the new president throughout the week, each minute detail was important.

The entire process was a revelation to me. I felt as if I could handle high-security-type situations, but the Secret Service agents are the best at it. I learned more about thoroughness in this work detail than in any other type of work I'd ever encountered. This event was going to be a part of history, and what the public would see was possible because of the tremendous behind-the-scenes work being done by our security team, among others. The objective was to make it look effortless. If it seemed routine to the average onlooker, then we had accomplished our task.

The official inauguration team received a number of outside monetary donations to help defray costs, as much as $400-500,000 at times. The security team was also in charge of banking and we would escort the money, alongside the Washington Metropolitan Police, to the appropriate financial institution for deposit.

I accumulated a substantial number of security passes to wear in order to gain access to various venues. After my initial invitation, I had to send an updated resume to the team since all my top security clearances from the past had expired years ago. I needed to send Sharron's resume, too, in order to obtain the badges for her as a member of the security staff. It took some time to get used to showing these and early on, when challenged, I would find myself flipping through the cards hanging on a chain around my neck looking for the appropriate one.

My specific assignments were the parade route and swearing-in areas, plus the ball to be held at the Hilton, the same hotel where President Reagan was shot while leaving a few years ago. I thought of that incident a number of times as I reviewed the security process for the event.

The morning of the inauguration, Friday, January 20, Sharron and I stopped off briefly at the congressional offices of Florida Representative E. Clay Shaw. He and his wife, Emilie, were hosting a party. Many familiar faces were in attendance including Wayne Huizenga, the owner of Blockbuster Video, located in Fort Lauderdale. There were danish pastries and coffee and lots of Republican chitchat, but soon it was off to work for me.

I didn't expect this to be a vacation. I also hadn't expected to be working most of every day and well into the evening, but we did what had to be done. Sleep was at a premium that week, but most of us were running on pure adrenaline anyway, especially on The Day itself. I walked the parade route a number of times and felt confident of its security. Everything that could have been anticipated had been addressed. Now it was up to President Bush.

The pomp and circumstance of an inauguration has to be seen to be appreciated. All the sights and sounds don't come across in newspaper accounts. Even television coverage can't convey the feeling of actually being there. Every American in the capital that day was a President Bush fan, whether they voted for or against him or not at all. This was a day of euphoria where everything was possible, like the opening day of a sports season when every team is in first place. It was a great day to be an American.

More than 300,000 people gathered to watch the inaugural parade in which soon-to-be President Bush started in his limousine but finished on foot. Having the president walk the last part of the route was inconvenient, security-wise, but it was his day; he could do as he wished. When the parade began, the limousine had been surrounded by Secret Service agents, moving along at a slow trot (I was not one of them), and their numbers increased as George Bush bounded up Pennsylvania Avenue like a kid headed to an ice cream truck in the middle of summer.

Barbara Bush joined the president for the last few steps and together they stood at the reviewing stands to watch the incredible number of floats and marchers parade by the White House, the Bushes' home for the next four years.

The Florida representation consisted of the Palm Beach Sheriff's Office Honor Guard, sporting its official banner displaying the Florida seal, and the Walt Disney calliope, dominated by Disney characters and pulled along by a team of Clydesdale horses. As I watched from my security position, I couldn't help but be moved by this tradition that had started with George Washington. This is a country proud of its roots that has orderly ceremonies when a changing of the guard occurs. Americans take the change for granted, but so much of the rest of the world does it in a far messier and less desirable way. As a native-born Cuban, I felt these minutes were proud ones, moments that I was lucky to have witnessed and to feel a part of.

U.S. Supreme Court Justice William Rehnquist administered the thirty-five word oath of office. The new President then says a few (some are longer winded than other, of course) words as part of his first address as the country's chief executive.

President Bush's speech was largely of a conciliatory nature. The last few years in Congress had been marked by a widening division between the two primary political parties, and as a result, it was extremely difficult to accomplish anything since getting both sides to agree was an almost insurmountable task.

The president didn't need to paint me a picture of the difficulties involved with partisanship, I knew them firsthand, but his tone was one of trying to put difficulties behind and pledging to work together in the future for the good of the country. "The people want action," he said. "They didn't send us here to bicker. They ask us to rise above the merely partisan." He was right, of course, but he faced an uphill battle trying to put the two parties together.

President Bush did get my attention with the next part of his speech. He railed against illegal drugs, telling everyone that we must be intolerant of them. "Take my word," the new president vowed, "this scourge will stop."

I might be wrong, but I don't remember any prior commander-in-chief discussing a war against drugs in his inaugural speech before. To hear the kind of commitment he'd just promised gave all law enforcement people a new hope, a new game plan to latch onto and take into the future. One can't go any higher than the president, and here he was saying he was ready to lend whatever support necessary to destroy this problem once and for all.

While generally gratified with the recognition the president was giving to our daily battle against drugs, it also put me in an awkward position.

Earlier in the week, I received a message through Florida Lieutenant Governor Bobby Brantley concerning the number two job in the newly created office of National Drug Control Policy. The head of this agency, William Bennett, was the nation's first drug czar. The offer to be the number two man was a very generous one and I was deeply honored and flattered to receive this type of recognition.

However, I had just been re-elected by my county's citizens and I truly felt like my work was unfinished in Broward County. They were expecting me to keep up the fight for another four years, and I wasn't about to let them down. While attacking the drug problem on a nationwide basis had its attractions, I was committed to my South Florida post for another four years. I was number one there. Besides, moving to Washington, D.C., wasn't at the top of my wish list this late in my career. I turned down the job.

However, with the president's full weight behind the program, the nation's drug problem had been taken off the back burner and placed out front as one of the president's four-year objectives. I thought a reconsideration of the job was in order. I decided to find out more about the specific duties of the position and the philosophy of drug czar William Bennett, the former education secretary. I would talk it over with Sharron again and see if the president's speech should change my mind or not.

When the speech was over, the president left - off to the first of many balls he would attend in his honor. I was on my way to the Hilton event, relieved that this part of the ceremonies was over. Now came more security checks and double checks, constant reviewing of our lists to be sure we hadn't forgotten anything. Do we need to bring dogs in to sniff for a bomb? Are the magnetometers working? How fast can we move people through while operating at maximum security efficiency? I could certainly be considered an expert, after the courthouse situation in 1987, on how slowly people can be moved through one door while using only two hand-held magnetometers. At any rate, all of our efforts were worth it; we didn't have a hint of a problem. I'd like to think it was because we were well prepared, but we knew we were lucky that no one picked today to try any crazy stunts.

The ball at the Hilton was an uneventful, extravagant, well-run affair; the dancing and the partying continued well into the next day. At that point, I was too tired to care about anything.

I had been in Washington all week working on behalf of the new president, but I didn't get to talk with him or even shake his hand. The president and I went back a few years, after all, although he may not remember with favor our difference of opinion on the status of the drug war back in the early 1980s when he was vice president and I head of the Broward County Organized Crime Division. The public expressed some surprise over our exchange then, but I didn't believe Vice President Bush wanted a "yes man" in the trenches but, instead, someone who told him the honest truth about what was really happening. He appreciated the advice then, and that probably helped me in being mentioned for the position in the new drug agency.

The president is a great statesman and, with his resume, one of the most qualified to take the executive office, but I decided, after thinking about it again, that my loyalty lay more with the citizens of Broward County. I had promised during my campaigns that the sheriff's office was my only interest, and I meant that. Flattering as it was to receive the Washington offer, I could hardly wait to get home and begin work on the next four years.

The week had finally come to a conclusion and Sharron and I were ready to return to Fort Lauderdale. It had been an experience I will never forget. To witness history as it's made is not an ordinary occurrence and I knew this was a week, and in particular, a day, that would be a treasured memory for me forever.

Fifteen

A Ride To
The Supreme Court

THE SUN HAD NOT YET APPEARED ON THE HORIZON IN THE EARLY MORNING of August 27, 1985, when a twenty-eight-year-old man named Terrance Bostick boarded a Greyhound bus in Miami, bound for Atlanta. It was a long stretch ahead, an all-day ride that was grueling on the body. As the hours passed, the miles disappeared blurring the all too familiar green foliage of Florida and Georgia.

Terrance Bostick's journey would not end in Atlanta but, instead, nearly six years later in the most prestigious courtroom in America. His decision to ride that bus triggered a review of law enforcement procedures used by my Broward County deputies that passed through several different courts before final verdicts were handed down by the nine justices who reside on the U.S. Supreme Court.

Bostick's first stop was in Fort Lauderdale's terminal, thirty miles north of Miami. There, two of my deputies were conducting a routine assessment of bus travelers, trying to decide if any of them fit the profile of a drug courier. The officers on this detail, Joseph Nutt and Steve Rubino, boarded Bostick's bus to carry out their assignment.

Rubino and Nutt spotted Bostick almost as soon as they boarded the bus.

The driver, George Black, had left the vehicle to get himself a cup of coffee. The officers walked to the back of the bus where Bostick slouched. Both men wore green windbreakers clearly identifying them as officers with the Broward County Sheriff's Office. Both deputies were also armed. They both reported that Bostick was awake as they approached, although Bostick would later deny this.

My officers identified themselves, explained why they were there, and asked if they could search the red carry-on bag that lay next to Bostick on he seat. Bostick agreed. As it turned out, the bag was not his but that of another passenger who had lent it to Bostick to be used as a pillow. There was no contraband in that piece of luggage.

Rubino and Nutt then noticed a blue bag stored above the seats. When asked, Bostick confirmed that the bag was his and, according to the officers, gave permission for this bag to be searched, too. This time, the exploration turned up nearly a pound of cocaine. Bostick was read his rights, handcuffed, and removed from the bus. So far, this was only a routine bust under the phase of the profile program we called "working the buses." When Bostick agreed to the search, it became legal. If he hadn't, Rubino and Nutt would have had little choice but to walk away. Without probable cause we would have simply wished him a good trip and went on to other passengers and other buses that August morning.

Bostick's bus continued its journey to Atlanta, twenty minutes late leaving the Fort Lauderdale terminal.

Bostick was detained in a local cell, awaiting trial. On the advice of a friend, he retained Max P. Engel as his attorney and pleaded not guilty. Bostick alleged that the officers did not ask his consent to search the blue bag and that he felt intimidated by the deputies who had, by the positions they assumed in the aisleway, effectively blocked any exit path should Bostick have desired to leave it. This allegation was in direct conflict with Rubino's and Nutt's testimony, in which the officers said they had done everything by the book, as they are trained to do in these situations. Bostick's bail was reduced to $10,000, which he posted, granting him release pending the court hearing.

Engel's colleague, Louis B. Stoskopf, filed a challenge to our drug charges and a motion to suppress the evidence, which was not only cocaine from the travel bag but also some marijuana found on Bostick after his arrest. The primary reason for claiming that the drug charges were invalid was the intimidating circumstances of being confronted by two armed deputies in a corner of a bus with no obvious point of escape. These circumstances made the consent nonbinding and the subsequent search illegal.

The judge handling this case, Russell E. Seay, Jr., agreed to hear the motion filed by Stoskopf, and all parties converged in his courtroom on the tenth floor of the Broward County Courthouse. Bostick reaffirmed that if he hadn't felt intimidated he wouldn't have consented to the search of the blue bag, especially since he'd been arrested before and he knew the bag contained contraband. The deputies gave the same testimony as before, that Bostick consented to the search and that they had not attempted to intimidate him in any way.

The judge discussed the case with the attorneys, conceding that the confining nature of a bus would make such situations somewhat intimidating, even if the deputies were as polite as they could be, but he also felt that the police have a right to ask anyone if they could search a bag. He conveyed this opinion on August 4, 1986, nearly a year after the arrest, by denying the motion to suppress the drug evidence. The trial would proceed.

Bostick's case was at a crossroads. The evidence was damning, and a court conviction for cocaine trafficking could mean up to fifteen years in jail. Faced with a case he would likely lose, Bostick and his attorneys opted for the easiest way out - a plea bargain arrangement.

As part of the plea bargain, Bostick's attorneys, Engel and Stoskopf, retained the right, on their client's behalf, to appeal Judge Seay's decision.

Obviously, Bostick had cocaine in his possession. The big question was, did we discover it through legal means or did we violate his rights by intimidating him into agreeing to a search? This question would be taken to the next judicial level, the Fourth District Court of Appeals for the state of Florida.

Unlike in some other states, in Florida, once someone has been convicted and sentenced, he or she is sent to jail, appeal or not. Elsewhere, Bostick might have been free pending his appeal, but not here. The case proceeded without his presence, even though filed on his behalf.

We continued to "work the buses" as before and were pulling a tremendous amount drugs off the street. In addition, we were seizing weapons and cash, which was used under the confiscated funds law. As long as our officers did their jobs by the book, we felt the arrests were being done properly.

Bostick's attorneys filed a brief with the three judges on the appeals court stating, in essence, that just being confronted by the police created an atmosphere in which the person being questioned did not feel at liberty to simply walk away and ignore an officer's request. The state reiterated that the questioning was pleasant, almost a social interaction instead of a confrontational one.

Both sides had the opportunity to argue their positions orally on March 27, 1987. Kenneth P. Speiller, from Max Engel's office, performed the honors for the defense, while Assistant Attorney General Georgina Jimenez-Orosa represented State Attorney General Bob Butterworth and Florida. The three judges, James H. Walden, Gavin K. Letts, and Barry J. Stone, returned their verdict twelve days later, favoring our law enforcement efforts. Bostick's appeal was denied.

Speiller wouldn't give up. He filed a petition for another hearing, which found a sympathetic ear in Judge Letts. The other two judges turned it down so the petition was denied, but with a caveat. All three judges recommended that the Florida Supreme Court review the constitutionality of "working the buses." While they felt defendant Bostick's rights had been preserved, there was concern over the way in which we apprehended drug criminals on the transportation system. On behalf of future defendants who might appeal a lower court decision as to the legality of our work, a ruling was needed.

In the meantime, all hell had broken loose back in Broward County.

ᴏᴎ

ONE DAY IN 1987, CAROL ANN KERWICK AGREED TO LET DEPUTIES SEARCH HER luggage at a local Amtrak station. The deputies found nothing except a small locked bag. What the officers found when they did open it was a kilogram of cocaine. The woman was arrested.

Kerwick insisted that she did not authorize deputies to open the smaller bag. She went before Judge Robert Andrews, the magistrate who had excused himself from the court case involving my switching political parties prior to the 1984 sheriff's election and whose wife tried to convince me to renounce my Republican status after I had won the election. Judge Andrews did not like this case and declared the cocaine that had been seized was inadmissible since it was obtained illegally.

We hadn't lost many of these cases and I make it a point not to second guess judges' courtroom decisions. Our officers must make their decisions within a split second; they don't have time to pore over case law in their mind. In a sense, it's the judge's job to decide if what we do is correct or not, within the framework of the law. If, in Judge Andrews's opinion our officers made a mistake in the incident involving Carol Ann Kerwick, then we would accept the judge's decision, try to learn from the mistake, and move on.

However, nothing had prepared any of us for the vehement attack Judge Andrews would unleash upon the Broward County Sheriff's Office in the course of rendering his opinion. In dismissing the cocaine obtained as evidence, Judge Andrews said he was concerned that we felt we could suspend a constitutional right in the name of fighting drugs. He went on to say that the founders of this country would be stunned by our random seizures. These methods, he noted, "evoked images of other days, under other flags, when no man traveled his nation's roads or railways without fear of unwarranted interruption, by individuals who held temporary power in government. This is not Hitler's Berlin, or Stalin's Moscow, nor is it white supremacist South Africa."

I was astonished at his remarks. To render a decision is one thing. To blatantly and unfairly attack my department was something else again. His remarks particularly shocked the officers in my department whose parents or family members were victims of Hitler's Third Reich. To compare our request to search a bag to the undeniably fear-inducing image of people being dragged from their homes in the dead of night was not only wrong but also totally out of line for a man in Judge Andrews's position. I'm not sure what inspired these harsh words, but they flew directly in the face of other court rulings, including the U.S. Supreme Court's, which consistently upheld random search and seizure.

The Fourth District Court of Appeals adopted Judge Andrews's opinion for its dispensation of these types of cases. In doing so, they also left intact the wording regarding Hitler's Berlin, Stalin's Moscow, etc. This infuriated me.

The local newspaper editorials were supportive of the courts, noting that "the reality of law officers randomly picking a traveler out of crowd to search belongings is chilling." They didn't equate our police searches with that of the Third Reich, but they clearly opposed the "working the buses" program. I had no problem with opposition, but comparisons to police states was another matter and one I would fight.

Steve Bertucelli, head of the Organized Crime Division, and I put our heads together to develop a different procedure for our searches to ensure they held up under court scrutiny. Using the court's ruling was a guideline, we made a few changes in our procedures but didn't release this information to the press. We worked to find the right balance between what we could do and a person's civil rights. The community had the right to travel freely and to see drugs and crime drastically reduced. The judge's decision simply ensured that defense attorneys would continue to chip away at a particularly successful endeavor. We would be ready for them.

In the meantime, the state was arguing the Bostick case, or, in actuality, the constitutionality of the "working the buses" program. The attorneys from the appeals case, Kenneth Speiller for Bostick and Georgina Jimenez-Orosa for the state, made their arguments all over again. In addition, two other lawyers shared their thoughts with the court, one representing each side of the issue. Speaking on Bostick's behalf was an attorney named Joseph S. Paglino, who spent his time arguing cases involving civil rights. He quoted some of Judges Andrews's wording concerning the Kerwick case. For the state, Edward A. Hanna, Jr., a former federal prosecutor, recounted our success rate at seizures using this program. The oral arguments were made to the seven Florida Supreme Court judges in March 1988, and they took more than eighteen months to render a decision.

When it came, their decision reversed previous lower court verdicts that had upheld the Bostick conviction.

The vote was a close four to three, and Justice Rosemary Barkett, a magistrate with whom I'd had my share of disagreements, wrote the majority opinion. She said the searches weren't constitutional and that we violated citizens' rights by boarding buses and randomly questioning passengers without "articulable reasons for doing so." She went on to say that a bus itself posed another major problem because it was a confined space and travelers didn't have a clear path to avoid the search or walk away once questioned. Like Judge Andrews, she compared us to Nazi Germany, Russia and, in this case, Cuba.

Well, I've been to Cuba, and the ability to travel freely here is light years away from the fear and trepidation that many Cubans take with them on a journey. I am an immigrant and believe strongly in the Bill of Rights and the Constitution. I doubted if Judge Barkett had ever been to Cuba and she wasn't likely to have visited Hitler's Germany or Stalin's Russia. What she was saying in her majority opinion was if you want to transport drugs through Broward County, it should be done by bus!

Terrance Bostick's conviction had been overturned. He would have been free to leave jail, except he had already done that in April 1989 when he was paroled with time off for good behavior. His best hope now was that a decision on his behalf would take the conviction off his record. The case, which began on a sleepy August morning in Miami in 1985, was nearly four years old, and our lawyers were now prepared to take it before the U.S. Supreme Court.

Since the issue was not just Bostick's conviction but the entire Fourth Amendment, we could take it one step higher than the Florida Supreme Court. Because a decision in such a case would have far-reaching effects (similar types of drug courier profiles were being used in D.C. itself, along with Georgia, New York, North Carolina, and Virginia), I thought the highest court in the land would take an interest and review this case.

Citing the fact that the Florida statute's search and seizure language was based on the U.S. Supreme Court's interpretation of the Fourth Amendment, the justices agreed to hear the case during their 1990-91 session.

It isn't often that one can be involved in a case that goes all the way to the top. This case was important to us. We had essentially stopped searches on buses, feeling that the original way was the most effective and efficient at collaring criminals. What the Supreme Court said would give us our guidelines for the foreseeable future.

The "heavy hitters" began lining up to argue this case before the nation's highest court. Terrance Bostick was represented by the American Civil Liberties Union and the National Association of Criminal Defense Lawyers. They were joined by a group that is considered pro-police called Americans for Effective Law Enforcement. This latter group had never filed against a law enforcement agency - until now.

Bob Butterworth, our Florida Attorney General, made the D.C. trip personally with Senior Assistant Attorney General Joan Fowler, who would argue the case along with U.S. Solicitor General Kenneth W. Starr from the Bush administration.

Bostick's lawyers were all working for free since he had no money to pay them, but one got the sense during all of this that Bostick was of little consequence to the defense attorneys. They simply did not want the Fourth Amendment tampered with.

Five and a half years after that hazy August morning in the Fort Lauderdale Greyhound terminal, each side had thirty minutes to make its arguments before the Rehnquist Court on February 26, 1991. On the bench that day, in addition to Chief Justice William H. Rehnquist, was Thurgood Marshall, Harry Blackmun, Byron White, John Paul Stevens, Anthony Kennedy, Sandra Day O'Connor, Antonin Scalia and the Court's newest member, David Souter.

The old discussions were rehashed, this time for a new judicial audience. The state argued that Bostick had every right to refuse the search and was given that opportunity. The defense pointed out that there was nothing that seemed routine about the approach by the officers and that Bostick didn't feel as if he had any option but to let the police search his bag.

In one hour, it was over, and the Supreme Court took the matter under advisement. It would be nearly four months before the justices would return with their verdict. In the meantime, based on the Florida Supreme Court ruling, we had drastically reduced the number of searches being made, making sure that all of the factors routinely checked pointed to the likelihood that an individual was transporting drugs.

On June 20, 1991, the Supreme Court handed down its decision on the Bostick case. By a six to three margin, the high court had ruled in favor of the state. The majority opinion in this situation was written by Justice Sandra Day O'Connor. She said that there was nothing unconstitutional or coercive about inquiring of passengers about searching their luggage, regardless of the mode of transportation. That included buses, much to Judge Barkett's chagrin, I imagine. Justice O'Connor wrote, "Bostick's movements were confined in a sense, but this was the natural result of his decision to take the bus."

Siding with Justice O'Connor were Justices Souter, Kennedy, Scalia, White, and Chief Justice Rehnquist. The dissenters were Justices Marshall, Blackmun, and Stevens. Marshall would write in his minority opinion that "the Fourth Amendment clearly condemns the suspicionless, dragnet-style sweep of intrastate or interstate buses."

This is where, I believe, the Florida court ruling against us was missing the point: we did not ask everyone about their bags, only a couple of selected individuals who seemed to fit our profile, and more often than not, we were right.

Not everyone consented to having their bag searched, either, further testament to the fact that some people did elect to exercise their right not to open their bags. Others, I believe, consented thinking we wouldn't actually search since they apparently had nothing to hide. This assumption was incorrect. We always searched as long as we had an affirmative answer.

Court analysts at the time said that this ruling was a continuation on the Supreme Court's part of limiting protection under the Fourth Amendment. This seemed to be an overreaction. We weren't trying to curb any part of the Bill of Rights. Nothing done in the name of law enforcement is meant to alter these rights at all. If we selected someone for a search that was innocent and the exploration revealed nothing, we thanked that person for his or her voluntary cooperation and moved on. Most individuals I know were glad for the extra security these detectives provided by being stationed in the bus and train terminals, especially late at night. The only ones with anything to fear were the individuals who were smuggling illegal narcotics, and they still had the right to refuse a search. To me, this was simply protecting good citizens, not violating rights. The Supreme Court agreed.

Life magazine did a special issue that year on the 200th anniversary of the Bill of Rights, and it featured the Bostick case as an example of how a case winds its way through the legal maze of the justice system. All of the participants, including Terrance Bostick himself, were pictured in the various sites where the courtroom "action" took place.

We weren't living in Hitler's Berlin after all, simply the nation's drug smuggling capital, a designation we were trying to do away with by conducting effective checks at all points of entry and pass-through. The amount of drugs seized continued to be substantial, and after all the years of taking this contraband off the street, I know we've made some drug dealers' lives a little miserable; there was great satisfaction in that.

The "working the buses" program continued to thrive under our Organized Crime Division.

Sixteen

"Organized" Crime

W HEN PEOPLE THINK ABOUT ORGANIZED CRIME, THE FIRST IMAGE THAT springs to mind is the Hollywood vision of the mob: gangsters, Edward G. Robinson, The Godfather. Somehow, the idea of organized crime has become synonymous with people of Italian or Sicilian descent.

Gangsters come in all shapes, forms, and backgrounds. When two or more people sit down to plot a crime, that's organized. This definition goes beyond the traditional "mob" idea, which is now just a myth. The Italians have been joined by Colombians, Jamaicans, Cubans, Koreans, and Chinese, all of whom have established their own organized crime gangs.

There's nothing glamorous about these people. As far as I'm concerned, these criminals are the lowest form of life. They have no respect for this country, the city in which they live, or the people that live around them. They're motivated by one simple interest: themselves.

There's only one way to fight organized crime - aggressively. As sheriff, the last thing I wanted to do was sit on my hands and try to wish the problems away. Organized criminals sometimes have friends in high places and pressures they may use to ease up on our vigilance as law enforcement officers. Such tactics wouldn't work with this sheriff. We spent a substantial amount of time trying to rid Broward County of these gangs through whatever legal means was available. Our own organized crime unit was focused on all aspects of these criminal conspiracies.

My own experience with gangs goes back a number of years. The best known of the gangsters who resided in South Florida was Meyer Lansky. He was an old-timer in criminal enterprises both in the United States and internationally. He helped Benjamin "Bugsy" Siegel set up casinos in Las Vegas, but he was into far more than that.

Lansky was a Russian immigrant who created an international crime ring, yet kept a low local profile in South Florida. He was a quiet, unassuming man, certainly not one you'd mistake for a notorious gangster, yet he was every bit as deadly as the worst of the lot.

In 1971, I was working for the Florida Department of Law Enforcement out of Orlando when I received a call from our chief asking me to come down to Miami to meet with some FBI agents, former associates of mine back when I had worked for what is now the DEA. The meeting was about Meyer Lansky.

Lansky had traveled to Mexico for a meeting with some of his "business" associates. The FBI had him under surveillance and noted that he had purchased some medicine during his Mexico stay. Lansky suffered from a stomach ailment and had bought an over-the-counter drug in Mexico for treatment. The problem for Lansky was that the drug was not approved for sale in the United States. In fact, it was a controlled substance here and very much illegal in the state of Florida. If Lansky brought that medicine back, we had a crime we could arrest him for.

The problem for the FBI was that they had no jurisdiction in this case since it was a state law being broken. They needed the FDLE's help to make the arrest. I was chosen for that assignment. Actually, the FBI's primary goal was not so much Lansky himself. The gangster carried a little black book that had phone numbers of Lansky's national and international contacts. This is what the FBI really wanted so they could begin to track the various illegal businesses Lansky managed.

Lansky came back to Florida following his meeting and went through Customs. As expected, he did not declare the medicine, but a Customs official noted it, didn't say anything and let Lansky pass through. We were notified that Lansky had brought the substance into the state. We went to a newly appointed judge, whom we felt would be untouched by any criminals so early in his career. We secured our warrant. It was time to make the arrest.

I bought a brand new pair of $14 handcuffs for this assignment. I staked out Lansky's apartment on Collins Avenue in Miami Beach. Lansky had a daily routine where he would walk his dog and stop at various pay phones to make his business calls. Once I had confirmed that he had the black book with him, I was ready.

After he had completed one of his calls, I stopped him, identified myself, showed him the warrant, and informed him that he was under arrest. He politely asked if he could return his dog to the apartment before going with me. I agreed and, with one of the FBI agents, accompanied Lansky back to his place.

He dropped his dog off with his wife and then asked a second favor - to change his clothes. This I couldn't let him do. I searched him, retrieved the black book, handed it to the FBI agent, and put the handcuffs on Lansky.

Lansky posted bail and tried to flee the country. He attempted to emigrate to Israel first, which denied him entrance, as did Argentina and several other places of potential refuge. He returned to stand trial, but it turned out to be a farce. A judge was brought out of retirement and, after the prosecution had presented its case, the magistrate moved for a "directed verdict of acquittal."

This power is seldom exercised by judges, but it is their right, even during a jury trial, to acquit the accused directly if they feel the prosecution has not made a strong enough case. I had never seen it happen before and have not seen it since. Lansky walked, but his power base had eroded. The FBI was successful, through the black book, in tracking down all of the various businesses that Lansky was involved in. The mere threat of an FBI investigation was enough to close down many of them.

The other major mob figure that I dealt with was Carmine Galante. He was one of the top New York mobsters affiliated with Carlo Gambino, the reputed head of all the New York Mafia "families." The word "families" is a newspaper description. I wouldn't defame the word by using it in context with a guy like Galante. Family, to me, has a wonderful connotation and I won't associate the term with these thugs. The so-called families were nothing more than gangs.

Galante was arrested in 1958 along with Vito Genovese and several other top mobsters in New York and had served prison time for heroin smuggling. He had been released in 1974 and returned to New York, where he was on parole.

Some friends of mine called me a few weeks later to tell me Galante was on his way to South Florida. I was head of Sheriff Ed Stack's organized crime unit at the time and I certainly didn't want someone like Galante even thinking about getting comfortable down here.

As a parolee, he had to make contact with a local probation officer within twenty-four hours of his arrival. We found out he hadn't told his parole officer in New York he was taking the trip. He checked into the Diplomat Hotel in Hollywood, Broward County, accompanied by his two daughters. He apparently was going to meet with other local crime figures, presumably to be organized under his direction.

We gave him twenty-four hours. When he didn't check in with any parole people, we had him for breaking his parole. I waited until just after 4:30 A.M. then went up to his room, knocked on his door, identified myself, showed him the warrant, handcuffed him, and walked him right out of the hotel in his pajamas and down to the sheriff's office for booking. He was livid.

I didn't want Galante to have any shred of doubt about how unwelcome his presence in Broward County was. He returned to New York after uttering a few vague threats, but he clearly understood that he could forget about organizing anything down here. He was shot dead in a Brooklyn restaurant a short time later.

Perhaps the biggest figure in organized crime that we didn't get was Robert Vesco, whom we had spotted on the Caribbean island of Antigua while we were conducting our Bimini "invasions" in the early 1980s. Vesco was one of the most wanted fugitives at the time. He fled the country in 1972 after diverting over $200 million from a Swiss mutual fund and making an illegal campaign contribution of some $200,000 to Richard Nixon's re-election effort in 1972. He had been conducting money laundering and other financial schemes for some of the world's worst criminals ever since, including Colombian drug gangs.

In 1982, once we knew where he was, I proposed a plan to shoot him with a tranquilizer dart and bring him back to the United States. Vesco lived aboard a yacht called *Halcyon* and often worked alone, so the "grab" would have been relatively easy. The problem was we couldn't get any federal agencies to take him into custody once we brought him back. While we had an extradition treaty with Antigua, its government was no more cooperative than that of the

Bahamas, so our chances of getting Vesco through the usual channels was virtually impossible.

I really wanted Vesco. We had pretty solid information that Vesco was a conduit for funds from Colombia to the prime minister's office in the Bahamas - payment for using the islands for smuggling drugs to the United States. We had made a dent in the drug traffic coming in from Bimini but could be more effective by clearing out the "money man," Vesco.

We already had the state department in Washington, D.C., in an uproar over the Bimini affair and the department was unwilling to sanction the effort to bring back Vesco. So, without federal cooperation, then Sheriff Bob Butterworth killed the plan and Vesco continued to operate.

When I took over as sheriff of Broward County in 1985, I expanded our organized crime unit. I wanted our OCD, headed by Colonel Steve Bertucelli, to explore all aspects of organized crime, not just the narcotics affiliations. Gambling, pornography, and finance were all areas organized crime was into, and I wanted OCD to conduct some long-term investigations into these activities.

Our best early effort was coined "Operation Cherokee" by the OCD. It was a complete two-year undercover effort that culminated in the arrests of nine high-ranking organized crime figures.

South Florida is considered neutral territory for organized crime gangs; no one particular group is in control. Instead, there is usually a cooperative effort to manage illegal enterprises. Into that loose structure walked a few of our undercover officers posing as gamblers, drug dealers, traders in stolen goods, and other criminal identities.

They joined an operation called Cherokee Enterprises, a catch-all for illegal operations run in South Florida. The officers were involved, undercover, in illegal bookmaking, drug deals, arms running, and liquor smuggling. Many of them participated in the various operations from planning to end and, as a result, learned much about the inner workings of the mob.

In two years, we had plenty of charges to bring in the top guys for indictment. It's relatively easy to pick off the underlings in this type of operation, but we wanted the planners, the thugs on top who gave the orders. Patience and excellent detective work paid off.

The problem was having enough resources in the state attorney's office to successfully prosecute the cases. Ideally, a state-wide grand jury made more sense since it could be given the resources and the criminal activities occurred throughout the state, anyway, not just in Broward County. Broward State Attorney Michael Satz dedicated two prosecutors to work exclusively on Operation Cherokee.

We followed up those June 1987 arrests with more in November of the same year. The second time, we concentrated on the illegal liquor aspect of the businesses, arresting six mobsters. Apprehensions of this nature sent a message to organized crime gangs: stay out of Broward County. If you run your operations here, we'll bust them.

The most successful task force we put together was the Blue Lightning Task Force, which combined forces from a number of law enforcement agencies to combat narcotics smuggling. We were well coordinated, well structured, and well equipped to fight drug running, and a lot of smugglers paid a high price because of our efforts. We arrested Colombians, Cubans, Panamanians, Costa Ricans, and Spaniards - it didn't matter to us. Drugs are a world-wide business, and we played no favorites. I'm color and race blind when it comes to law enforcement. A person is either a lawbreaker or not. It was as simple as that.

The Asian community had set up a large gambling ring around the United States and Broward County was no exception. From 1990 to 1992, we conducted several raids on various Asian businesses, uncovering millions of dollars in gambling operations. Many of the arrested criminals were associated with some of the Chinese tongs. Illegal weapons were in abundance and we seized these as well. The extent of the gambling was incredible; there were dozens of small operations, all well coordinated, that raked in millions of illegal profits.

These gangs are typical of what prevails today. Asian gangs are interchangeable with Jamaican gangs and Colombian gangs and others. They all have their specialties, but what they share in common is a general disdain for the value of human life. Intimidation, terrorism and murder are commonplace with these individuals. There isn't a semblance of conscience or feeling in these thugs, and gang killings have proliferated here and elsewhere in the country. Drive-by shootings, one gang evening a score with another gang, is as ordinary as picking up the morning paper.

It wasn't all that easy to infiltrate and break up youth gangs with the average undercover cop. Since we couldn't recruit minors as informants, we had to use a different method of enforcing the law against these kids before their gangs grew into a more deadly type of operation.

In the Broward community of Tamarac, we had a police officer named Bennett that we suspected of selling drugs to minors. He knew we couldn't use minors to testify against him. I looked through our files of officers, searching for someone who could pose as a minor in a sting against this disgrace to the badge.

I found a twenty-two-year-old female who looked even younger in person than in her photograph. She looked about fourteen or fifteen and was, I believe, the perfect answer for our undercover problems. We set her up as a high school student and arrested Bennett when he tried to sell her some drugs. It was hard to believe that while we were trying to reverse a deteriorating pattern of youthful crime, one of our own was making the problem much worse. He received a fifteen-year sentence as a result of our undercover officer's excellent work.

This case was the beginning of our undercover youth assignments. We found a number of other young-looking officers who could be put into schools as both a positive influence and a spotter of illegal activity. In this way, our officers started making some inroads into youth crime.

During our undercover operations, we found a sixteen-year-old Coral Springs student who ran a sports betting operation out of his locker. He would take students' money - any amount from $20 to $3,500 - to bet on professional football and baseball games. He used his profits to buy baseball cards.

One of his practices was to use an imaginary enforcer to collect his bets. He would make the phone calls himself, threatening those that hadn't paid up. One scared youth told his father and he tipped our office.

What was more amazing was that the kid didn't appear to be working with anyone else. This was a one-person operation dealing, in some months, with thousands of dollars. About a dozen students bet regularly with the young bookie, who, like any in this profession, had to pay out some large amounts when a heavily favored team would lose to an underdog. The baseball card collection that he poured his winnings into was valued at more than $10,000.

We asked the kid who had been threatened to pay off the young bookie with marked bills. Once the student accepted them, we arrested him on two felony counts of bookmaking and the misdemeanor counts of gambling and conspiracy.

Parents need to be on the watch for any type of unusual behavior in their children or an increase in the amount of personal goods. If we don't increase our vigilance, the result will be a further drop in the quality of our society. This is not a legacy I want to leave.

Organized crime comes in all types of packages. Our officers at the Broward County Sheriff's Office worked long and hard to break up these rings before they became too widespread. The increase in youth crime is a frightening statistic. Much more work remains to be done in this area if we wish to continue to enjoy the communities in which we live.

Seventeen

Bad Rap

O N NEW YEAR'S DAY 1990, A MIAMI-BASED ATTORNEY NAMED JACK
Thompson received a copy of some lyrics to a rap album entitled As
Nasty As They Wanna Be, recorded by a Miami-based band called 2
Live Crew. The lyrics had been mailed to Thompson by a group known as
Focus on the Family, located in Pomona, California. Thompson was a born-
again Christian who had left a law firm to pursue a vigorous and controversial
crusade against people he commonly referred to as "vulgarians." After reading 2 Live Crew's lyrics, he angrily denounced them and took up a brand new
cause. "A society that allows this material," he said, "is one that doesn't take
seriously the brutalization, rape, and even murder of women."

Thompson was already well known for his crusades and had attained a certain amount of notoriety in South Florida for his personal attacks on Dade
County State Attorney Janet Reno and South Florida radio talk show host Neil
Rogers. He had gone so far as to openly accuse Reno of being a lesbian when
he ran against her for state attorney in 1988. Reno, naturally, denied the
charge, replying that she was attracted to "strong, brave, rational, and intelligent men." The attack on Rogers grew out of the types of songs the radio personality played such as "Boys Want Sex in the Morning." This resulted in messy
lawsuits on both sides, as well as wide-ranging publicity.

2 Live Crew was his next target. Armed with the song lyrics, Thompson

immediately went to work to ensure that the album was declared obscene and pulled from distribution. The same day he received the lyrics, he fired off a letter to Janet Reno demanding that she prosecute the rap group on obscenity charges. When she chose not to investigate, Thompson said it was because 2 Live Crew, curiously enough, had released a rap song the year before entitled "Janet Reno," which praised her efforts to collect child support payments from deadbeat fathers. Reno (now U.S. attorney general) said Thomson's charge was absurd, as she couldn't even understand the lyrics.

Having no help from Reno, Thompson decided to try another strategy. Two versions of As Nasty As They Wanna Be were released, one labeled for adults only, and the other a less vulgar version intended for sale to the general public. Thompson decided to enlist the assistance of a sixteen-year old who was sent into a record store to see if he could purchase the adult version. He was successful, and Thompson documented these results and sent them to Janet Reno, noting that minors have easy access to these lyrics. When the youth declined to get further involved in helping to prosecute the record store owners, Reno referred the matter to the Metro Dade police, which in turn alerted all area record store owners that the "adults only" version of the rap album was labeled as such for a reason and that they should check identification before selling it.

Thompson did not stop there. He wrote to Governor Bob Martinez and asked that he consider the matter. He also sent letters and copies of the lyrics to every sheriff in Florida's sixty-seven counties, including me. My office receives numerous citizen complaints concerning films, music, tape recordings, and the like that individuals feel are pornographic or obscene. When a complaintant says that the material enclosed is not in compliance with the First Amendment, we follow a certain procedure.

As sheriff, I have nothing to do with what is considered obscene or not. Since the 1973 landmark obscenity case of Miller v. California, only a judge has the ability to classify material as obscene. In the ruling, the U.S. Supreme Court said that "community standards" should govern what is labeled obscene and that a federal judge was in the best position to determine this. (Apparently, when that individual dons the black robe, a special light shines down from above that gives the judge insight into making this decision.) I am certainly entitled to my opinion that the 2 Live Crew lyrics were offensive in depicting brutal treatment of women, but my judgment has no legal clout whatsoever. When this type of complaint comes in, we process it, even when it comes from a crackpot like Thompson, who had sent us material before. Every American has the legal right to ask for a review of any media for an obscenity evaluation, and Thompson was no exception. A judge would decide on the merits of the grievance, not me.

Bill Kelly, formerly the lone FBI agent in South Florida assigned to pornography and obscenity cases, had been hired by me to handle this type of request. He asked an undercover cop to purchase a copy of the 2 Live Crew tape. He then filed an affidavit for order of determination or probable cause of obscenity in court. This is our routine with the majority of these complaints. After filing, it was a matter of waiting for the judge's order to determine how we would proceed.

The affidavit was filed in late February 1990. Governor Martinez, in response to Thompson's request, had reviewed the lyrics, found them "disgusting," and turned them over to statewide prosecutor Peter Antonacci. On March 7, Antonacci concluded that any investigation into whether these lyrics violated obscenity laws should be left to the local authorities. We were local authorities and we followed our standard procedure. It was not the first nor would it be the last time we received a complaint from Jack Thompson.

The Broward circuit judge who reviewed our affidavit was Mel Grossman, husband of County Commissioner Nicki Grossman. A long-time magistrate, Judge Grossman had a reputation of being fair and not letting personal feelings interfere with his interpretation of the law. Over the years, he had handled numerous cases without complaint from any party. On March 9, after his review, he found probable cause that the lyrics violated community standards. He stated that he'd listened to the entire album before making his decision and also cited a story that appeared in a local newspaper that said many of 2 Live Crew's lyrics are so filled with hard-core sexual, sadistic, and masochistic material that they could not be printed. One of the lyrics Judge Grossman did cite as being among the tamest was "I'm like a dog in heat, I freak without warning. I have an appetite for sex 'cause me so horny'." Judge Grossman felt these lyrics were not protected under the First Amendment.

I admit to being surprised. No lyrics that were ever submitted had been considered obscene. It was a ground-breaking decision. These lyrics, the judge felt, seemed to advocate that a woman was a tool to be used and discarded, and thus violated community standards.

Once the judge made his ruling, it was up to my office to enforce it. I distributed copies of the judge's statement to my district commanders and asked them to notify all music shops that those selling the record risked prosecution on a felony charge if the record was sold to a minor, a misdemeanor if sold to an adult.

Executives of the record company, Luke Skyywalker Records of Miami, were naturally outraged by the ruling. They insisted that Governor Martinez had singled out 2 Live Crew and that no one had ever had a problem with rap music until white kids started buying the albums. American Civil Liberties Union lawyers said it was a clear violation of free speech rights under the First Amendment, although they acknowledged the lyrics to be "sexist, violent, and tragic." A black owner of a radio station said that he had already made a decision never to play 2 Live Crew on the air, saying that something this extreme would lead to decay in the community: it was the kind of material that contributed to an environment in which killing and maiming could occur.

2 Live Crew's record label, Luke Skyywalker Records, was already feeling persecuted since filmmaker George Lucas was taking legal action to prevent Luther Campbell, the rap group's leader and owner of the record label, from continued use of the Luke Skyywalker name, claiming it was a copyright infringement on Lucas's movie Star Wars. Campbell would eventually change the label to Luke Records.

Some people noted that other albums were far worse than As Nasty As They Wanna Be," so why weren't they being banned from record stores? The answer is we react to citizen complaints; we do not seek out pornographic material. We utilize the same procedure on all complaints and we rely on a judge for guidance. If the judge to whom we sent the album had said there was no probable cause for obscenity in 2 Live Crew's case, there would be no story. Since he did consider the lyrics obscene, my office had the task of enforcing the law. I did not single out 2 Live Crew, nor did Jack Thompson make the band his only target. But the law is the law, and our duty was to see that it was upheld, regardless of the flak I knew we would take. In the entire criminal justice system, law enforcement officers are arguably the most visible. We receive the most criticism. We are seen as people who deprive others of their liberties, who handcuff individuals and march them off to jail. We may not like being the object of critical attention, but we accept it as part of the job.

Bruce Rogow, the attorney who represented the Democratic Party in 1984 over the constitutional question concerning my candidacy for the sheriff's office and represented me in the courtroom security case, was retained by Skyywalker Records to represent the company and the members of 2 Live Crew. He filed a suit on their behalf on March 16 seeking to block obscenity arrests for sales of the album as a result of Judge Grossman's opinion. As one of the area's leading authorities on the Constitution, Rogow was a natural selection, and a good one, to defend 2 Live Crew and the record company. In his suit, he questioned the constitutionality of what our office was doing in following up Judge Grossman's probable cause findings.

In the meantime, a judge in Lee County Circuit Court, Isaac Anderson, also ruled that As Nasty As They Wanna Be was obscene and ordered it removed from store shelves. 2 Live Crew's leader, Luther Campbell, labeled the judge a racist, a hater of black people, and a probable Ku Klux Klan member. As it turned out, Judge Isaac Anderson was black. Luther Campbell had never seen him nor knew anything about the man. The charge of racism was to echo throughout this case as a prime issue. Such a charge was also mistakenly directed by Campbell toward our office. If 2 Live Crew had been a white group, the matter would have been handled the same.

In Broward County, the record had virtually disappeared from stores after distribution of the ruling to record store owners, but this didn't seem to settle any questions. Rogow's lawsuit named me as the defendant, and my attorney, John Jolly, and I agreed that the best way to resolve this matter was to bring it to court. We filed a counter suit on Tuesday, March 27, seeking a trial by jury to declare the album obscene - or not - and settle this issue once and for all. A jury's conclusion of what the community standards are for obscenity would have much more force than one judge's probable cause determination. A jury trial would also permit 2 Live Crew the chance to present evidence that the material is not obscene, something the band was not able to do with our earlier affidavit filing. The suit filed by Rogow for the band was handled first.

The case was assigned to U.S. District Judge Jose Gonzalez, who agreed to hear evidence in mid-May. By now, national publicity being accorded this case was beginning to heighten. 2 Live Crew had already sold more than a million copies of this album before Judge Grossman's ruling and countless thousands more after it, which underscored the risk in calling more attention to the material. While other areas in Florida and the rest of the country were taking similar actions to Broward County concerning this album, the publicity was very likely furthering the rap group's career.

The hearings began on May 14. Over the next couple of days, Bruce Rogow brought in a number of witnesses to testify on 2 Live Crew's behalf and to defend its lyrics under the First Amendment. Several individuals attested that As Nasty As They Wanna Be was a true representation of black culture, that this type of music was a message from the entire black community.

I could only shake my head to that. For years, I had spent a lot of time in all of our communities, and I couldn't imagine that the message in these lyrics represented the majority of blacks.

Books, magazines, and films from X-rated stores were presented as evidence that in Broward County, we had accepted this type of media as part of our community and should not, therefore, single out 2 Live Crew in enforcing an obscenity law.

It was a well-prepared, well-orchestrated and well-presented defense that Bruce Rogow had put together. After the defense rested its case, my attorney, John Jolly, stood up and presented only one piece of evidence, the tape itself. He gave it to Judge Gonzalez and asked that he listen to it in its entirety. As magistrate, Judge Gonzalez had the power to render a decision as to whether the material was obscene or not.

The judge took the tape, thanked everyone for their cooperation, and advised that he would return at a later date with his findings. We went back to business as usual.

Judge Gonzalez called us back to court on June 6 to hear his decision. Numerous editorials and features had appeared in local newspapers, and there had been ongoing television coverage debating the issue for weeks. Virtually everyone felt that the judge would not rule the material obscene. No other musical recording had ever been labeled obscene by a federal court.

The courtroom was jammed. The great majority of people were media, and when the judge entered, he ordered the doors locked. He didn't want, he explained, people rushing in or out of the place until he decided everyone could go. He admonished all in the room to keep calm, to not make any unnecessary noise, and to maintain the decorum of the court. He then proceeded to distribute copies of his findings, a sixty-two page document that he handed to all the affected parties. Everyone was completely still.

Rogow had been smiling all day. He was very congenial before the judge came in and seemed completely confident that the decision was going to go his and 2 Live Crew's way. He was still smiling when he received the judge's document. He sat there and began to read. He flipped a page, then another. The smile began to disappear from his face and, as more pages were turned, his face grew serious. I thought to myself, we won, the judge has ruled against 2 Live Crew. I then thought, what next?

In his decision, Judge Gonzalez said that this was a case between two ancient enemies: Anything Goes and Enough Already. He noted that Judge Oliver Wendell Holmes Jr. had observed that the First Amendment was not absolute and that it did not, for example, permit one to yell "fire" in a crowded theater. Today, the judge said, the court had to determine whether the First Amendment absolutely permits one to yell another "f" word combined with graphic sexual descriptions anywhere in the community.

In Florida, he continued, obscenity is a crime. Violation of the laws against obscenity is as much against the law as assault, rape, kidnapping, robbery, or other forms of behavior that the legislature has declared criminal.

The Judge said he used the U.S. Supreme Court's three-part measurement of obscenity. According to this test, before material is banned, an average person applying community standards must find that it appeals to prurient interests, is patently offensive, and lacks serious artistic, political, or scientific value. Judge Gonzalez defined the community as Dade and Palm Beach Counties along with Broward since they share the same geography, culture, news media, and transportation network and declared that he was qualified to comment on community standards since he had lived in Broward County since 1958.

As to the rap group's defense that their album was comedic art, the judge advised that it could not be reasonably argued that the violence, perversion, abuse of women, graphic descriptions of all forms of sexual conduct, and microscopic descriptions of human genitalia contained on this recording were comedic art. He said that in a society where obscenity is forbidden, it is human nature to want to taste forbidden fruit. It is quite another thing to insist that this aspect of humanity forms the basis for finding that As Nasty As They Wanna Be has serious artistic value. The evident goal of this particular recording was to reproduce the sexual act through musical lyrics. It was an appeal directed to "dirty" thoughts and the loins, not to intellect and the mind. Based on the deluge of graphic sexual lyrics about nudity and sexual conduct, the judge said that the court had no difficulty in finding that As Nasty As They Wanna Be appealed to a shameful and morbid interest in sex.

The judge concluded that the Philistines are not always wrong, nor are the guardians of the First Amendment always right. He said that what began as a dispute between two ancient enemies concludes with the hope that they are reconciled by a mutual friend - the Constitution of the United States.

It was a first. No federal court had ever done it. Judge Gonzalez had listened to that tape and came to the same conclusion that Judge Grossman had reached. Judge Gonzalez then took a moment to ask me to cease the sheriff's office current procedure of filing an affidavit with a judge to render an opinion about probable cause for obscenity and then warning store owners that they could be arrested if caught selling the specific item the judge thought obscene. An opinion is not the final word of law. Judge Gozalez felt we were violating the Constitution in our process, because the authors of the specified material were not given a chance to offer a defense of the material in question. These comments came through loud and clear to me and I changed our procedures accordingly.

Another request from the judge also stood out in his court order. He said that the sheriff's office should vigorously enforce the county's obscenity law. The words were emphatic.

What began as a simple misdemeanor had now blown into a full-fledged media circus. When the judge opened the doors, the courtroom resembled a beehive with all of the media swarming outside, hoping to obtain some commentary from Bruce Rogow and 2 Live Crew's Luther Campbell. They weren't disappointed.

Rogow said he would appeal the decision. He was surprised by it and felt that it was a retreat from the notion that adults should be free to decide for themselves what was obscene. He said other entertainers, such as Eddie Murphy and Andrew Dice Clay, would also be in trouble in Broward County after this ruling. The government, he warned, could now be "as nasty as they wanna be" in cracking down on pornography. He also predicted a further increase in record sales for 2 Live Crew.

The trial had been my first meeting with 2 Live Crew's leader, Luther Campbell. He had come across as an arrogant, conceited loudmouth, typical of many people I had encountered in my profession. He tried to intimidate people, but I sensed he was trying to suppress an inferiority complex. A tall, slender, flashy dresser, he spent considerable time drawing attention to himself and he clearly liked the limelight here.

Campbell made his reaction known on the steps of the courthouse when he held the judge's decision aloft, declared it to be no more than toilet paper, and claimed that the judge didn't understand his culture. He also said he didn't think Dice Clay would have any problems here because he's white. At any rate, he noted, his band's next album, Banned in the U.S.A., was going to be even raunchier and he predicted big sales, though he probably wouldn't sell many in Broward County.

It really bothered me to see Campbell treat the judge's document with that much contempt. Those sixty-two pages represented a considerable effort on the judge's part to make the right decision. Campbell's actions were typical of the attitude he would display in the weeks to come.

My own reaction was one of trying to decide how I was going to "vigorously enforce" this law. I certainly wasn't going to use this court order as the means to pursue a major crackdown on all forms of pornography in the county. For now, it was just As Nasty They Wanna Be that carried the illegality tag, and my office would do all it could to uphold the federal ruling, but I wasn't going to have my deputies spend any extra time on this, nor was I going to assign extra people to the vice squad. We weren't going to use the decision as a reason to routinely check record stores unless there was a specific complaint. If we had to make an arrest as a result of this ruling, then it was very likely a jury would decide whether a violation of this law had occurred. The ruling said that this album was obscene and its sale and distribution banned in Dade, Broward, and Palm Beach Counties. I sincerely hoped I would not have to make any arrests.

The media went crazy. They called and interviewed as many people as they could before press deadline that evening, soliciting opinions from individuals ranging from nationally known lawyer Alan Dershowitz (who called the decision preposterous) to failed Supreme Court nominee Robert Bork (who thought the decision would make Tipper Gore very happy). They interviewed music industry executives who certainly didn't agree with Judge Gonzalez, and the American Civil Liberties Union, which echoed the music industry's feelings. It was an emotional subject and the media was stoking the fire as much as they could.

After this interesting day, I went home as usual and Sharron and I watched the six o'clock news. One of the first individuals shown was a man named Charles Freeman who said he owned a bookstore and also sold cassette tapes. He carried copies of 2 Live Crew's As Nasty As They Wanna Be and would continue selling it from his location in Broward County. I groaned. Only a few hours had passed and someone was openly defying the law. Sorry, Charlie, I said to myself, I have a court order to enforce and intend to do just that. I would decide in the morning how to handle the situation.

Some of my deputies had seen the same news clip and went to Freeman's store on Thirty-First Avenue and Sunrise Boulevard in Fort Lauderdale early the following day. There were television trucks and cameras in front of the store already. One of the officers went in undercover to see if Freeman was, indeed, selling the tape. He was, and my undercover cop bought one. He then called me at the sheriff's office where I was talking to Sam Price, my senior legal advisor and an African-American, who suggested we both go down to the store before Freeman was arrested to make sure everything was done exactly by the book. With camera crews and news reporters already there, it was sure to be a high-profile event and we couldn't afford to make any mistakes.

We arrested Freeman. He was not happy about it, calling me a Communist from Cuba. He told reporters that someone has to stand up and say that the judge's ruling was wrong, that we should never be banned from selling anything in this country. We charged him with the appropriate misdemeanor for selling obscene material, a charge punishable by a maximum sentence of one year in jail and a $1,000 fine. The courts could decide his fate.

Luther Campbell held a news conference promising to give moral, legal, and financial support to anyone selling his record. He said the retailers were the ones who had to take a stand. Everything Campbell did seemed calculated to give him the most publicity he could generate. He knew the media would cover his every move and he counted on it.

A resident of Davie (a town in Broward County) who was spending the summer in New York organized a campaign called "Radio Free Broward" and vowed to mail copies of the record to anyone who wanted it. This individual had also campaigned at one time to be Florida's commissioner of education, advocating prison terms for students who couldn't pass the state's functional literacy test. This whole thing was beginning to get a little crazy.

2 Live Crew performed that night in Miami Beach, reportedly taking some verbal shots, spiced with profanities, at both me and Governor Martinez. They had also scheduled a pair of shows at the Club Futura in Hollywood, which was in Broward County, for Saturday night, vowing to perform pieces from their banned album in the second show. The concert was predicted to be a sellout.

My Organized Crime Division (OCD) handled this case as any other, sending undercover cops into the club with mini tape recorders to collect evidence. An adult not familiar with the rhythms of rap might understand one out of every five words, while a person used to this kind of verbal delivery could hear and discern every word. The noise in the nightclub was deafening, which, when combined with the natural difficulty in understanding the lyrics, made the lyrics somewhat difficult to record in their entirety.

Luther Campbell, Chris Wongwon, and a third band member were booked and then freed without posting bond. Bruce Rogow, their attorney, said the arrests amounted to police harassment, but this was no different than the Freeman case, one of complete contempt for the law. As sheriff, my job was to arrest everyone that I caught breaking the law, not to selectively ignore some people and handcuff others. I didn't arrest them for their profanities against me, either. I've been called every name you can think of over the years: a few more or less didn't make any difference. These men had said on television that they were going to perform pieces from As Nasty As They Wanna Be regardless of the court order. Now they were as arrested as they wanted to be.

Broward County was not the only place where 2 Live Crew was banned from playing. In Texas, record stores were being warned about selling the album. In Huntsville, Alabama, where 2 Live Crew was scheduled to perform on June 16, the city council voted to expand its obscenity ordinance to include live performances. Only 300 tickets had been sold for the concert at an arena that seats 8,000. For some reason, Broward County was singled out for ridicule, but 2 Live Crew was not welcome in these other communities. Broward is where the case was initiated, so I was labeled the "father of censorship." It was a bad rap all the way around, as far as I was concerned.

The case went international. Police in Toronto, Canada warned record store owners about hefty fines and jail time if they sold copies of As Nasty As They Wanna Be. A news team from Tokyo, Japan, showed up in Fort Lauderdale to interview me about the case. One of Florida's U.S. senators, Connie Mack, took issue with Judge Gonzalez's ruling, declaring that words are protected under our freedom of speech. It seemed as if everyone wanted to get in on this act.

The national talk shows had a field day. Nightline and Geraldo Rivera managed to put Luther Campbell and me on their shows to discuss the issue. Campbell also did the Phil Donahue show, which I declined. I only did Rivera's show because he was a friend. The show was a nightmare for Rivera, as Campbell filled the airwaves with four-letter expletives. He directed his rage at me for singling him out because he was black and again said that I wouldn't arrest Andrew Dice Clay since he was white. I calmly replied that I didn't single anyone out, I was merely enforcing a court order that was openly defied. If Andrew Dice Clay's work was declared obscene, I would enforce the ruling in exactly the same manner.

Rivera asked Campbell during one of the breaks to stop using profanity since it would make editing difficult. As Rivera walked away, Campbell said something under his breath about Rivera's heritage and that Rivera was lucky he had agreed to be on the show. I wanted to shout, "Hey Geraldo, did you hear what he said?" but it wasn't worth it.

The shows included a remote telephone interview with a lieutenant from a sheriff's office in Texas, where they were warning record store owners about selling the rap group's album. Campbell went on a tirade, calling the officer, among other things, a racist. The lieutenant replied that the accusation wasn't fair, that Campbell did not know him, that he was, in fact, also an African-American. It was the second time Campbell had unknowingly accused an African-American of being a racist.

Someone wrote to me after the show and asked me how I could resist turning to my left and punching that "foul-mouth idiot" in the face. Really, I was never tempted to do any such thing. I just wanted to get in my side of the story and then go home.

Mail poured in from all over the country. While I was being criticized by the majority of media outlets in South Florida, people in other parts of the United States seemed to be on the side of law and order. I have never received more mail on any issue in my life. The 2 Live Crew fracas had definitely struck a chord. One woman quoted the Bible, saying, "I tell you the truth, no prophet is accepted in his own hometown" (Luke 4:21). She was on the money there. A letter from a black female attorney in Saint Petersburg said she was personally offended by 2 Live Crew's lyrics and music and that it didn't represent black culture at all. A singing group called The Davis Brothers & Sisters commended us for upholding the law. George Will published an article in Newsweek, noting that "America today is capable of terrific intolerance about smoking or toxic waste that threatens trout. But only a deeply confused society is more concerned about protecting lungs than minds, trout than black women. We legislate against smoking in restaurants; singing "Me So Horny" is a constitutional right. Secondary smoke is carcinogenic; celebration of torn vaginas is 'mere words.'"

A woman from Forestburgh, New York, summarized the issue for me when she enclosed a quote from Abraham Lincoln. In 1862, he said, "If I were to read, much less answer, all the attacks made on me, this shop might well be closed for any other business. I do the very best I know - the very best I can; I mean to keep doing so until the end. If the end brings me out all right, what is said against me won't amount to anything. If the end brings me out wrong, ten angels swearing I was right would make no difference."

This is just how I felt and all of these thousands of letters were much appreciated at a time when support for the sheriff's office was thin.

The media continued to explore every aspect. Judge Gonzalez and I were even asked what our favorite music was. For the record, the judge liked the symphony and the opera and had an extensive collection of Pete Seeger and Woody Guthrie records. I liked a lot of different music: classical, country, easy listening, and Middle Eastern music. I even enjoyed listening to a local FM station in the morning that frequently did parodies of me. They were good at them, and they always gave me a laugh.

With all of the attendant publicity that surrounded this case, it was important for me not to lose sight of what it was about. In July, a local writer, John Underwood, noted that his newspaper, The Miami Herald, had published two

articles on the same page that made a bizarre pairing. The first was a columnist's attack on me for ignoring "real" crime and arresting 2 Live Crew on
obscenity charges for performing rap songs that celebrated the brutalization
of women, including slapping the "bitches" around, forcing various forms of
sex on them, "makin' em' bleed," and so forth. On the same page was a story
reporting the opening of the trial of several New York City youths who had cornered a Central Park jogger, slapped her around, and forced sex on her. She
bled so much from being hit with bricks and a lead pipe that her blood vol-
ume was down to about 20 percent. One of the youths said they were just having some fun. This was the so-called "wilding" incident and a dramatic example of the potential influence of the philosophy prevalent in As Nasty As they
Wanna Be.

Perhaps the most thought-provoking letter I received was from an inmate
in a Texas penitentiary who was convicted of rape in 1984. He wrote, "Thank
you for your efforts to prosecute 2 Live Crew. I lowered myself to the standards
of that group's message when I committed my crimes. I hope that you will
never cease to enforce the law in such matters, because you are the last bastion
between innocent victims and men such as I was, who actively lose control of
themselves by partaking of destructive pornography, music, etc."

In August, a three-member, white, Scarsdale, New York, band came to the
same Hollywood club Luther Campbell had played in, Club Futura, bragging
that they were going to perform the same songs 2 Live Crew did when that
band was arrested. One of the members, Timothy Quirk, said he had told
Luther Campbell that he was going to prove whether or not the sheriff of
Broward County would arrest a white band for the same offense. The group,
Too Much Joy, came down on August 10 and performed the songs after a few
obscene Navarro "cheers." I had undercover cops there who recorded the
lyrics and, after the concert was over, arrested the group members. It never was
about race and never will be. If someone crosses the line, I look at the act, not
the color of the person who performed it. Also detained and told to appear in
court was the club owner, Ken Geringer, who was charged with promoting an
obscene act.

A group of individuals bought some advertising space in the Miami
Herald. They wanted to actually publish 2 Live Crew's lyrics so that the public
could judge for themselves what all the fuss was about. When the newspaper

executives found out what the advertisement was going to include, they refused to publish it and returned the group's money. Talk about censorship.

The trials of 2 Live Crew and Charles Freeman were coming up. Freeman's was the first week in October. Jury selection yielded an all-white, six-person jury that the media claimed would have potential difficulty understanding the plight of a black record store owner. Five of the jury members were women. The jury listened to the album, which was played during the proceedings. The defense attorney for Freeman, Bruce Rogow, was concerned that these jurors had no understanding of black culture and would be biased in their view of As Nasty As They Wanna Be. The real issue, of course, was a man deliberately flouting the law who virtually dared us to arrest him. The case went to the jurors for deliberation on October 3 and they spent two hours debating it. When they came back, they returned a guilty verdict. In doing so, they agreed with Judge Gonzalez's opinion that the material was obscene.

Charles Freeman was outraged and blamed the verdict on the color of the jurors. So did Bruce Rogow and Luther Campbell. The newspapers questioned the value of a jury system that could put an all-white jury together for this case. In truth, blacks represented only 8.5 percent of the registered voters in Broward County, from which jury pools are assembled. For the Freeman trial, thirty-five potential jurors were considered, only one of which was black. From this pool, six individuals were chosen.

The 2 Live Crew trial was next. Between the two trials, Vice President Dan Quayle flew into town to stump for Republican candidates for the November 1990 elections. Naturally, he supported the efforts of the sheriff's office, citing our willingness to provide moral leadership.

Bruce Rogow and Luther Campbell both made public pleas for a jury that included more blacks and younger people than the group that judged Charles Freeman. Rogow said he would ask Broward County Judge June L. Johnson to expand the pool of potential jurors to include people that are more likely to understand rap music.

Jury selection took five days. When it was over, there was one black among the four women and two men chosen. The jury consisted of an office clerk, a retired cook, an assistant principal, a retired administrative assistant, a mechanic, and a retired sociology professor. Although none of these individuals described themselves as rap fans, they were all at least familiar with this type of music. Bruce Rogow and the defense team seemed pleased by the choices.

Luther Campbell and company didn't escape the first week of the trial without a blemish. All three members who ended up being charged (the fourth, David Hobbs, was not charged as he did not rap any of the lyrics) strolled in thirty to sixty minutes late on Friday, October 12, leading Judge June Johnson to threaten them with contempt of court if they were late again. The judge then banned people under eighteen years of age from attending the trial.

Judge Johnson was one of the magistrates who had agreed to spend a night in the new Broward County jail when it had opened in 1985. She had also created a stir once when she initially refused to go through the magnetometer as part of court security procedures - she told surprised security officials that she had an eight-foot aura around her and didn't want it disturbed. After a few moments, the guards realized that she was joking, and she eventually went through the machines. When I saw her every so often, I always checked to see if her aura was visible.

The trial itself began on October 16. The prosecution suffered an early setback when Judge Johnson ruled that transcripts our office had made of the tapes from the micro-recorders used that night in Hollywood would not be permitted because they contained comments (exchanges between our undercover officers) that might confuse the jury. That left only the tape recordings themselves, which were difficult to understand because of the noise and the quality of the tapes. Thus, many of the lyrics that had caused the record to be declared obscene would not likely be heard clearly by this jury.

Bruce Rogow contended that 2 Live Crew's performance must be understood in the context of the type of black popular music that had arisen in the last few years. He said that some of the four-letter words reflect exaggeration, parody, and humor, even about delicate subjects such as sexual practices. The words, he pointed out, though crude, can have artistic value when one has an understanding of the lyrics and have, in effect, decoded them.

The defense brought in a Duke University English professor named Henry Gates, an expert on African American culture, who called 2 Live Crew's work a brilliant expression of the black American experience. He went on to describe the art form of "signifying," which he dated back to the sixteenth century. Signifying is a form of rhythmic teasing that is often loaded with lewd remarks and profanity that can be meant as either insults or compliments. It was the way black people could fight against the oppression of their slave masters, he said. Rapping was its contemporary form. In 2 Live Crew's case, the lyrics to made fun of the stereotype that black men are oversexed. The only reaction to have, he said, was to burst out laughing.

That's exactly what the jurors did when the tapes were played or excerpts from the album were recorded for them to hear because of the poor quality of the tapes. One of my deputies, Eugene McCloud, who was undercover at the concert, had to translate and explain what was going on, a process that was embarrassing to him and during which one of the jurors dozed off.

The case closed on October 20. The jury deliberated for about two hours and came back with not guilty verdicts. The jurors claimed to be more disgusted with my office's detective work (because of the garbled tape) then they were with the group's sexually explicit lyrics. They said they found the show to have both artistic and political value and that it was not offensive to community standards. They also said that the sheriff's office shouldn't be wasting its time with this band but should be out tracking down real crime.

This thinking was undoubtedly influenced by the media, even though one juror had told the judge and the court that she would not read any coverage of the event. Still, the verdict wasn't much of a surprise. I did not attend the trial but felt that everyone had done the best they could, given the limitations of the tape. Jack Thompson was upset, although I didn't know why he should be. As an attorney, he should realize that one of the things in life you cannot predict is the finding of a jury.

The lyrics were still considered obscene in Broward County as this verdict did not reverse Judge Gonzalez's ruling. If the member of 2 Live Crew expressed their intention to perform these songs again in Broward County, my deputies would respond accordingly. The law was to be "vigorously enforced." Luther Campbell said he wasn't anxious to play again in this county unless doing so would guarantee I would be impeached as sheriff. The South Florida media would have liked nothing better.

In December, Charles Freeman lost his appeal for a new trial and was fined the maximum $1,000. Broward County Court Judge Paul Backman chose not to impose any jail time (he could have given Freeman up to one year).

Freeman had, at one point during the hearings, shouted a profanity at the judge. His attorney, Bruce Rogow, was less than pleased at the outburst, but the judge didn't let it bother him. He told Freeman that in October, he had received a good old American trial that was fair in every respect. The problem was, he continued, that Freeman didn't like the result. Sour grapes is not the order of the day, the judge added, if you don't like the law, work to change it.

Also in December, the Club Futura in Hollywood closed. The owner, Ken Geringer, blamed it on me, saying that I had made millions for Luther Campbell and became the most talked about sheriff in the United States, while he, Geringer, had lost everything.

Geringer had no one but himself to blame for his club's dwindling attendance. I didn't book his acts. After the New York band had been arrested along with Geringer in August, people stopped showing up.

Also in December, 2 Live Crew pulled more of their usual antics out in California. The band booked a club there that sold out tickets for the show within twenty minutes of offering them for sale. The rappers initially threatened not to take the stage because the crowd wasn't large enough, even though it was a sellout. When they did take the stage, patrons complained and said the show wasn't worth the money they'd paid. People were tiring of this act. This club eventually closed its doors a short time later.

Charles Freeman's store closed in January 1991. He eventually had to sell his stock at reduced prices. He claimed he had attempted to obtain financial assistance from Luther Campbell but was unsuccessful, even though Campbell had promised help back in June. Campbell had no comment. Naturally, Freeman also blamed me for his record store's demise.

Too Much Joy was acquitted by a Broward jury on January 17. The jury found that the lyrics and the performance were not obscene. The state attorney's office then elected to drop charges against Club Futura owner Ken Geringer.

Finally, in May, the Eleventh U.S. Circuit Court of Appeals overturned Judge Gonzalez's original ruling and declared that 2 Live Crew's lyrics were not obscene. The three-judge panel concluded that Judge Gonzalez had used his own standards and not those of the Supreme Court's in reaching his decision. In the end, 2 Live Crew had, so to speak, beaten the rap.

Since so much hinged on the lyrics themselves, now that they've been declared not obscene, I will reprint portions of them for you here as they were written in our original affidavit submitted to Judge Mel Grossman. This way, you can decide for yourself what artistic value they possess.

"Me So Horny"

Chorus

Me so horny (repeated several times)
Sitting at home with my dick all hard
So I got the black book for a freak to call
Picked up the telephone, then dialed the seven digits;
Then I arrived at her house, knocked on the door,
Not having no idea of what the night had in store.
I'm like a dog in heat, I freak without warning,
I have an appetite for sex 'cause me so horny.

Repeat chorus:

Girls always ask me why I fuck so much.
I say, "What's wrong, Baby Doll. with a quick nut?'
'Cause you're the one and ya shouldn't be mad.
I won't tell your momma if you don't tell your dad.
I know he'll be disgusted when he sees your pussy busted
Won't your momma be so mad if she knew I got that ass?
I'm a freak in heat, a dog without warning,
My appetite is sex 'cause me so horny.

"Bad Ass Bitch"

Let's get butt booty naked and do the wild thing
First she took off her panties, snatched off her bra.
I popped the biggest tits I ever saw -
They were big enough to knock a man down,
They were shaped like grapes in my favorite shade of brown
My dick was hard and she was hot like a heater,
By the look of her mouth, she was a dick eater.
I said, "You raggedy bitch, don't play dumb!
Put my dick in your mouth and make this mother fucker cum!"
Ya! Yo! This bitch is on!
Bad Ass Bitch.

"Break It On Down"
When they say 2 Live, your momma gets worried.
When they speak of us, the negatives get mentioned.
But we don't care, thanks for your attention,
An underground sound, taling straight off the street,
That ghetto style with a hard ass beat.
Our explicit lyrics tell it like it is,
If you don't like what I say,
Get the fuck out of here...

"Put Her In the Buck"
Now put her in the buck
(Female sexual groans)
There's only one way to have a good time,
Fuck that pussy and make it mine
Lay a bitch on the bed flat on her back
Throw the legs up high, make the pussy splack
You can put her in the buck by sitting on a sink
Wrap her legs behind you, now take this dick, dick, dick
(Female sexual groans)
Now put her in the buck.
(Female sexual groans)

- From the affadavit filed in February 1990 with Judge Mel Grossman
Now, you be the judge.

Eighteen

Cinema Verite-Cops

IT IS NIGHTTIME IN FORT LAUDERDALE. A TRUCK DRIVER IS ENGAGED IN A DRUG buy with a pusher the police have had under surveillance for some time. The transaction completed, the two criminals are about to part when drug task force agents burst out of a box stowed in the back of a truck. One of the men tries to make a break for it, but he is quickly caught and handcuffed. The truck driver simply gives up. Miranda warnings are read. No bullets are fired.

If this were a scene from the television series, "Miami Vice," the cops would have blown away one or both of the perpetrators in a stylish, slow-motion shoot out, delighting viewers. After the gunfire, one of the cops might have even blown the smoke away from the gun's barrel. This isn't "Miami Vice." Welcome to the world of Fox-TV's "Cops," reality-based television showing police officers - Broward County police officers -as they really are.

When I was a federal narcotics officer in New York, I worked with a man named Ike Wurms. He lived in New Jersey with his wife, Rose, and their three children. When I left to join the Florida Bureau of Law Enforcement in 1968, Wurms was transferred by the feds to Miami, so we continued to see each other and occasionally work together. One of his sons, Jerry, expressed an interest in following in his father's law enforcement footsteps in the late 1970s. He wanted to work with me in the Broward County Sheriff's Office, where I was heading up the Organized Crime Division.

Jerry Wurms passed all the required tests and was getting ready to attend the police academy when he telephoned me with some news. It seems he had grown up in New Jersey with a kid named John Travolta, who had just hit it big in the film Saturday Night Fever, following a successful television stint in the comedy series, Welcome Back, Kotter with Gabe Kaplan. Jerry had received an offer from Travolta to be his manager. It was his one chance to become involved in show business and he decided to go for it, with my blessing, although I was sorry to lose such a promising young police recruit.

Ike eventually retired from the DEA and moved to Los Angeles. I didn't hear from Jerry, although I did see his picture now and again. I remained close to Ike; we were both members of the Association of Former Federal Narcotics Agents, and like many of the other old-timers, we stayed in touch.

Jerry Wurms popped back into the Broward County Sheriff's Office in connection with the Geraldo Rivera special for television "American Vice: The Doping of a Nation," which was to show the real drug problems in the country to counter the images portrayed on shows like Miami Vice. Jerry had parted company with John Travolta but was still plying a show business trade, trying to put together shows for Rivera, with producers Malcolm Barbour and John Langley, that included the Al Capone vault break-in and this show on drugs in America.

Wurms, Barbour, and Langley had gone to several police departments across the country and had done some filming. None of them was overly pleased with the results to date, neither with the action or with the lack of arrests associated with the filmed "busts." Jerry called Ike and asked if he would phone "Uncle Nick" about the Broward County Sheriff's Office participating in the filming. "Uncle Nick's got a reputation for action, maybe there's something filmable there." Ike called me and I told him to have Jerry come in and we could discuss it. There was always something going on in South Florida in the way of narcotics raids and arrests, and I was fairly certain we'd have something for them.

We did. Another officer in our department had worked as a cameraman for Rivera, so the television folks were predisposed to liking us. The producers, Barbour and Langley, seemed like reasonable people as I laid down the guidelines for the filming, mostly for the safety of those behind the cameras. Shooting footage of a real drug raid comes with an obvious downside: the criminals wouldn't be working from the same script. They were unpredictable and I wanted to minimize the risks involved to the bystanders, while still capturing the action of a true-to-life bust.

The case we selected for filming was one close to wrap-up involving a Bahamian drug dealer named Nelson Scott. Scott had been running a significant amount of cocaine out of his house, where he and his family were the only blacks in a white neighborhood. When the first complaints were called in, we had to decide if they were valid or if the motivation for reporting Scott lay elsewhere. The initial investigation turned up nothing other than a white community that was upset because a black family had moved into the area.

Unknown to me at the time was that Scott had been friendly with some of my deputy sheriffs before I'd taken office. The officer who made the initial report misread the situation entirely, although not intentionally. More complaints came in and I assigned the matter to OCD, which built a probable cause case that necessitated surveillance and a raid. We secured a search warrant and took Rivera and the cameras along on the bust, which was a success and led to Scott's arrest. As it turns out, this was the best part of Rivera's show and the only arrest in all of the raids he'd filmed across the country.

At this point, Jerry Wurms decided he wanted to leave show business behind to pursue his first career choice - law enforcement. He asked me for a second chance. I heartily agreed as Jerry had the makings of a good cop. It was probably in his blood; like father, like son.

The Rivera show was my first contact with the television production team of Barbour and Langley, and I was surprised to hear from them only a few weeks after the "American Vice" taping. I met them for lunch and they explained an idea to me they had for a regular television series.

Malcolm Barbour, who was from England, recounted to me the popularity of some British television shows that were cinema verite, true-to-life situations captured on film. The "Most Wanted" concept there developed into America's Most Wanted for U.S. television viewers. Their idea was to take this reality a step further and follow police officers around with cameras to film them live in their daily war against crime. They asked if I was interested in showing America what real police work was all about.

Damn right I was interested. Like many police officers, I was not pleased with the image films, books, and television portrayed of law enforcement officers. Say "cop" and the average American might imagine "Dirty Harry" blowing away ten or fifteen punks a day. Cops in the movies and television shows violated so many people's rights that if those scenes were transferred to real life, the police officers would all be behind bars. As Barbour and Langley talked, it became clear to me that these men were offering me (and my fellow officers) a chance to show cops as they really are. This would not be just about Broward County police officers but about law enforcement officials everywhere.

People needed to understand that at the end of a working shift, these officers face the same problems everyone else does: family disputes, money matters, mortgage payments, credit card debts, health concerns, and the other parts of normal daily lives. We have to perform every day, within the law and without the aura of overaggressiveness in which a cop is viewed as a trigger-happy individual putting notches on his or her gun after each kill.

Barbour and Langley understood this, and I followed my gut instinct to do the taping and see what developed. In agreeing for my department to be filmed in the summer of 1988, I laid down certain conditions.

First, there were to be no re-enactments. The filmmakers had to be honest in their portrayal of my officers and how they really are, on and off the job. I told them, "If we do it right, you show it. If we do it wrong, you show it, too. We all make mistakes, we're not superhuman, and our blemishes should be displayed along with our positive feats."

Second, I didn't want them to concentrate on one specific deputy sheriff. I wanted several people followed and filmed. These are cops, not movie stars, and I didn't want my officers to convince themselves otherwise. Spreading the filming around, I felt, would likely prevent this from happening.

Third, and last, I agreed that the BSO would be the first department filmed, but I wanted assurances that if the series was successful, the producers would go on to other cities and other law enforcement agencies. If the ratings were high and viewers enjoyed this look inside the lives of real cops, a number of other police departments would open their doors. I assured both Barbour and Langley of this and they agreed to limit their filming of Fort Lauderdale to one season. Of course, if the ratings were dismal, I didn't have to worry about the cameras following my officers for too long.

Barbour and Langley agreed to all of my conditions and we had a deal.

They asked about money and I told them that no one was going to receive compensation for this but that I would like a donation from Fox-TV to my youth and victim-assistance programs. All told, Fox-TV would eventually give more than $430,000 to these worthy causes.

The producers went right to work interviewing and selecting deputies to be involved in the filming process. Naturally, they chose Jerry Wurms, their former associate, who, though a rookie, was already demonstrating his abilities as a professional law enforcement officer. (I knew it was in his blood.) Also picked for this unusual duty was Ron Cacciatore, an O.C.D. agent; Vicki Cutcliffe, Leo Callahan's daughter, who was working undercover at the airport; and Jerry's live-in girlfriend, Linda Canada, mother of two and one of our many promising young police officers. Also featured were Sergeant Bob Deak and his county-wide drug task force along with several other deputies. Even I was tapped for a couple of episodes.

Under the blistering summer sun, mobile camera crews joined the daily rigors of police work. Armed with lightweight Betacams, Hollywood West met Hollywood, Florida, and some of the other towns in Broward County. There were no scripts, no narration. All the crews did was film day in, day out, in the squad car, at the office, at a crime scene, at a stakeout, and at home at night. They even filmed me in my bathrobe at home - Nick Navarro as you've never seen him before, I guess. (With any luck, that segment would probably hit the editing floor.)

Their first turns with us produced about fifty hours of raw footage that would be edited down to fifty minutes of film for the series pilot, set to air in January 1989. They captured some great police work, and a few screw-ups, but in all the filming that was done, not one weapon was ever fired. This was what I wanted America to see.

The officers involved had to adjust, naturally, to the presence of cameras. There was a certain tendency to showboat at first, knowing the cameras were rolling, but after a time, real instincts took over and the officers virtually forgot about the cameras being there. The crews' presence was always at the back of their minds, however, as everyone was concerned about doing their jobs by the book and not embarrassing their department.

During early filming, rookie Jerry Wurms once displayed a gun in a way that violated some of our own internal rules and he was chastised, rightly, for it. This was captured on film as it happened. That was the deal, though, warts and all.

Broward County had a mixed reaction to the filming as publicity leaked out about the show. As one might expect, Broward County tourism officials were not enthusiastic about this portrayal of its community as one of the nation's major crime areas. However, the county commission was all for it, noting that all big cities have crime and Cops would publicize Broward County doing something about it - positive publicity, in their opinions. Reactions would be more judgmental after the first episode aired.

Pleased with the editing for the pilot, four additional half-hour episodes were pieced together from additional footage shot in the latter part of 1988. Like it or not, the Fox-TV producers had ripped the veil, and as a result, American television viewers were about to get their first taste of Broward vice as it truly happens. It was a big gamble for FOX, as well as our department, but I liked what I saw of the footage edited for the series and felt that it would be well received.

I had the option to prevent anything that I wished from being aired, but I left intact what Barbour and Langley had done. There was a drug bust involving multiple arrests, the catching of a murder suspect, and a bust at the airport where Deputy Cutcliffe, acting on a tip, stopped a passenger, seemingly at random, and asked him if she could search his bags. His consent led to the discovery of illicit narcotics.

The first episode aired on January 7, 1989. It was a surprising overnight success, with excellent ratings measured in New York, Boston, Washington, Chicago, Dallas, Houston, and Los Angeles, in addition to our own South Florida stations that ran the telecast. Additional episodes were ordered immediately to round out a thirteen week initial season.

Personally, I wasn't surprised. I think people were tired of the car chases and make-believe violence that dominates much of the cop media today. I was proud of our team after the first show, which portrayed us as we are, not violating criminals' rights but instead contributing to a better quality of life in our community. That's what we do day to day. Law enforcement wasn't only about busts but also about service. Cops weren't Dirty Harry loners but real people with families and personal problems. Episode one, to me, was an unqualified success.

The South Florida media was somewhat less enamored. "Cops shows South Florida's ugliest side" ran one newspaper column. Some people interviewed thought the show was brutal, citing a scene where we cleared and leveled a crack house. One person complained that all of the drug dealers in the first episode were black and felt that wasn't realistic. I was called a grandstander by a local television critic who said that I never met a camera angle I didn't like.

The biggest local complaint was the portrayal of Fort Lauderdale as South Florida's "heart of darkness," even as the tourist bureau was trying to lift up Fort Lauderdale's image. We were "working at cross-purposes," critics said. Fort Lauderdale had gone from being the "Sun N' Fun" capital of the world to "Sun N' Gun" country.

I had some news for those people. Fort Lauderdale and Broward County had changed. I know. I worked in South Florida in the late fifties to early sixties when it was nothing but sleepy little towns. A population explosion and a natural interception point for international drug cartels altered the landscape here. My department was on the right track to take the county back through the only means available to us - the law. And that is what Barbour and Langley's cameras captured.

The pilot was followed quickly by the half-hour shows that had already been filmed. Americans continued to watch, most notably in Los Angeles, where the episodes ran for a straight week during television's "sweeps" period, and helped make Fox-TV a part of television history. For the first time in Los Angeles, the second largest television market in the country, an independent station finished first in a prime-time slot for a full week, while competing against the likes of The Cosby Show and Growing Pains, two popular shows on network television. Naturally, Fox-TV was elated.

I received several requests to travel to promote the show. Since I believed in what we were doing and knew the added exposure would be short-lived for Broward County, I took the tour, stopping in major cities to give interviews and talk about the show. I re-emphasized the fact that we were not television stars but, instead, hard-working police officers trying to bring crime under control. No one was a celebrity, especially me. I had been a cop for thirty years and I will always be a cop, not a television personality.

We did not anticipate the avalanche of mail that poured into the Broward County Sheriff's Office as a result of this show. Fan letters are quite uncom-

mon for police officers or departments to get, but the word from the public
was overwhelmingly positive. Typical of the letters we received are a couple of
paragraphs from a woman who lives in Newport News, Virginia:

Sometimes the programs are funny and sometimes they are quite sad, but
always they are most fascinating. It is refreshing to see real police persons in
action as opposed to the phony police programs that are on weekly.

To all of you who put your lives on the line every day, and who show you
truly care about your fellow man, you are to be commended for your profes-
sionalism and for allowing us, the public, to see your department in action.

We were accomplishing the objective we'd initially set, that of trying to
bring the community and the police closer together in the war against crime.
We can't really do it without each other, and our best chance for success lies
in a successful merger. I hoped that the people would realize that the type of
law enforcement we practiced in Broward County was likely used in their own
hometowns, too. I felt as if we were bridging a gap with this show.

A few people were upset about an Everglades segment. To the masses, the
Everglades is simply a national park of immense value for the natural flora and
fauna that flourish there, but it is also the drop shipment point of choice for
drug smugglers. On any given evening, amid the swamps of the Everglades,
one can find alligators, snakes, smugglers, and crazy cops. It's unfortunate, but
true. We don't disturb that area except for laying traps for incoming contraband. One of my hopes for this show was that the criminal element would tune
in to see what we were doing and decide to go somewhere else. If we discour-
aged just one smuggler, the show would be a success.

The Cops episodes provided compelling drama for the viewer. No, we
weren't firing any guns, but we had some lengthy and riveting foot races, elaborate crack stings, random seizures at the airport, and assaults on known crack
houses. The camera also went along after hours with us, to our homes, into
our personal lives. Ron Cacciatore was seen arguing with his wife, for whom
the long hours of the job had taken their toll. Jerry Wurms actually proposed
on camera to Deputy Linda Canada and audiences roared their approval.

I said I didn't want stars, only cops, but inevitably the celebrity was hard for
some of the officers to keep at bay. Linda Canada, who could have chosen a
modeling career rather than law enforcement, was naturally photogenic and
was featured in issues of People, USA Today, and T.V. Guide. Staff from

Entertainment Tonight followed her around with cameras. The interviews were a distraction, but she was pleased with the episodes in which she was filmed. She told reporters that Fox-TV had done an admirable job portraying life on the streets for the average cop. It helped people to see what cops really do and it was far from the images of a cop sitting in a doughnut shop, never available when really needed.

Jerry Wurms, whose continued improvement during his rookie year earned him a promotion to deputy, was somewhat disappointed that more of the sensitive side of police work wasn't portrayed, but he was also in a better position to understand Fox's choices of what to televise. As a former television employee, he knew that ratings still go up based on action. Even if routine is more true to life, a half-hour of filming police doing paperwork or sitting in a surveillance car was not going to interest anyone.

The question of an individual's right to privacy was also raised by the show. A search warrant covers the police's actions, of course, but doesn't extend beyond that. We were going on busts and raids with cameras in the background, so each of the individuals arrested was given a release to sign stating that his or her image could be used. To my knowledge, no one refused to sign it. If someone had, Barbour and Langley wouldn't use the piece or, if it was otherwise useful for the program, they would digitize the person's face so you couldn't identify him or her. The American Civil Liberties Union was not very happy with all of this and predicted there would be a number of mistrials as a result once the cases went to court. The predicted mistrials didn't happen.

This show aired long before the Rodney King tapes or the O.J. Simpson freeway chase, where videotapes were seen as admissible evidence. Still, in 1988 and 1989, we didn't have a problem with an accused's rights. Most of the evidence we had was solid before the bust was ever carried out. We didn't even attempt to introduce the television show footage in court.

The local media continued to give us so-so reviews about our police work. One cartoon ran in the Fort Lauderdale Sun-Sentinel showing a man with movie-star looks saying to a BSO recruiting officer, "Hey, doll, I'm applying for Sheriff Navarro's elite crack cocaine task force." The recruiting officer asks, "Qualifications?" The man replies, "Walk-on in 'Cagney and Lacey', stunt double in 'Police Academy IV', personal friend of Clint Eastwood's." The officer says, "You're hired. Report immediately to makeup and wardrobe." Obviously, these folks had missed my message that Cops was getting away from the old television image of police officers

In May 1989, Fox-TV bid goodbye to Broward County. It would take a few of the deputies some time to adjust to having no cameras pointed at them, but it was best for the department. We had done our bit. The producers were off to Portland, Oregon, while crime continued in Broward County and we continued to rein it in. At the same time, the press ran a story about all my travel time and wondered who was running the department. Inferred, of course, was that taxpayer dollars were likely paying for the trips. Buried in the story was the notation that Fox-TV picked up the expenses of any trip promoting Cops. Virtually all the rest of my travel, other than vacations, was to attend task force gatherings and other police-related business. These trips promoted Broward County and allowed me to recruit better personnel, attract state and federal grant money, and be a public relations person for the county. I didn't think much about the story at the time, but it was the beginning of a four-year-long media blitz of inference and supposition that I had interests other than in law enforcement and the well-being of the law-abiding citizens of Broward County.

Fort Lauderdale's Chief Joe Gerwens was openly critical of the show Cops and his comments were presented in full for people to read. He claimed that "most law enforcement professionals find this kind of show inaccurate, and even offensive." I'm not sure who he meant besides himself, because the show was endorsed by both the American Federation of Police and the National Association of Chiefs of Police with high praise, not to mention the heavy load of positive mail we'd received from law enforcement people around the country.

Cops received an Emmy nomination for the best information series on television, an honor that Fox-TV sincerely enjoyed. It started as an interesting idea and blossomed into a show that took off on its own and spawned numerous spin-offs of new "reality-based" television shows. Cops has continued to do well and a number of police departments have participated. From the standpoint of showing people what real cop life is like, the series is an unparalleled triumph. I will always be proud to have my name associated with it.

Nineteen

Nick-Picking

P UBLICITY HAS ALWAYS MANAGED TO FIND ME. BACK IN THE MID-1970S, WHEN Sheriff Ed Stack asked me to answer reporters' questions about a particular investigation or procedure, I had no idea what a powerful medium the press could be. In those early media days, newspaper and television reporters sought me out, knowing that my Organized Crime Division was newsworthy.

In the latter part of the 1980s, the media interest changed from positive to negative. My unlimited accessibility, which I had always been proud of, was turned against me by the same people for whom I had made good copy in the past. Suddenly I was a grandstander, a showboater who couldn't read his name in print often enough. The reporting turned vicious.

What happened? Throughout my entire career, I was focused on one thing only: proper law enforcement. That never changed. What did change was the amount of exposure my career received. As sheriff of Broward County, I had a higher profile than at any time since I went through the police academy in 1959. With that territory came significant outside scrutiny. I understood and welcomed it. I had nothing to hide. There was a natural increase in the number of stories bearing my name.

In my first term of office (1985-88), I received some criticism over my handling of the Broward courthouse security scare following a shooting inside

another courthouse in the Florida panhandle. Some of that criticism was jus-
tified.

It was following my overwhelming victory at the polls in 1988 that the stories began to constantly focus on any negative aspect of the Broward County
Sheriff's Office that could be found or, worse, implied. I called this process of
media coverage "Nick-picking" for obvious reasons. Somehow, somewhere, I
had touched the sacred cow and offended someone in high places. The reporters never looked back in a relentless drive to place me in the worst possible light.

Throughout this ordeal, I had to maintain and build on our law enforcement successes. The people liked what they saw in the Broward County
Sheriff's Office, and maybe it was this popularity that caused the news media
to react. Whatever it was, "Nick-picking" was in style.

Politics is, largely, a game of insiders. My predecessors in the Broward
County Sheriff's Office, particularly Ed Stack and Bob Butterworth, were very
effective at this type of backslapping. At times, law enforcement actions were
dictated by political rather than practical considerations. To a lesser extent,
George Brescher wore the political hat, too, although he was much less flam-
boyant than the others.

I could never play the game. What's more, I didn't aspire to learn how to
do it and wasn't interested in whether a program was politically correct or not.
When considering a program, my main question always was, "will it help somebody?" If the answer was yes and the Broward County Sheriff's Office could
afford it, we implemented the program. Politics was not allowed in as a factor
in the equation.

This was not a popular stance and was viewed with disdain by even my own
Republican Party. I didn't care. I answered to the people who elected me, not
to party officials.

This led to another problem: the debate about the sheriff's office being an
elected position. The news media and the political insiders, primarily
Democrats, wanted the sheriff's post to be appointed, not elected. This
became clear to me as far back as 1984, in my first run for office. It seemed
the political destiny of the office of sheriff to be appointed, leaving the sheriff
to answer to the county manager and commissioners instead of the people. If
George Brescher had been re-elected in 1984, it is more than likely the sheriff would have been appointed in 1988.

I was an inconvenience in this preordained process. In 1984, I received support from Republicans and Democrats alike. They gave me a mandate. I was the first career police officer ever installed as sheriff and people wanted to see results. Our citizens should always have this option. Freedom of choice is what this country was founded on. If the people didn't like what I was doing, then they could dump me in 1988. If the position became an appointed one, the people's voice would be silenced.

My 1984 election changed the plot. Initially, I was still popular with the press. I had been, after all, the underdog in the campaign, something the media feasts on. My victory was a statement from the people and, as such, good copy that sold newspapers, but the underlying resentment remained and a "waiting game" of sorts began.

My 1988 landslide victory sent a message the media and the political folks didn't want to hear: the citizens of the county were happy with their sheriff's office. The 1988 reelection was an affirmation that the people had made the right choice in 1984. That proclamation must have sent shivers down the backs of those that hadn't expected a Cuban immigrant with a pronounced accent to be successful. It was clearly time for a new type of war to be waged if control of the sheriff's office was to be wrested from me.

Since I do not really understand politics all that well, I cannot explain the media's link with political insiders or why the media chose to be the platform for the negative press campaign that followed the 1988 election. While I was always willing to talk to reporters and answer their questions, I didn't frequent the watering holes where both the media and politicians could often be found. I wasn't that type of insider in any case. Naively, I believed the media was supposed to tell both sides of a story objectively. Opinion was to be saved for the editorial page.

In the four years from 1988 to 1992, it was clear the editorializing had spread to much more of the newspaper than just the op-ed section. Sometimes the power of the pen lies not in what is written, but in that which is omitted. Stories that slant by omission are the cruelest kind of trick to play on readers. The reporter is not actually lying he or she is simply not telling the entire story. This allows readers to take the path toward a wrong conclusion, cleverly pushed forward by the tone of the written word. Nothing slanderous. Nothing factually incorrect. Today, this is know as "spin." I call it manipulation.

The media seized on any bit of news that could be construed as negative. Any time our Internal Affairs department conducted an investigation, the media was there, hoping for something to report. During my tenure, only one police officer under my direct command was indicted, and the charge was not police-related, but corruption makes good print and an allegation is better than nothing if you're trying to make a point. The opportunity to exploit a story came unexpectedly with the drug bust involving Nelson Scott, filmed by Geraldo Rivera's crew. Scott, during his arrest proceedings, inferred that there was widespread corruption within the department. His defense attorney focused on these groundless accusations as did, to my disappointment, our own prosecutors.

While I was certain that there was no corruption within the department, we conducted our usual investigation and turned up only a deputy who had committed the "crime" of being a lousy police officer, unable to recognize a drug dealer like Scott when he should have.

Scott's insistence, combined with the word of another deputy who had been fired, provoked an unprecedented investigation into the Broward County Sheriff's Office that not only was totally unjustified but also would cost the Broward County taxpayers a small fortune. The witch hunt had begun.

Most stories about the Broward County Sheriff's Office during that time included a note in the first paragraph along the lines of "currently being investigated," which meant absolutely nothing. But reading it day after day, week after week, month after month, even the most trusting citizen in Broward County would begin to wonder if the story wasn't true.

Our office sent boxes and boxes of files and papers to the federal investigative team. Team members combed through every conceivable record for six long years. They found nothing. It was "Nick-picking" to the highest degree, but they couldn't find anything because there was nothing to find. We ran our departments with the goal of maintaining the highest possible ethical standards. The results of the investigation proved that. Meanwhile, the media had what it wanted: a tag line to play over and over again: "the Broward County Sheriff's Office, currently under a corruption investigation."

There was some remorse. A Fort Lauderdale Sun Sentinel reporter named Jonathon King wrote an article in July 1993 saying, "One of the sorriest outcomes of the story I wrote in 1987 is that for six years taxpayers have been billed for federal investigations of the BSO which were spin-offs of the Scott case. Nothing has come of these investigations. No proof of corruption or pay-offs or protections. Nelson Scott liked to talk, but someone should have recognized that's all it was: talk."

Nick-picking wasn't confined to the corruption investigation. My budget was a constant newspaper fixture. It had grown significantly during my tenure. However, a substantial portion of the increase was not within my control. When more jail space was commanded, we had to build and maintain it, all within my budget. We had added numerous towns to our BSO jurisdiction and the cost of providing services to them came out of my budget. What wasn't reported was that we were paid by each district that hired us, generating revenue of around $30 million dollars, but this revenue didn't go to my departments; it went to the county's general fund, and my budget showed only expenses.

I hear criticism about police officers, that we have the right to take away liberties, put handcuffs on them, send them to jail. That's a lot of power and responsibility, and we have to answer to a set of laws that govern the procedures for conducting this process. The public expects us to perform at a super-human level and we try our best.

In law enforcement, we police ourselves. We have drug tests, we have polygraphs, we have Internal Affairs units. We evaluate outside complaints and do what we can to clean up the ranks if needed. Nothing like this is done in the newsroom. How do we know what type of influence a writer is under when he or she reports a story? Retractions are never made, acknowledgment of factual mistakes or omissions rarely done, and no apologies made if a life or two is ruined in the interest of a free press.

When the power of the press is abused, we must be emphatic in our protest that the media police itself better. The type of handcuffs they can shackle people with can't be seen, but that doesn't mean they aren't just as effective as metal handcuffs. The worry about a police state in this country is unfounded, but by giving the press unlimited rights, are we creating something far worse? The ability of a few people to shape how we think and react to a given subject is a scary thought, if that privilege is abused. The news media has lost its objectivity. I understand there is competition for the public's attention from electronic media. I know headlines sell, but when the headlines are designed to do more than sell, to alter the perception of the people, to make myth a reality simply by repeating it often enough, we have a corruption that must be stopped.

By the time 2 Live Crew showed up, the Broward public was reading that our office was under investigation, that our budget was out of control, and that I was eager for publicity of any kind. The news media always seemed to know when I was out of town so that they could break some story or other and write, "Nick Navarro could not be reached because he was out of town." The implication, of course, was that the citizens of Broward County had elected an absentee sheriff. The truth was that most of my trips were county-related and necessary to function on the number of tasks forces I chaired or worked on.

The 2 Live Crew affair gave the media one more tangent to run with - Nick Navarro, trampler of human rights. I was against the First Amendment; I was against free speech; I was a censor; I was against rap music; I was anti-minority.

Depicting me as being against human rights was the unkindest cut of all. I had left a country where human rights carried far less meaning than in the United States. I was proud to obtain my American citizenship. I was living proof that an immigrant, a minority, could make it to the top of my profession, and I did it as a protector of human rights, not a violator. The law-abiding citizens of Broward County were the people most important to me. Yet the Miami Herald ran an advertisement about the sale of a T-shirt that said, on the front, "See Nick Censor, See Nick Arrest, See Nick Lose Election" and, on the back, "Don't Be a Nick." This same newspaper, however, would not print the song lyrics from the 2 Live Crew album that a Broward judge had found obscene. There was only one view that this newspaper wanted to portray: that I wanted to dictate to people what they could buy in record stores.

That campaign was very effective. Day after day, new stories surfaced mentioning corruption, censorship, and higher property taxes to pay for the sheriff's office. Attention also focused on the number of employees in the sheriff's office who were related.

Every law enforcement agency I know encourages relatives of officers to join the police ranks. It's often a tradition to have several generations of a family in the police force. This tradition wasn't unique to our office. In many police agencies all over the country, fathers and sons, husbands and wives, work within the same arena. The only constraint was that one relative couldn't supervise another.

Frankly, we encouraged this type of hiring as long as the relative was qualified. Many police officers have trouble with their home lives. Family members don't understand what it's like to put one's life on the line every day. The long hours and the stress take their toll and divorces are common. When a spouse joined the force, it often improved at-home relationships. There was a clearer understanding of the pressures of the job and an empathizing that would otherwise not have been present in the relationship.

In our office, I had hired Leo Callahan early on. Leo was a good, capable officer who I needed in a position of importance to help run the office. He had two daughters, both of whom were on the force, both of whom were excellent police officers. The two women had met their husbands in law enforcement and both of Leo's sons-in-law worked here as well. My second in command, Ed Werder, was not the only Werder family member working for the BSO. His wife worked in the detention department. I was the only one who could not have relatives in the office. My wife, Sharron, was working for former Sheriff Ed Stack when I met her.

All of this was portrayed as a department that returned favors with jobs. The inference was that these individuals wouldn't have been hired if they didn't have "connections." Over and over again, the media painted a picture of the sheriff's office as one big family-related group. This was nonsense. In fact, I had the opposite reputation with the political bigwigs - that I wouldn't trade favors with anyone when it came to law enforcement. But media perception was becoming reality in the minds of the public.

While my budget and salary were prime focal points, the political power base of county commissioners received no such attention. Intrepid reporters would have had a story of some interest if they had looked at the numbers.

My salary was set by Tallahassee. In 1992, I was paid $98,000 to supervise some 3,200 personnel. County commissioners were paid $55,000 a year in 1992, well above the going rate for this position around the state. There are seven of them for a total salary of $385,000. At the time there were 4,500 employees in the county. Somehow this math doesn't add up. Commissioners nearly always voted themselves a raise every year, which is likely how the salaries grew out of balance. It sounded like a good story, but it isn't one that was written as long as I was in office.

In 1990, the media ran a report on my community involvement staff. This staff was a fulfillment of a campaign promise. The people employed in this unit provided information on crime prevention, services for the elderly and children, neighborhood improvement programs, and similar ideas. The purpose was to forge a positive link between officer and citizen.

This unit was depicted as a "slick publicity machine" for me. The article indicated that the shcriff held the most powerful political office in the country. The implication was that I was making it even stronger, feeding a hidden political goal.

What was my goal: To be governor? Senator? President? No one, especially the cynical media, can accept that one seeks a political post simply because he or she wants to perform in that job and only that job.

If anyone was to blame for the amount of media attention I received, it would have to be the fourth estate itself. The media dictated the column inches I would receive every day, long after I stopped talking to certain reporters who never reported what I said anyway.

The best example of this was an incident associated with my and Sharron's attendance at a fund-raiser for "Ducks Unlimited." One of the auction items was a pig, with yellow and brown stripes, who would be held on a farm for a couple of months, fattened up, killed, dressed and ready for the barbecue. Well, Sharron and I are both animal lovers and that pig looked too cute to be served up as a family dinner. We bid on it, and won, at the cost of $350. Instead of packing the pig off to the farm, we took him home.

We had a travel container that we'd used for our pets and we put some paper down in it for the pig. At about 1:00 A.M., Sharron suggested that the pig may have to do his necessities and a walk was in order. I took the pig out back, where our house borders the Middle River in Fort Lauderdale, and let him go. I figured he wouldn't head for the water and there was no other place for the little guy to go.

So what does did do? He headed straight for the water and dove in. We both thought for a few moments that he'd drowned, but suddenly we saw him, swimming like Mark Spitz down the river. I was worried about him because of the lengthy sea wall. Where would he get out of the water?

I retrieved a flashlight and we started looking for him, but he was long gone. We got the car out and drove down to the end of the street to see if he had somehow come ashore. No pig. I called our police dispatcher to put a call in to the woman in charge of our animal unit. She came on the line and said she thought the pig was probably still in the vicinity. Just as she said this, the pig appeared in my headlights. He let me get close, then took off again. By now, the dispatch calls had been picked up by several area Fort Lauderdale police cars, which surrounded me, offering to help. I suppose crime could have run rampant that night with half of Fort Lauderdale's force looking for a pig.

We searched until 6:30 A.M. when a jogger finally alerted us to the pig's location. A couple of police officers used a net to capture the little guy and we had him back. It was Monday morning and, by a strange coincidence, we were having the house tented that day for termite extermination. We were booked into a local hotel that night. What to do with the pig?

Sharron took it to her real estate office on a leash while I called Bob Gill, the proprietor of the hotel. He gave me permission to bring the pig in as long as I did it as unobtrusively as possible, since pets weren't normally allowed. In view of the circumstances, he said, we could make an exception that night.

The pig spent the night in a Fort Lauderdale hotel with us. The next day, Tuesday, we started getting phone calls from the news media, which had somehow stumbled onto this non-story.

We were never looking for any publicity, simply trying to save an animal from a barbecue spit. Suddenly, the office wanted to have a name contest ("Hambo" won). The Fort Lauderdale police then stole the pig in honor of our annual fundraising event called the "Pig Bowl." Instead of being a modest human interest story, there were pictures of me holding the pig, the football game received more attention than ever, and all of the publicity was attributed to my love for the camera.

While my office was roundly criticized by the local media, we were well known and respected around the globe as one of the world's premier law enforcement agencies. Rather than take pride in that, our local media reported it as a waste of local taxpayer money when a domestic or international police agency sent a representative to South Florida for training by our staff. This training never cost us a dime; the other agency paid for it, and we received a tremendous amount of information about what these agencies were doing that we might apply to our own law enforcement techniques.

I compare the situation to a kid whom the rest of the neighborhood parents covet because they often see him mowing the lawn, taking out the trash, and performing other chores. At home, though, his own parents aren't satisfied. The kid didn't cut the lawn right or didn't take the trash out as often as he should. He is criticized far more at home while the rest of the neighborhood is saying, "I wish my kid was like that."

A source at one of the local newspapers told me that by 1991, a bounty system of sorts had been set up for news articles about me. Extra money would be paid for any article that provided negative information about either me or the Broward County Sheriff's Office. We sent press releases that were never printed, stories that were never told. We had to write columns in smaller local publications to tell the citizens of Broward County what we were doing. It was a travesty.

The culmination of all the bad press occurred in 1991 when our officers raided a bar frequented by homosexuals. The raid was done as a result of undercover police work that turned up illicit drug dealing. All of it was strictly routine, but because it was a bar that catered to gays, the media (and the local gay community) latched on to the story.

We had investigated two establishments, Club 21 in Pembroke Park and Copa Cabaret near Port Evergaldes, as a result of an anonymous tip. When the investigation was completed, the raid was planned and conducted as any raid would have been. Illegal aliens were discovered, as were illegal firearms and underage patrons. We handled these crime "spin-offs" as we do in any raid. We made arrests and confiscations.

This raid was not, apparently, a politically correct thing to do, but my job isn't to sort out political correctness. I could have avoided negative publicity by not conducting the raid, but this was not my practice. I treat everyone the same.

As expected, there was unlimited news about the raid, all of it negative. This, combined with the avalanche of coverage associated with the budget, the corruption investigation, family members in the department and the amount of publicity I apparently sought, was all for one purpose - to get rid of Nick Navarro. It was such an effective campaign that I had no idea who I was reading about in the papers. The name in the article was Nick Navarro, but the thoughts, motivations, intentions, and aspirations of the man they wrote about weren't mine. They belonged to a character the media created for its own devices. How could I fight something like that? I was trained to deal with law-breakers, not muckrakers, and I was clearly overmatched.

I did the only thing I could do; I kept doing the job I was elected and paid to do. Throughout the media ordeal, the thing that kept me going day after day was the knowledge that we were making this a better community to live in. I believe most of the people knew that, despite what was printed. I was not a political puppet. I was not seeking a higher political post. I ran an ethical office, and more importantly, I was slowing down the criminal element in Broward County.

The media, however, was to create one final spin, revolving around the case of Jeffrey and Kathy Willets.

Twenty

The Nympho Defense

IN 1991, THE YEAR THE BERLIN WALL FINALLY CAME DOWN, THE BIGGEST STORY in South Florida wasn't the global demise of communism. Instead, the local news media turned its frenzied eye on the fall of Broward Sheriff's Deputy Jeffrey Willets. With Manuel Noriega on trial in Dade County, most of the interest centered on our Broward county court system as one of the more bizarre cases I've been associated with was winding its way through the legal system's maze.

It began with a newspaper advertisement in the Fort Lauderdale *Sun-Sentinel:*

> Frosted Blond. Great tan, hot body, very sexual, turquoise eyes, romantic and sensual, seeking generous, affluent executive male, for day/evening interludes. Fun loving & hot. Enclose business card. Postal Center USA, 8209 N.W. Pine Island Road, Tamarac, 33321 Suite 217.

Tamarac is a small town west of Fort Lauderdale in Broward County, and it was there that Jeffrey Willets was employed as a deputy in the Tamarac police office. Tamarac was one of several Broward County towns that had contracted the Broward County Sheriff's Office to provide police services for its community. Willets had been with the Tamarac police office since 1982. The BSO assumed control in 1989. No information was found that would disqualify him, so Willets and several of his fellow Tamarac police officers were officially sworn in as Broward Sheriff's deputies.

In July 1991, a call was placed to the Tamarac police substation reporting that one of our deputies had left a threatening message on an individual's answering machine. The message was a warning to the person to stay away from Willets's wife, Kathy. The man reporting this incident said he had answered the advertisement (detailed above), had sex with the woman, and continued to see her afterwards, by mutual consent. Her husband had apparently found out about it and left the warning on the man's answering machine.

The Tamarac office contacted our Internal Affairs division since this case apparently involved a police officer and his wife. Internal Affairs in turn involved our Organized Crime Division since prostitution appeared to be involved. The informant who had called in about the threatening message gave us other details to work with, namely that Kathy apparently engaged her customers with the full knowledge of her husband. Further, it appeared that Willets also watched his wife's affairs from the bedroom closet.

A check of his recent work record revealed nothing substantial, but there was a notation about a lack of initiative on Jeffrey's part with little or no participation in arrests, crime scenes, interrogations, or even traffic tickets. Much of his time, it seemed, was being spent at home. With the information provided by the informant and a confirmation that the voice on the man's answering machine tape was definitely Willets's, we now knew why he was such a homebody.

We had enough information to show probable cause and a search warrant was obtained. Deputies went to the Willets household on a Tuesday evening in July 1991. They found more than they bargained for as one of Kathy's encounters had just been completed and the customer was caught sans pants when deputies entered the house. In the kitchen was a card file of customers' names and a pile of unanswered mail. In the bedroom was an appointment book listing individual clients along with a few other details: how much they paid (from $50 to $150 per hour), what they did, and how well they did it. Several entries were followed by the one word: "Watched."

In a briefcase found in his squad car, Jeffrey Willets had a copy of the advertisement that included a 900 phone number, which gave this recording:

"This is Julie. I'm everything my ad says and much, much more. I'm 32,

5'4," 115 pounds, 36E - 23 - 32. I don't smoke or anything like that. I'm a very nice, nice person. Send a business card to the P.O. box and I look forward to talking or maybe getting together. And, by the way, I am very hot."

It seemed that one of our deputies was also a part-time pimp. Based on the entries and fees found in the appointment book, Willets was adding $2,000 per week to his paycheck with his wife's activities.

When a deputy makes an arrest, it is often the satisfying culmination of a lot of hard work, the arrest being an end to the labor-intensive process of putting together a case. But the arrest of Jeffrey Willets that evening was unsettling for several reasons. It isn't often that a uniformed police officer is the subject of a warrant, and any arrest involving a fellow deputy is difficult to accept. This was much more than a straightforward "cop involved with prostitution" case, since it concerned an officer turned voyeur who was making the arrangements for his wife. This case had all the makings of an event the media would publicize heavily, and even our office wasn't ready for what followed.

Kathy apparently had entertained at least fifty clients, including executives, attorneys, and other professionals. The bedroom had been decorated and included a fireplace, small bottles of champagne, and an assortment of candles. Willets had taken notes while inside the closet and also filmed a few sessions. Our informant had told us that Willets had fallen asleep in the closet one night during one of Kathy's encounters and began snoring so loudly it scared the customer right out of the house.

The notes provided small details: 5/27, Gary, $150, 2 times, good; 5/31, Steve, talked too much; 6/9, Paul, $150, 2 times, almost caught. No wonder Jeffrey was falling asleep. Working as a police officer by day and videotaping his wife at night made for very few hours of sleep.

The Willetses had three children, two from their own marriage and one from an earlier marriage of Jeffrey's. All three children were living in the house. What the youngsters knew about their parents' home business was anyone's guess at that point. Jeffrey was taken to the Tamarac office and charged with living on the earnings of a prostitute, suspended with pay pending further investigation, booked at the Broward County Jail, and released on $1,000 bail. Kathy was not arrested that evening. It should have been a routine case, other than the detail that it involved a police officer.

Enter attorney Ellis Rubin.

Someone had put the Willetes in touch with this high-profile Dade County attorney. Rubin had a reputation for constructing novel defenses for his clients and he announced yet another original idea at the press conference he arranged three days after Jeffrey's arrest. Nymphomania, Rubin proclaimed, would be the cornerstone of his defense of the Tamarac deputy. "What we're going to do," Rubin told reporters, who were just warming up to this case, "is turn the courtroom into a classroom. We're going to learn about nymphomania and surrogate sex." He went on to say that he would provide medical testimony to the effect that Kathy Willets suffered from this disease, which gave her an uncontrollable desire to have sex.

Rubin contended that what her husband was doing by providing her people to have sex with was a therapeutic way of treating the disease. Displaying copies of the books Disorders of Sexual Desire and The Female Orgasm, Rubin said that the Broward County Sheriff's Office was trying to make a case against Jeffrey because of his wife's compulsion. He also accused me specifically of leaking information to the media to sensationalize the case and win it in the newspapers.

Rubin obviously had not been paying attention to the papers lately. I had been taking a consistent beating from the press, especially in the case of 2 Live Crew, and the last thing I or the BSO wanted was any press on the arrest of one of our own deputies.

I had to admit the nymphomania defense was unique. It hadn't occurred to me that it could be a disease and that Kathy Willets may have been a willing participant in the entire affair because she was unable to control her sexual urges, but it didn't answer every question.

Why, for example, were the Willetses charging her sexual partners for their encounters with Kathy if they were just a part of her therapy? Why would Jeffrey hide in a closet and not only take notes but also videotape the sessions? What form of therapy was that?

Well, Rubin would have time to work on the balance of his defense. What interested us more at this press conference was that Kathy Willets had changed her story about Tuesday night's search, saying that she only had a gentleman visitor over to talk, that there were about twenty officers banging down her door, that an officer had held a gun to her head and ransacked the house without telling her anything.

Actually, there were seven male and two female police officers involved in the search, which was done as neatly and methodically as possible. No one held a gun to Kathy Willets's head. It was the gentleman himself that advised us he'd just had sex with Kathy and showed us the $150 he'd left on her dresser.

The next couple of days, investigators pieced together a list of names of Kathy Willets's sexual partners who had paid for the privilege. Culling information from the appointment book, letters, business cards, and Jeffrey Willets's notes, we came up with a list of about 150 names that included, unfortunately, a prominent local politician. If this information became public record, which I felt certain it would be, this individual was going to suffer miserably in the press. There appeared to be irrefutable proof, based on all of this material, that Kathy Willets had certainly been trading sex for money for the past several months.

On the day warrants were issued charging Kathy with four different counts of prostitution, she and her husband had an argument outside a Fort Lauderdale office, during the course of which Jeffrey injured his back. Neither of them cooperated with the officers who were called to the scene; in fact, Kathy treated the officers to a lengthy profane discourse. Ellis Rubin told the media that Kathy would surrender the next day.

Reporters, however, were focused on the list. They were anxious (naturally) to get their hands on it. Our office refused to release it. The list was evidence at this point, but not public record. Inevitably, however, the name of the prominent politician was secured by the media.

It was Fort Lauderdale Vice Mayor Doug Danziger, who owned an insurance business in northeast Fort Lauderdale. He had been a crusader of sorts, campaigning for family values and against establishments like nude bars. Naturally, Danziger denied any association with Kathy Willets, but the press wouldn't accept that story. The Fort Lauderdale Sun-Sentinel immediately called for Danziger's resignation, saying it would be in the best interests of the city. The newspaper got its wish - Danziger resigned on July 29 - less than a week after Jeffrey Willets's arrest.

The Danziger connection was yet another bizarre piece of this increasingly weird case that was taking on a life of his own. It was now front-page material, pushing the historic Bush-Gorbachev accords off the top of the headlines. A crew from the tabloid television show A Current Affair showed up to question the mayor about Danziger's resignation. Danziger denied the allegations, citing personal reasons for his resignation.

Kathy Willets surrendered as Rubin had promised and was booked at the Broward County jail on four counts of prostitution. The whole process took twenty-five minutes and she was freed on $2,000 bail. Any other case of this size would have gone unnoticed and unreported, but Kathy was photographed going through the jail metal detector.

She was potentially facing sixty days in jail and a $500 fine for each count if convicted of the four misdemeanors. Jeffrey faced a stiffer sentence of a $5,000 fine and up to five years in prison. He had accompanied Kathy to the booking. While Kathy declined to talk, Jeffrey said he would be willing to speak after his trial where, he told reporters, everything would come out, meaning the names on the infamous list.

The press found our original tipster, a fifty-four year old man from the Broward County town of Weston named Foster McAllester. He told reporters essentially what he had first told us, namely, that he had been emotionally involved with Kathy Willets, but he declined to discuss the case further with them and referred the press to our office. We were continuing our investigation and had nothing more to say.

The state attorney's office had drafted a plea bargain deal for both Willetses, and was ready to proceed with its offer when this case took an ever farther turn off the normal path. A reporter from the television show Inside Edition, Steve Wilson, alleged that Ellis Rubin's son Guy offered to sell him the videotape that showed Kathy Willets having sex with the now former vice mayor, Doug Danziger. Wilson said he viewed the tape, which contained sound as well.

Assistant State Attorney Joel Lazarus took off on two different tangents. First, if the videotape contained sound as Wilson claimed, this filming, unbeknownst to the person being filmed, was like recording a phone conversation without someone's consent. This violated state wiretap laws and stepped the charges against the Willetses up a notch. Second, Lazarus notified the Dade state attorney's office about the possible misconduct of the defense attorneys.

Ellis Rubin naturally denied nearly all of Wilson's statement. He did admit a tape existed and that it had been given to him by his clients, but he declined to name Danziger as being the subject of the film and he further stated that he had turned the tape over to the Willets's civil attorney, Guy Seligman.

The court hearing that day attracted over 100 reporters and citizens who crowded inside and outside the courtroom. They heard the plea bargain withdrawal and the prosecution's contention that the videotape constituted evidence of a new crime. For her part, Kathy took a moment to chastise me for my relentless pursuit of the Willetses in the face of real crime on the streets. She told reporters that taxpayers should complain about my wasting their money on this case.

By now, television talk shows were extremely interested in this case and Jeffrey and Kathy quickly became national personalities. Rubin added another twist to his nymphomania defense with the news that Kathy's disease was a side effect of her taking Prozac. He cited the *Physician's Desk Reference* for pharmaceuticals as a source, along with other medical testimony that would be given in court.

Playboy and *Penthouse* magazines ran their stories on the "carnal couple." T-shirts were printed with Kathy's picture on them. The couple was due to appear on Oprah Winfrey's show in September 1991 but backed out at the last minute because Oprah had another guest, one of the Willetses clients, who was joining the show live via remote in South Florida. A London reporter, in Florida to cover the Noriega trial, phoned our office to speak with me because he found the Willetses' case much more fascinating than the "boring" case involving the former Panamanian dictator.

The clients from the Willetses' list also began to express themselves, mostly through an attorney hired to protect their names from being released. That list was the subject of endless speculation for months and there were widespread guesses as to who could be on it that would create a further sensation.

A newspaper article ran accusing me of using the case for more publicity. I swear that someday someone will accuse me of sinking the *Titanic*, too.

There are maybe four or five cops out of 3,000 that end up succumbing to the temptation of corruption. Most likely it would be graft or drugs that led to their undoing. This type of situation rarely warranted any media publicity and certainly nothing of the size and scope of the Willets case.

Sadly, an officer who makes the supreme sacrifice for his country is not nearly as notable as an officer who videotapes his wife having sex with others and collects money in exchange. Why should we be surprised at people who commit crimes for the resulting publicity? Today they are relatively assured of receiving it.

In October, Kathy Willets put a brand new 900 number into effect. For a mere $2.99 per minute, Kathy offered listeners her side of the story. The advertisement said, "If what you read in the paper doesn't satisfy you, call Kathy today." Her former "stage name," Julie, was apparently gone.

In December, Jeffrey and Kathy finally pleaded guilty to operating a prostitution business out of their home and illegally videotaping customers. They finally agreed to enter these pleas after the months of endless publicity this case had generated. Kathy pleaded guilty to twenty counts of prostitution and thirteen charges of illegally taping phone conversations of her clients and was given three years' probation. Jeffrey pleaded guilty to living off the earnings of a prostitute, thirteen counts of taping phone conversations, and one count of illegally taping the words of Doug Danziger while he was with Kathy. The sentencing wouldn't be until February 4, but as a convicted felon, Jeffrey would no longer be able to serve in this state as a police officer. He would lose his certification immediately.

He tried to formally resign from the Broward County Sheriff's Office following his pleas, but there wasn't any way I was going to let his record reflect a resignation. We formally fired him, so that any state checking Jeffrey's past work record would see the notation on his chart. That should be enough to prevent him from resuming a law enforcement career. As far as I was concerned, he could look for any other job he wanted to, but his police career was finished.

Kathy publicly stated at the time that they simply wanted to put the case behind them. They wanted to get on with their lives, not ruin any others. Ellis Rubin's nymphomania defense was history.

Ellis Rubin still had to answer some questions from the Dade state attorney's office concerning the videotape in his possession that reportedly showed the encounter between Kathy Willets and Doug Danziger. In addition to this ethical question, Rubin had stretched the "attorney-client privilege" issue as far as it could go. Normally, a defense attorney doesn't divulge any information that could hurt his or her client, but if it is evidence of an illegal activity, the withholding of that information subverts the justice system.

Rubin also crossed swords with the "Son of Sam" law, named after famed New York City serial killer David Berkowitz. This law states that in Florida it is illegal for anyone convicted of a felony to profit from the crime. The

Danziger tape was certainly part of this case and accepting money for it ($60,000 was the figure negotiated) even before a conviction subjected the money to seizure.

Finally, Rubin had to contend with the possibility of a conflict of interest since he represented both Jeffrey and Kathy. If the case had gone to trial, one party may very well have testified against the other. I can picture Ellis Rubin in the courtroom, scurrying back and forth between a client as a defendant and a client as a hostile witness. I'm sure that Rubin was sorry he'd ever received the phone call involving him in this tangled affair.

Jeffrey was sentenced to 364 days in the Broward Detention Center for his part in living off the earnings of a prostitute. Kathy was given a three-year probation that did not include any jail time. This case had already received more publicity than it deserved and it should have ceased with the convictions, but there was much more to come.

Kathy continued to visit Jeffrey at the Detention Center until he was moved to the Broward County jail because Kathy had been trying to smuggle things in to him. Later, he was put on a work-release program, but he violated the terms of it and ended up back in jail to complete his sentence. When released in September 1992, Jeffrey attacked Kathy and tried to strangle her. He was booked, tried, and sentenced to three and a half years. His animosity toward his wife did not abate with this new jail term and while inside, he tried to hire a man to beat up Kathy's new boyfriend. Jeffrey's obsession with Kathy had been his undoing and continued to shape his actions a year and a half later.

Kathy took a step backward at the end of 1992. She violated the terms of her probation by showing up inebriated at the probation office. She was initially sentenced to an alcohol rehabilitation program in jail, which she concluded, but she then asked the judge presiding over her next sentencing to put her in jail rather than back on probation. The judge concurred, giving her a three and a half year sentence. Now, both Jeffrey and Kathy were in jail and, according to Kathy, broke. Their house was in foreclosure and she had declared bankruptcy.

The other central part of the case revolved around whether the Willetses' list of clients should be published. Several of the "John Does" had hired an attorney to plead their right to privacy in the courts. That legal fight went all the way to the Florida Supreme Court, which ruled that they had lost their right to privacy when they answered the Willetses' ad, looking for a relationship with the hot body.

The mainstream newspapers in South Florida didn't publish the list after the Florida Supreme Court ruling. Interestingly enough, the name of an employee of the Miami Herald was on the infamous list. An alternative South Florida publication called XS, however, did make the list public in February 1993. Other than Doug Danzinger's name, the other names listed would be recognized only by a listed person's immediate circle of family and friends.

The videotape of Doug Danziger and Kathy Willets was also released in February and viewed by the local media. The interest in this story was still amazingly high.

Jeffrey was released from jail in May 1993 and went to work as a doorman at a strip joint in Pompano Beach, a town in Broward County. Kathy was released because of prison overcrowding a few weeks later, after serving six months of her sentence. It was time for them to rebuild their lives. Since Jeffrey couldn't return to police work, he needed to find a new profession. They decided to let Kathy perform. Jeffrey became her manager and they began to cash in on their fame. Kathy worked out with a personal trainer and started dancing at topless clubs. The couple planned to venture into X-rated films, too.

The Willets had lost their home, custody of their three children, and Jeffrey's chosen career as a result of this episode. They were made celebrities by the press, but only attorneys and talk shows realized any benefit from the entire affair.

Early in 1994, Ellis Rubin was finally cleared for his part in the "sex tape for sale" scandal that set back his original nymphomania defense. The case was dropped when prosecutors decided the tape was not illegally recorded since Doug Danziger had waived his right to privacy when he answered Kathy's advertisement.

It did seem clear that Rubin and his sons had crossed some ethical lines when they advised Jeffrey Willets that his videotape was a money maker and represented the couple in negotiations with television tabloid shows. Rubin called the decision by the courts not to call this an ethics violations a victory for him and threatened to sue Inside Edition over the entire matter. I doubted that would happen. Rubin should have been glad it was over and moved on.

One last footnote: In July 1994, Kathy was arraigned on charges of lewd-

ness and violating Palm Beach County's lap-dancing ordinance. Her performance included sexual acts with a flashlight and having customers shave her.
Palm Beach County Judge Deborah Pucillo ruled that Kathy's strip club performance was not a form of constitutionally protected expression. She will
now have to stand trail on these charges.

She just can't seem to get enough of the court system.

Twenty-One

Swept Away With Andrew

W HEN I WAS ELECTED TO OFFICE IN 1984, I HAD MENTALLY DECIDED TO run for only one additional four-year term. If re-elected in 1988, I could groom someone to run in my place in 1992, another experienced law enforcement professional that would continue to keep Broward a safe community in which to live. These ideas turned out to be naive. It became more difficult to let the office go than I had believed as there were so many people who were counting on me to continue. We'd brought Broward County law enforcement to the brink of the twenty-first century and it seemed premature to step down in the face of these achievements. Nevertheless, the decision to seek a third term was strictly an emotional one.

Deep inside of me burns a pride that was sending a signal to not let the bastards run me off without a fight. I succumbed to the challenge. I established a re-election campaign fund and, as in the past, Sharron volunteered to run the campaign while I went about the business of running the sheriff's office. It was round three of my election experience.

What's more, I already had an opponent. Al Goldstein, the publisher of the pornographic magazine Screw, had promised to run against me after I had arrested Charles Freeman, the record store owner who openly defied a judge's court order not to sell copies of As Nasty As They Wanna Be. It appeared that he was keeping his promise.

Goldstein generated a lot of early publicity and gave the media yet another angle on negative publicity for me. Goldstein called me incompetent, a Nazi, and an incompetent Nazi. The press printed these words. The reports on Goldstein, whom even the media couldn't have taken seriously, simply dovetailed with the type of publicity I was getting. The next wave of assaults attacked the size of my re-election campaign fund.

In April 1991, a cartoon ran in the local paper making fun of my "war chest." Headlines ran, "Navarro is soliciting donations from out-of-state." A lot of campaign contributions came from out-of-staters at that early time because they supported of my arrest of 2 Live Crew. While the letters were welcome, they were hardly solicited.

In July 1991, a man named Alfred LaManna of Coral Springs filed fundraising papers to run for sheriff as a Democrat. He was a twenty-eight year veteran of the FBI who was working in a private investigation capacity for a consulting firm. Despite his law enforcement experience, his filing seemed half-hearted. He told reporters he would step aside if a better Democratic candidate emerged.

It was about this time, well over a year before any primary would be held, that the race started to take on a deja vu aspect. Gil Gesuldi, who had run on the Democratic ticket in the primary in 1988, decided to run again. Jim Howard, my 1988 Republican primary opponent, declared his intentions to run against me in the 1992 primary. Ron Cochran, Jim Howard's 1988 campaign manager and former Fort Lauderdale police chief, was rumored to be considering a run after talking with the Broward Democratic Executive Committee chair, Russ Barakat. Cochran was currently a Republican but was considering a switch to the Democratic party to avoid having to run against me in the primary. I had no problem with his switching parties, having done it once before.

What was bothering me was the recycling of the same people who ran against me back in 1988. Howard and Cochran, once allies, had divided up in an effort to oust me from office. I was sure they would receive some good press over the next few months, as sure as I was that I'd be hit with as much negative publicity as possible.

Cochran switched parties in August, although he wasn't officially declaring himself to be in the race for the Democratic nomination for sheriff. There seemed to be no question, though, that he was the candidate the Democratic party wanted for the office. "Mr. G," Gil Gesuldi, said he would bow out if Cochran ran. I suspected that LaManna would do the same.

The National Inquirer newspaper also got into the act in September 1991, by printing an article about Al Goldstein's run for the sheriff's office. This article ran next to a piece about a girl in England who was attacked by a giant rat - all the news that's fit to print.

By December, Al Goldstein had officially filed his fundraising papers as had two other Democrats, Gary Steinberg, a club-toting Buford Pusser type who was a former police officer, and Howard Fox, another veteran of the 1988 campaign. Gesuldi had dropped out, as promised, once Cochran made his campaign official. Al LaManna remained in the race for now.

One more Democratic candidate would be added before Christmas. Craig Glasser, a deputy in our car theft unit, announced he would resign January 3 in order to campaign full time for sheriff. His mother, Diane, a Democratic state committee member, was planning to run for mayor of Tamarac in March 1992 and knew the political machine quite well. The media cautioned the Democrats saying a united Democratic effort was needed to beat Navarro, not a divisive primary campaign. Glasser said he wanted to bring respectability back to the department and rid the place of "cronyism" and "taking care of friends."

I'm not sure why Glasser apparently felt like he didn't fit in, but I respected his right to make his feelings known. Those feelings weren't shared by the great majority of his fellow officers.

In January, the media gave the usual Navarro war-chest update: it stood at $300,000 including contributions from Blockbuster magnate and Florida Marlins baseball team owner H. Wayne Huizenga. That month, a limit of $500 per contributor went into effect in the state of Florida; the limit had been $1,000. Many of the generous contributions I received were for the maximum legal amount.

I admit to still being taken aback by the number of well-wishers who were willing to actually donate money to my campaign. I have never been able to adjust to this since police officers are trained not to accept monetary gifts, which could always be construed as bribes. I was glad for the financial help, especially the additional fund-raiser in 1985 to help pay the legal fees of fighting the Democratic Party lawsuits. Grateful and comfortable are two different feelings, though, and I suppose I would never be at ease with this part of the political process.

In February, the Democrats had another candidate: Woody King, a Margate police officer. This brought their total to six with Cochran, Glasser, Fox, Steinberg, and LaManna. Only Jim Howard was running against me in the Republican primary. While there was concern among Democrats that too many candidates were running, which could dilute the advantage the party had in the number of registered voters in the county, the themes of their campaigns were similar. Rather than talk about the contributions they could make, the candidates seemed satisfied to stand back and blast my nearly eight year record as sheriff. Taking their cues from local newspapers and radio stations, their speeches repeated the rhetoric associated with a Cochran catch phrase: "End the Nick-tatorship."

Cochran was getting the best of early media ink and appeared to be the front-runner for the Democrats. The newspapers portrayed him as very low key and low profile, in contrast to what the papers deemed my "newshound" image. Cochran was careful to maintain this image and took his cues from the media. If articles were running that criticized my budget, Cochran emphasized that. If stories were written about the "corruption" in the sheriff's office, Cochran would talk about low morale in a department that was, in his words, "out of control." Cochran was confident that he would be the Democratic challenger that emerged from the now-crowded field. He'd also assumed that I would be his Republican opponent, although I still had Jim Howard to beat again.

The media remained nervous about my ability to raise campaign money, equating a solid financial position with the best chance of election success. Editorials were published that suggested limiting campaign contributions and reforming campaign finances. Of course, this hadn't been an issue in the past with other individuals more to their liking who had raised substantial amounts of money.

Howard Fox quit the campaign in May and threw his support to newcomer Lou Lupino, the former chief of forensics in Palm Beach County, just north of Broward. Lupino criticized Ron Cochran for taking a leave of absence from the school board job he held rather than resign and let someone fill the seat during the long campaign for the sheriff's office.

In June, the media couldn't find anything current to focus on, so reporters brought up one of our older operations, an undercover fencing operation that resulted in the recovery of $3 million in stolen property, more than 70 arrests, and the breakup of a major auto theft ring. The headline ran "BSO Sting Put Public at Risk."

What the media focused on was that our investigation into the operation was not as well run as I would have liked. The press spent a lot of time researching our work during the operation, most of the investigation being done by the Miami Herald.

In July, the newest criticism was of the number of take-home cars we allowed for employees, virtually all of them necessary for sheriff's office business. A number of our people were involved in community involvement work, a key ingredient in our Neighborhood 2000 program, but the implication was obvious: perks and wasted tax dollars.

The next headline was "Sheriff's employees feel office is tense." The survey was conducted by the Broward County Police Benevolent Association, which had given its early support to Ron Cochran. Supposedly seven out of ten BSO employees said morale was bad, even though most of them still liked me as sheriff.

Following that was an article about the net worth of county politicians, calling Broward officials "fat cats." Naturally, I was one of those depicted as "fat" with a $500,000 net worth, 80 percent of which was the house on the Middle River that Sharron and I had bought several years ago. Property on the water in South Florida was now at a premium and our home's value had risen accordingly. I was hardly a "fat cat," and these numbers should have been disappointing to those who expected me to have my hand in the till after reading about the "corruption" in the BSO. Apparently I was a better cop than a crook.

Another 1988 campaigner joined the Democratic fray, Walter Ramsdell. Along with King, Glasser, Cochran, Steinberg, and Lupino (LaManna had withdrawn), the total appeared to be staying at six for the Democratic nomination. No one else had joined Jim Howard in the Republican challenge. Al Goldstein was an Independent candidate.

A flier circulated around the BSO offices in July slamming candidate Ron

Cochran. It made allegations about past and present alcohol abuse and a plan Cochran had to privatize the operation of the county jail. The purpose of this piece was to point out to the Police Benevolent Association members that they had endorsed a man who would likely take their jobs away if he won. I never condoned any political piece being sent around the office and certainly not one that make unsubstantiated allegations. Cochran clearly had his enemies, though, but I informed my close campaign committee members that we would not be a party to any of this type of literature.

Later that month, Al Goldstein called it quits, from his campaign as well as his fourth marriage. He needed 18,000 signatures to get his name placed on the ballot and could muster only 7,000. He also vowed to back my candidacy if it would hurt my re-election chances. He ended up being more of a talker than a doer.

In the meantime, the avalanche of Navarro negative publicity continued: our 911 operators were slow to respond to calls; I neglected to record meal discounts at fund-raisers as "in-kind" contributions to my campaign; the BSO steered sequestered-juror business to a favorite hotel; a theft sting we ran cost the taxpayers unnecessary dollars, and on and on. Accuracy never seemed important, only the inference. I was beginning to have my doubts that I could survive this onslaught. It was a well-conceived, hard-fought effort by the media and it was beginning to take its toll on all of us. Did I really want to listen to this crap for another four years?

The slate of candidates was finalized in July. On the Republican primary ticket was myself and Jim Howard, a repeat of 1988. Howard was running a hobby store business and a campaign at the same time. He was a former BSO employee who left under a cloud of suspicion, though no charges were ever filed against him. In my mind, he was not a good candidate for the top office, because he lacked the leadership skills and knowledge necessary. I had beaten him easily in 1988 and didn't have any reason to think the outcome would be different this time, although I felt the results would be closer because of all my bad press.

The Democratic side was an interesting collection, much as it had been in 1988. There were no Ralph Finnos this time, but Walter Ramsdell, who had worked closely with Finno in the past, was back. Ron Cochran was well known and had a substantial amount of experience in the Fort Lauderdale police department. Lou Lupino had selected a man convicted of murder a few years earlier as his campaign manager. Gary Steinberg walked around with an ax handle he nicknamed "Justice," but the Buford Pusser act was not likely to play well in Broward County. Elwood "Woody" King, a nineteen-year veteran of the Margate police force, had a lot of experience. Craig Glasser had filed rebuttals to his personnel evaluations in the BSO, which labeled him as a competent, if unremarkable, officer. Glasser had the most political connections other than front-runner Cochran. It was a packed slate, but Cochran had the advantage of having more funds available to promote himself.

September 1 was primary day, the first Tuesday of the month. The election was rarely held on the first day of the month, and some people were bound to forget about it. My campaign staff worked to remind people all August that the primary was on the unusual date of the first of September and hoped for the best. Also, a substantial amount of redistricting had occurred this year and county residents were a bit confused about where their polling places were and what district they were now in. This situation had the makings of a low turnout, as most primaries muster, but the question was becoming, will the registered Republicans get out and actually vote?

Meanwhile, the media was mobilizing around the gay bar raids we had done at the request of and in conjunction with the State Beverage Department. One radio talk show host called me a homophobe on a daily basis and flatly stated that I hated gays. He encouraged gay voters to switch party affiliations from Democrat to Republican to vote in the primary. Plain and simple, he wanted Navarro out at any cost. That I had no record of being anti-gay in my thirty-three years of law enforcement also had no influence with the media.

This storm of negative publicity I had foreseen, but no one could have predicted what was about to hit South Florida one week before the September first primary.

On August 24, the unthinkable happened. A category five hurricane named Andrew, which had been tearing up the Caribbean, came ashore just south of Miami and ripped through Dade County, leaving billions of dollars of damage in its wake.

It had been so long since a hurricane had struck this part of Florida that people had generally relaxed about the annual threat. Hurricane David had created problems in 1979, but there had been no serious storms since then. Until Andrew.

Bad weather had been battering our coast for a couple of days. Even in Broward County, the wind and rain had created havoc and power failures. During the worst of the storm, many of us had simply huddled in closets, praying for the best. But it was Dade County that got hit the hardest. Thousands of residents were left without homes, more without water and power. When the sun came up on Sunday, the cleanup started.

Suddenly, the election was the farthest thing from my mind. All of the sheriffs in the state had a mutual aid pact. If something happened in Broward County, I knew I could count on the other sheriffs, especially those from Dade and Palm Beach Counties, to help us out. Now it was our turn. We had escaped the worst of the damage. Our comrades in Dade needed help.

We mobilized quickly, assigning deputies to details involving food and water distribution, shelter, general cleanup, and whatever else needed to be done. I lent Dade County a number of our deputies as Dade officers were struggling with the loss of their homes.

The Dade police force had lost its helicopter, housed in a hangar in Homestead. We gave them our helicopters, which were initially used to rescue some of the more isolated victims needing medial attention. We gave Dade County everything we could. Luckily, this was toward the end of our fiscal year and we had about $2.5 million marked to be returned as unspent from last year's budget. We would not be able to turn in as much now, but the money would be spent on a good cause. We transported food, water, supplies, equipment for the police officers, anything we could.

We set up a temporary shelter for those police officers and their families who had lost their homes, and many of our deputies volunteered their own homes for people to stay in. With crime being down overall in the county, we had a surplus of jail beds at the time and we converted them into temporary housing. Everyone in the department offered to do extra work, to help in any way possible. I was extremely proud of the BSO's efforts in response to this tragedy.

The devastation the storm brought to the Dade County cannot be expressed in a matter of a few words. It would be months before the county would be restored to normalcy. It was the worst mess I had ever seen in South

Florida. It was time to pitch in and help each other out and the BSO was a big part of that.

I spent the last week of the primary campaign - arguably the most important week - in Dade County. The campaign continued without me, but was hampered by the fallout from the storm. Television commercials we had shot didn't run, but they were hardly important in comparison to the critical information that was passed on to residents, many of whom had lost everything in the storm. A week later it was primary time in Broward County (Dade's was postponed), but it was the farthest thing from most people's minds, including my own.

The hurricane had interrupted mail service, and many Broward residents had no idea where to vote. Many that did know had lost their enthusiasm for the election - it was only a primary, after all. The general election wasn't until November.

The primary was held and about 32,000 Republicans turned out. When the votes were counted, Jim Howard had more votes than I did. On the Democratic side, Ron Cochran buried his opponents. That was as surprising to me as the Republican results. Usually, with six candidates running for an office, one candidate doesn't get a 50 percent majority of votes. Cochran did.

I am a great believer in fate. Everything that happened over the last year was a message to me that I didn't receive until the September 1 election. The message was, it was time to leave. The voters had made their choice; it was time to move on.

I had been a public servant for so long that, this was going to be a welcome change. I would do the best possible job as sheriff until January, but that was it. Democracy is a wonderful power that we give the people. It's one of the primary reasons we are the melting pot of the world. The people had spoken and told me eight years was enough. I accepted their mandate.

I received hundreds of calls over the next day or so from people protesting that they hadn't been able to get out to vote. They called the whole process unfair and said that Broward County should have postponed the primary by a week because of Andrew, the postal service delays prevented many residents from knowing where their polling places were, and most of my supporters had stopped reading the newspapers due to the negative publicity I was accorded daily and missed the rundown of new precincts.

I appreciated all of their solicitousness. I briefly considered filing a protest but decided against it. What was the purpose even if successful? To prolong this anti-Navarro campaign? I didn't need it and the residents of the county didn't, either. It was time to finish up the job and move on. I was sixty-two years old, eligible for full retirement and looking forward, at long last, to private enterprise. I figured the press would celebrate and leave me alone after a week or so.

Naturally, Al Goldstein was elated. He was quoted as saying that my defeat was as good as finding a twenty-year-old Playboy playmate who loves you.

There was endless analysis by the press as to why I lost the primary, something even my worst critics in the media didn't expect. They essentially attributed it to an informed public. I would have said the exact opposite was the case. At any rate, their glee would likely keep my name off the front pages for a while.

There was still Dade County to help, which would keep officers busy from now until the end of the year. There was also an election for sheriff to be held, but I suspected that Cochran would have no problem beating Jim Howard. All of the information that surfaced back in 1988 about Jim Howard would probably rear itself again now. Cochran was clearly the press's choice.

In October, the Fort Lauderdale Sun-Sentinel editorial headline was "Enthusiastic support for a thinking man's police officer," a flowery ode to Cochran unlike any accolades they had given a sheriff in the past. Good luck, Jim Howard.

Cochran went to a meeting of MADD (Mothers Against Drunk Drivers) in October and gave a short speech, thinking that there would be plenty of questions to answer. However, the room was filled with BSO officers being honored by the MADD organization for their efforts. Not a question was put forth. Our officers were not looking forward to a future with Ron Cochran.

A report was released in October about Jim Howard owing a former business partner $28,000. This was not new information, but the press ignored the story until after the primary. For a candidate who criticized how I handled the office and the budget, this was not the kind of publicity desired as the general election drew near.

Cochran made some heavy campaign promises to reduce the budget of $196 million that had been approved for the BSO recently. He also promised not to pursue any more city contracts. Three or four additional municipalities were set to join the BSO in January, but these additions were doubtful now. It would be interesting to measure Cochran against his promises, but I doubted the press would bother.

When the election was held on November 3 Cochran pulled in more than twice as many votes as Jim Howard. It gave the press another chance to throw a few cheap shots in my direction, but otherwise the affair was unremarkable. Many BSO deputies were not happy about the result, but I don't think the election of Jim Howard would have been cause for their celebration either.

A local magazine, XS, which had labeled me in the last year as anti-gay, ran a contest to see what jobs I would be suited for in my post-sheriff days. The most popular choice was a dog groomer in the BSO canine unit. The only problem with that, of course, was that Cochran would have to hire me for that occupation. Not likely.

I stepped down on January 4, 1993, after eight years as the sheriff of Broward County. So much was accomplished, so much done on behalf of Broward residents, I couldn't ask for anything more. Together, we in the BSO had changed the face of law enforcement in this county. We were one of the most envied and copied agencies in the world. Nothing would come of any of the allegations made against the agency in the past couple of years. I was proud of the BSO and my only regret was that it would likely fall apart under Ron Cochran.

My last message to my BSO deputies and staff summarized my feelings for the people that had helped make my years as sheriff great ones:

"At times the going was tough, but I was always able to count on the best efforts of true professionals to bring us through. We have all had the experience of contributing to the development of this agency during its greatest growth period ever. I am grateful for that experience and I depart now with the same message that I delivered when I was first sworn in as Sheriff in 1985: Never forget that we are public servants and that we have been vested with special authority, not for our benefit but for the good of the community at large. Many thousands of people depend upon us daily for the maintenance of peace and order in their lives.

I am proud to have been a career law enforcement officer and extremely proud to have served with some of the finest I have ever been associated with - the men and women of the Broward Sheriff's Office. I am sure you will continue the high standards we have set as you prepare to enter 1993.

Additional Information

If you are unable to obtain a copy of *Cuban Cop* from your local bookstore, you may send $24.95 plus $3.50 shipping and handling to:

TransMedia Publishing
6001 Broken Sound Parkway, N.W.
Boca Raton, Florida 33487
(561) 998-4888
(561) 998-5661

If you would like to contact the author, you may write to
him at the above address.

Other books from TransMedia are:
Rexall to Riches by Carl DeSantis
Spin Man by Thomas J. Madden
The Bloat Blitz Diet by Krescent Thuringer

Visit our website at: www.prpluspublishing.com